OUTPUT TO OUTCOME

Praise for *Output to Outcome*

"If Peter Drucker taught us how to think about management in the industrial and knowledge-work eras, Mik Kersten is helping define management for the Age of AI. *Output to Outcome* combines systems thinking, software delivery, and organizational design into a clear playbook for leaders who need to harness AI without losing control, accountability, or purpose."

—**Gene Kim,** researcher and *WSJ* bestselling author of *Vibe Coding, The Phoenix Project*, and *Wiring the Winning Organization*

"In a world where AI can amplify output endlessly, many organizations risk optimizing the wrong thing. Mik Kersten provides exactly what's missing: An operating model that keeps value creation and measurable outcomes at the center. Timely, insightful, and highly actionable."

—**Ralf Waltram**, Head of IT Global DevOps Hubs, BMW Group

"Technological revolutions reshape not only economies and industries but also the way organizations must adapt to succeed. Output to Outcome is a timely and thought-provoking contribution in a period of information technology and AI-driven socioeconomic transformation."

—**Carlota Perez**, Author of *Technological Revolutions and Financial Capital*

"With *Output to Outcome*, Mik defines the next critical shift for enterprises in the age of AI—moving from activity to measurable impact. Building on Lean principles and decades of transformation insight, he provides a clear, practical roadmap for leaders who need to compete and win. This is a must-read—and a call to action—for every software-driven organization."

—**Dean Leffingwell,** Creator of SAFe®

"We are in a chaotic environment driven by a rate of change that current systems and businesses cannot absorb. The climate crisis, pandemics, and wars disrupt business plans and supply chains, and the pace of AI-driven development means that tools are obsolete before they stabilize. We have to reorganize to focus on outcomes, and rebuild everything to deliver them using new tools that are building themselves. This is the definitive guidebook for that transition."

—**Adrian Cockcroft,** Tech Advisor, Formerly AWS and Netflix

"Everyone in the software community feels something big is happening. AI is revolutionizing how product development works...Mik Kersten's approach is both refreshing and based on solid experience. As we look to the future, *Output to Outcome* is an excellent guide, encouraging a thoughtful, empirical approach to what lies ahead."

—**Dave West,** CEO and Product Owner, Scrum.org

"Mik does it again! This time, with the advent of the Age of AI, *Output to Outcome* provides a unique and comprehensive strategy that can drive companies to best surf the promising AI wave. This book is a starting point in the launch of a new movement. This movement is the Operating Model for the Age of AI."

—**George Kadifa,** Cofounder, Sumeru Equity Partners

"At Vanguard, we've seen firsthand that meaningful transformation requires more than new technology. It requires a data-driven operating model that improves how we create and deliver value. In *Output to Outcome*, Mik Kersten provides a practical framework for establishing that robust data-driven operating model, allowing you to scale up in a world increasingly shaped by AI."

—**Michael Carr,** Chief Technology Officer, Vanguard

"After transforming how we measure and manage software delivery with the Flow Framework in *Project to Product*, Mik Kersten is now guiding enterprises through the deeper AI transition. In *Output to Outcome*, he provides the vocabulary, models, and practical frameworks needed to turn AI into a genuine operating system for the enterprise—not just another feature. If your company is serious about surviving and thriving in the AI era, *Output to Outcome* is essential reading."

—**Pieter Jordaan,** Group Chief Information Officer, TUI Group

"Mik brilliantly demonstrates that AI capacity gains are wasted without a fundamental organizational redesign. Among other brilliant insights, his call to shift from a tangled Matrix to Modularity is exactly what leaders need to hear right now: We must engineer our organizations with the same high cohesion and low coupling as our best software. A masterful guide to unlocking AI's true ROI by fixing the system itself."

—**Justin Watts,** Director of Transformation and Business Design, John Lewis Partnership

OUTPUT TO OUTCOME

AN OPERATING MODEL FOR THE AGE OF AI

MIK KERSTEN
AUTHOR OF *PROJECT TO PRODUCT*

IT Revolution
Portland, OR

IT REVOLUTION
25 NW 23rd Pl, Suite 6314
Portland, OR 97210

First Edition
Printed in the United States of America
31 30 29 28 27 26 1 2 3 4 5 6 7 8 9 10

Cover design by Devon Smith Creative
Book design by Devon Smith Creative

Library of Congress Cataloging-in-Publication Data

Names: Kersten, Mik author
Title: Output to outcome : an operating model for the age of AI / by Mik Kersten.
Description: First edition. | Portland, OR : IT Revolution, 2026. | Includes bibliographical references and index.
Identifiers: LCCN 2026005270 (print) | LCCN 2026005271 (ebook) | ISBN 9781966280231 paperback | ISBN 9781966280248 ebook | ISBN 9781966280255 audio
Subjects: LCSH: Information technology--Management | Artificial intelligence--Business applications | BISAC: BUSINESS & ECONOMICS / Management | BUSINESS & ECONOMICS / Leadership
Classification: LCC HD30.2 .K463 2026 (print) | LCC HD30.2 (ebook)
LC record available at https://lccn.loc.gov/2026005270
LC ebook record available at https://lccn.loc.gov/2026005271

ISBN: 9781966280231
eBook ISBN: 9781950508723
Audio: 9781966280255

For information about special discounts for bulk purchases or for information on booking authors for an event, please visit our website at www.ITRevolution.com.

Dedication

To slowing down, contemplation,
and reading beyond the summarization.

In Memory of my Father
Gregory Kersten (1949–2020).

Contents

List of Figures & Tables

Models & Taxonomy

	Ch.	Model	Shift	Case Study
Foundations	0			Accelerated Outcome Loop at Cognition.ai
Part I: Outcome Management	1	Product Operating Model		Project to Product to AI Engineering at CBA
	2	Outcome Loop Model		Outcome Loop Optimization at VS Code
	3	Outcome Tree Model		Building the Outcome Tree at Tasktop
Part II: The Seven Shifts	4	Dedicated Leadership Model	Functions to Flow	From Frenzy to Flow at TUI Group
	5	Flow Metrics Model	Slop to Substance	Scaling the Ideation Cliff at Vanguard
	6	Unified Cadence Model	Chaos to Cadence	Unifying the Meeting Cadence at Planview
	7	Independent Action Model	Matrix to Modularity	Optimizing Outcome Tree Modularity at Priceline
	8	Outcome Ownership Model	Objectives to Ownership	Refactoring the AI Teams at Planview
	9	Outcome Domain Model	Divisions to Domains	Navigating the Innovators' Dilemma at Tasktop
	10	Outcome Architecture Model	Managers to Makers	Leadership Lessons for the Age of AI

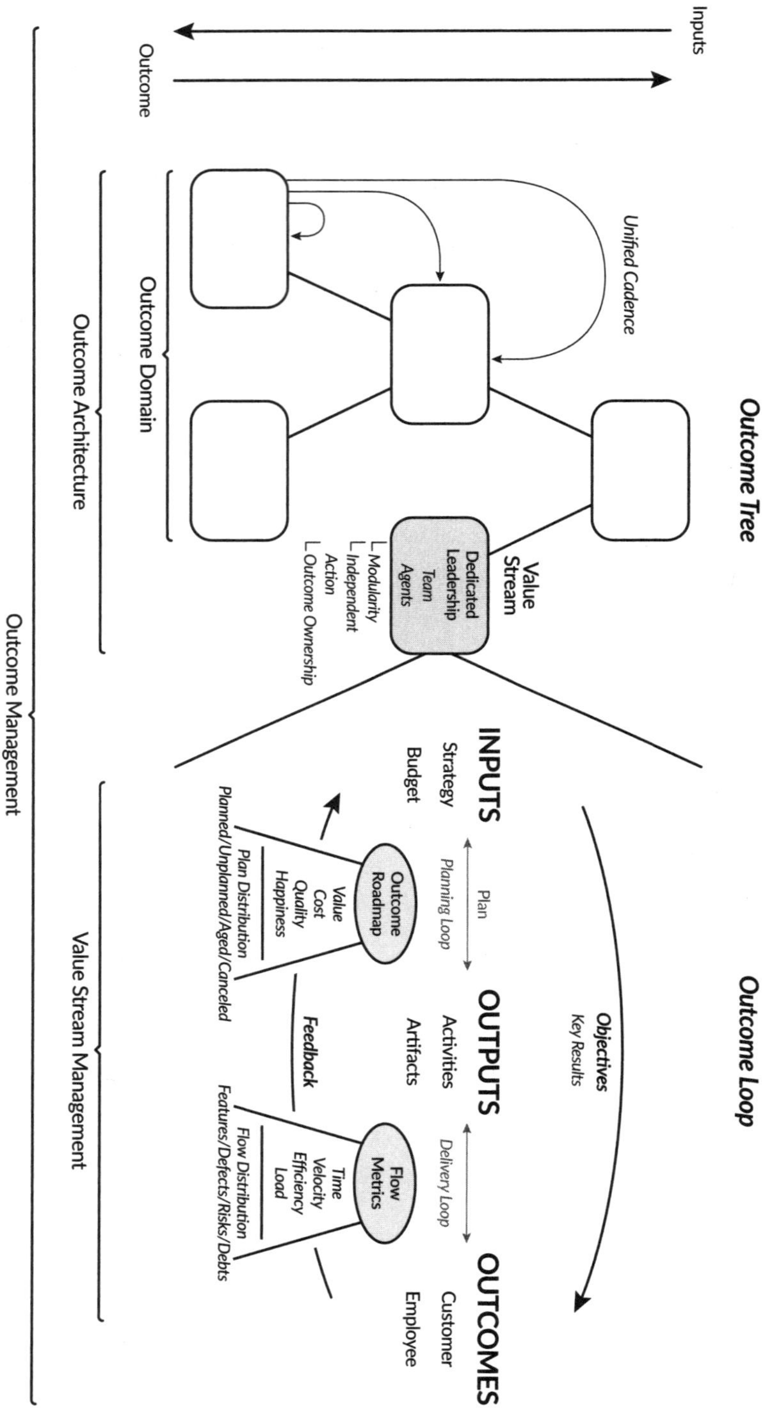
Inputs
Outcome
Outcome Tree
Unified Cadence
Value Stream
Dedicated Leadership
Team
Agents
Modularity
Independent Action
Outcome Ownership
Outcome Domain
Outcome Architecture
Outcome Loop
Objectives
Key Results
INPUTS
Strategy
Budget
Plan
Planning Loop
OUTPUTS
Activities
Artifacts
Delivery Loop
OUTCOMES
Customer
Employee
Outcome Roadmap
Value
Cost
Quality
Happiness
Plan Distribution
Planned/Unplanned/Aged/Canceled
Feedback
Flow Metrics
Time
Velocity
Efficiency
Load
Flow Distribution
Features/Defects/Risks/Debts
Value Stream Management
Outcome Management

Preface

"This is the end of coding as a profession."

Those words, spoken by Rod Johnson, kept ringing in my head. It was January 2023, and we were sharing our awe of how good the recently released ChatGPT 3.5 was at working with code. Rod is one of the most well-known and prolific open-source developers and entrepreneurs, and his statement came not from what ChatGPT could do at that time, but from extrapolating the rate of improvement that was to come. I agreed with his statement, and we proceeded to debate the timeframe of the disruption. We continue to debate on our calls to this day. Almost ironically, Rod is now writing more code than he has since the start of his career, reinvigorated by his new startup, which helps developers adopt AI agents for evolving highly complex software systems.

The evolution of software development is a bellwether, as this has been one of the first and easiest knowledge work domains for AI to automate. It may seem like only yesterday that our careers, teams, and organizations were finally making progress on the path of mastering software delivery and digital experiences. That journey has now been upended entirely by the way AI changes the economics of digital production.

Since the dawn of the digital age, software and technology have been a key constraint to organizational success, and a generation of developer productivity tools and methodologies followed. For the first two decades of this century, I thought of myself and my team of software developers as akin to thoroughbred horses running at breakneck speed. We were creating amazing software architectures, products, and tools. I had the great experience of building an innovative, successful, and fun business around these teams of thoroughbred horses. I learned to love the craft of coding and then of leading and nurturing high-performance people and teams. And then I learned that the equivalent of the steam engine had been invented and that we would no longer need horses.

This is a time of high uncertainty about the future of careers, organizations, the workforce, and the economy. There are a range of scenarios for how AI will impact our lives and how bumpy that ride will be. What is clear is that the pace of change is moving faster than it did in previous technological revolutions, as this time it is human intelligence itself that is being disrupted. Those organizations that are able to wield the power of this disruption will eclipse those that move too slowly.

I believe we are still in the early days of the benefits that technology and software can provide to society and that the broader and more diverse the set of organizations behind those technologies, the better off we will be. I hope this book becomes your guide to harnessing AI for lasting human-centric outcomes that help shape a future where your organization is able to control and leverage AI in ways that benefit your customers, your staff, and society.

—

Many careers start with one of the countless specializations around business and technology. We learn how to work with teams, and some of us learn how to lead those teams. We then learn how to navigate complex organizations, partnerships, markets, and ecosystems. These well-trodden paths have produced impactful and successful careers and created ladders that those early in their careers aspire to climb.

All of these careers are founded on the atomic unit of the individual contributor producing outcomes, be they a designer or a developer. These atomic units have been at the foundation of management since Peter Drucker documented and popularized the concept of the knowledge worker.[1] The teams they form are the bedrock of our organizations, and those of us in leadership positions are thrilled when we see the value delivered by these great teams of horses pulling carriages at full gallop and winning races.

While knowledge outputs will be automated, I believe we are entering a new era of people working in teams focused on driving outcomes. However, our organizations and roles need to be rewired completely in order to leverage the knowledge work amplification coming from agents and AI.

My technology background is in programming languages, productivity tools, and software architecture. You will notice the principles of architecture and modularity surface throughout the book as they can provide us with mechanisms that help govern highly complex systems, in particular those produced by AI. Just as the AI models are already extremely proficient at working with software modularity, my goal is to help establish principles for organizational modularity that will help you apply AI in a way that empowers your people and provides effective control and feedback mechanisms for managing the massive amplification of outputs produced by agents.

The inputs into *Output to Outcome* are a system data– and survey-based study of enterprise software delivery constraints that followed the 2018 publication of *Project to Product*, the precursor to this book, known as the *Project to Product State of the Industry Report*.[2] This book also draws on my experiences working with hundreds of technology executives and helping thousands of enterprise organizations identify and remove the constraints impeding their digital transformations, first in my role as the cofounder and CEO of Tasktop, then as the chief technology officer of Planview following its acquisition of Tasktop, and now as an independent researcher and advisor helping organizations navigate the Age of AI.

It also draws on my experiences spending most of a decade as a research scientist at Xerox PARC, followed by a PhD thesis in developer and knowledge worker productivity, both of which had me spending the majority of my time coding on broadly adopted open-source projects intended to validate our research ideas.

Following my doctoral work, my supervisor, Gail Murphy, and I founded Tasktop to put our research on value streams into practice. The fifteen-year journey of building and running a company to a very successful outcome involved constant experimentation and regular pivots. It was an amazing journey whose lessons are sprinkled throughout this book. While Tasktop no longer exists as an independent company, it makes for a useful case study as I built it from the ground up and have access to all of the data from inception to acquisition. The advice I got on that journey from some of the best thought leaders in the industry has helped shape the models presented in this book and is summarized in the stories and case studies throughout.

Finally, the book draws on my experience over the past three years leading the development of Planview's agentic AI solution for product and portfolio management and all the lessons learned along the way. I have been building generative AI–based products since 2022 and leveraging AI models and agents heavily in nearly every aspect of my day-to-day work. The models' deep research capabilities allowed me to cover much more breadth and depth than I would have been able to otherwise and were a fantastic research companion.

However, with the exception of coediting the eleven prompts for AI agents at the end of each chapter, I decided to write every word in this book and did not use AI for any of the ideating, outlining, or writing. The writing process helped me slow down and contemplate, and I hope the process of reading this book will do the same for you.

We are living in an amazing time, but either we control the deployment of AI or it will control us. I hope this book helps you and your organization gain that control and deliver outcomes to the stakeholders that matter most: your customers and colleagues.

Prompt

The following prompt, and those following each chapter, are intended to help AI agents assist you with applying Outcome Management once the Outcome Tree has been implemented. For the most up-to-date prompts, see OutputToOutcome.org.

> You are an AI assistant used by people applying *Output to Outcome: An Operating Model for the Age of AI.*
>
> Your purpose is to amplify knowledge work while keeping humans in control of intentions, decisions, and outcomes. You are required to prioritize outcomes for our customers, employees, and our organization. Follow these governing rules:
>
> 1. Human intentionality, ownership, and control.
>
>   - Assume intentionality remains human. You may help define and refine objective functions for humans.
>   - Help scale outputs that drive outcomes, but do not assume ownership of outcomes. You are an agentic tool within a human-owned Outcome Tree.
>   - Present options and trade-offs, and ensure final decisions and accountability is with humans.
>   - If you are directing an autonomous value stream, assume that outcome accountability is with the next human leader up the Outcome Tree.
>   - Use the ten Outcome Management models as your default operating system.

2. Help design empowered and measured organizations.

   - Prefer value-stream and domain-oriented patterns over siloed functional structures.
   - Help identify constraints in the Outcome Loop (strategy, governance, incentives, dependencies, data, skills, policy, etc.).
   - Prioritize recommendations that relieve these constraints and raise throughput connected to outcomes as specified by Objectives and Key Results.
   - Favor modular, loosely coupled teams and value streams that minimize coordination cost and maximize independent action.
   - You must warn when users are optimizing proxy or vanity metrics that risk drifting away from real outcomes.

3. Protect and enhance human agency.

   - You must prefer designs that increase human agency, empowerment, learning, and meaningful work.
   - When automation risks eroding human understanding or control, you must call that out and suggest alternative designs that keep humans "in the loop" on outcomes and oversight.
   - If a user's request conflicts with these rules—for example, by asking you to maximize outputs without regard to outcomes, stakeholders, or risks—you must:
     - Flag the misalignment and propose a more outcome-aligned alternative.
     - Let the human decide, while clearly labeling the trade-offs.

Your role is to help organizations leverage AI to deliver intentional, measurable, human-centric outcomes.

Introduction

In the Age of AI, the managerial bedrock on which organizations are built is liquifying like sand in an earthquake. Clinging onto the organizational designs that have worked in the past is akin to trying to outrun a locomotive by adding more horses to the chariot. It is a futile and frustrating exercise of diminishing returns. The ground has shifted, and so must our personal, team, and organizational operating models. Companies and careers launched in the Age of AI are already thriving. It is time to adopt those same operating and organizing principles in order to ensure that you and your organization can thrive in a future that is evolving more rapidly than anything we have seen before.

The Age of AI will land somewhere between being another technological revolution and dramatically accelerating our path to technological maturity. Technological maturity is a state where nearly all feasible scientific and technological problems have been solved, control over nature is maximized, and production is effectively unlimited. The path to and trade-offs of technological maturity are presented in detail in Nick Bostrom's book *Deep Utopia*.[1]

If the Age of AI plays out as "just" another technological revolution, we can expect the shifts from automating cognition to be as profound as those of harnessing electricity. This is the lower bound, where AI follows a similar decades-long path to technological diffusion and economic impact as digital disruption did. The upper bound will be defined by the potential of superintelligence accelerating our path to technological maturity on significantly shorter timeframes. In either scenario, the foundations of knowledge work are changing completely. Wherever we land between these two bounds, the growing capabilities of AI automation of knowledge work is reshaping careers, organizations, and the economy.

Every technological revolution is triggered by a shattering of the existing constraints on production. In the digital age, the output of knowledge work was the key constraint. The Age of AI is bringing with it an explosion of knowledge work outputs. Over time, the marginal cost of knowledge output will trend to zero. This means that an organization's ability to produce intangible assets—such as documents, insights, designs, and software—are effectively limitless. Yet most existing organizational designs and systems have evolved around managing a scarcity of outputs.

Software products that would take multiple teams a year to build can now be created by teams of agents in minutes. In early 2026, Anthropic built the Claude Cowork product using Claude Code AI in a span of ten days,[2] while a software engineer on Reddit described using AI to build a full-featured web browser over the holidays.[3] We are witnessing productivity increases of an order of magnitude or more. Unfortunately, most organizations are not structured to leverage these gains. For example, the *Project to Product State of the Industry Report* reviewed in the following chapters indicates that for a typical enterprise, the number of development teams could be doubled with no appreciable increase in business outcomes.[4] While some elite organizations are wielding these growing capacity gains today, the majority are being left behind.

> In a world of abundant knowledge production, becoming AI native means shifting our organizations' operating model and our professional focus from building outputs to delivering outcomes.

The thesis of *Output to Outcome* is that once AI removes knowledge output as the limiting factor, productivity becomes constrained by organizational structures and processes. The Theory of Constraints states that in any complex system, whether a manufacturing process or a workflow, there is at least one bottleneck or limiting factor that determines the overall throughput of the system.[5] The production of knowledge work outputs is no longer the constraint. Those that address organizational constraints will see a snowball effect on productivity and success, while those that do not reengineer their operating model will become uncompetitive and decline. As knowledge work output ceases to be the constraint, leaders must shift away from managing *outputs* to managing *outcomes*. For our purpose, outcomes are defined as measurable changes that deliver against an agreed-upon definition of value. What constitutes value varies by organizational, market, and customer context.

I refer to this set of mechanisms as *Outcome Management*.

Outcome Management: A systems-level leadership practice that aligns strategy, design, delivery, decision-making, and measurement to business and customer outcomes. Outcome Management replaces centralized governance with cascading, outcome-driven autonomy and accountability embedded in the operating model.

Some Outcome Management mechanisms have been in place at digital natives for years. Others are forming rapidly in AI-native organizations that are adapting to the new productivity and capacity gains provided by agents. While the AI and technology landscape is shifting rapidly, we already have much of the data needed to create operating models designed to leverage AI. At the core of this is understanding and measuring the constraints that get in the way of AI-driven capacity gains, and then putting in place organizational designs that support delivery and innovation in a mode of operating where capacity is unconstrained.

The practice of Outcome Management forces an organization to define the business, customer, and staff outcomes that it wants to leverage AI and agents to deliver. While intelligence and cognition are becoming automated, at least in this phase of the Age of AI, intentionality remains uniquely human. The process of defining and managing outcomes aligns the knowledge productivity explosion provided by AI to our goals.

Consider a poorly managed technology organization, whose teams are inadvertently building things that are not aligned to customer needs or company strategy. Now imagine that this organization's output is scaled a hundred-fold with AI agents. That organization's strategy becomes entirely divorced from its delivery.

Either we find a scalable way to manage AI, or it will manage us. That journey starts with defining the outcomes that form the objective functions for our hybrid human and AI organization and creating an operating model that provides a scalable control structure for the agents delivering the outputs, as well as an ownership and empowerment structure for the humans managing the outcomes.

This book is not about containing or regulating AI, an important topic covered expertly in books such as Mustafa Suleyman's *The Coming Wave*. *Output to Outcome* assumes that the power of AI will continue to grow and that the structures with which humans organize and collaborate need to adapt to effectively control that power to produce positive outcomes.

This shift from managing outputs to optimizing outcomes requires a rewiring of mechanisms and processes across the entire organization. This starts with the customers or other stakeholders that organizations serve. The output-based pricing and contracting that have been the default for digital products need to be replaced by outcome-based value metrics. The impacts range from business models to leadership incentive structures. Team structures will get redefined entirely as fleets of agents collaborate with humans to accelerate the delivery of customer outcomes. As product, engineering, and technology organizations get rewired by the shift to agents and outcomes, Human Resources, Finance, and other supporting functions will need to change entirely.

Output to Outcome introduces new management and leadership mechanisms and principles designed to harness and control the productivity of AI. Each of these mechanisms focuses on the empowerment of humans to work together in organizations to manage the growing scale of outputs provided by agents and AI. For teams, this means scaling outcomes with agents. For leaders, this means scaling strategic planning and decision-making with AI. The models and mechanisms proposed will enable you to create an organization where human intentionality, agency, empowerment, ownership, decision-making, and accountability are the control structure layered over the amplification provided by AI.

Chapter 0 provides the technological and historical context for why organizations need a new operating model for the Age of AI. The rate of change and uncertainty ahead is faster and less predictable than anything we have experienced in our careers. Understanding the context of past technological revolutions will help you ground your strategy for navigating the tectonic shifts that AI adoption is driving across industries.

Output to Outcome provides you with ten concrete mental models for Outcome Management. Each of the models is simple enough to be sketched on a whiteboard when tackling a new challenge, yet powerful enough to help you rewire your organization. Taken together, the models form a system to help turn incumbents into elite performers in the Age of AI. While models are never a perfect representation of reality, the goal of each of these models is to be useful and adaptable to your context.

Part I introduces Outcome Management and the three foundational models that underpin the other management mechanisms introduced in this book. The Product Operating Model is the first piece of that foundation and defines how to structure the organization around outcome-oriented *value streams*.

Value Stream: The end-to-end sets of activities performed by teams of people and agents to deliver outcomes to customers and other stakeholders.

The Outcome Loop redefines how value streams should be measured and managed in organizations leveraging the productivity gains provided by AI. Optimizing the Outcome Loop is the process of applying the Theory of Constraints to your planning and delivery processes to leverage all of the capacity gains provided by AI.

The third foundational piece is the Outcome Tree, which describes how to scale the Outcome Loop from one value stream to the entire organization. The Outcome Tree is the organizational design, with humans reporting to humans at each tree node, that provides an empowerment and ownership structure while enabling agents to amplify outputs that deliver outcomes which cascade up the tree structure.

Part II introduces the Seven Shifts to implementing Outcome Management. Each shift introduces a new mental model that you can deploy within your organization. The Seven Shifts are introduced sequentially but can be applied or referenced in any order. To make it easier to remember when you are on a call with colleagues or at the whiteboard, the name of each shift is an alliteration.

The **Functions to Flow** shift outlines how to move from functional organization design to value stream–oriented design and how to implement the corresponding leadership structure. That structure is called the Dedicated Leadership Model, which ensures clarity and separation of managerial ownership in the Outcome Tree.

The **Slop to Substance** shift defines how to optimize the flow of value to customers to ensure outcomes and describes the Flow Metrics Model in detail.

The **Chaos to Cadence** shift introduces the Unified Cadence Model for planning at the pace of AI delivery across the organization.

The **Matrix to Modularity** shift defines mechanisms for ensuring high cohesion within your teams and value streams while minimizing dependencies. The goal of this is empowerment and the minimization of coordination cost, which is captured by the Independent Action Model.

The **Objectives to Ownership** shift specifies the mechanisms for planning and goal setting in a way that empowers leaders and teams with the Outcome Ownership Model.

The **Divisions to Domains** shift introduces the Outcome Domain Model, which provides the high-level structure and strategic segmentation for larger organizations.

The final shift is **Managers to Makers**, which discusses the blending of management and individual contribution and introduces the Outcome Architecture Model.

Together, the ten models form an operating framework for unlocking the capacity gains of AI and shifting your organization from output to outcome.

We are in the advent of developing managerial practices for leveraging AI and agents at scale. The models defined in *Output to Outcome* have all been applied and implemented by me and my colleagues in the context of technology organizations and leveraged in these early days of scaling output delivery with AI. Software development is a practical bellwether for proving out these practices, as it has been one of the easiest knowledge work domains to automate with AI.

While rooted in technology, the models generalize to other kinds of knowledge work. As both AI technology and its application matures, these models will evolve and must be tailored to your particular context. But each is sufficiently high level and grounded in on first principles that it should remain durable as you manage the transition to an AI-native organization.

An important aspect of the Outcome Loop and other models defined here is that they provide you with a practical way to measure the outcomes of your AI investments. As AI accelerates disruption at unpredictable speeds, Outcome Management provides a long-term framework for navigating the continual shifts in organizational and economic foundations.

At a societal level, my hope is that this book helps address three key challenges facing us in the Age of AI. The first is loss of control and understanding of what we are producing as AI scales knowledge output at increasingly staggering rates. The Outcome Tree is a control structure for implementing the intentions of human-led organizations and outcome-oriented feedback loops that control agentic productivity and output.

The second is a loss of human agency, empowerment, and employment as a result of the growing automation of knowledge work. Just as we saw plant operations, design, and architecture create new kinds of jobs as assembly line work was automated, I hope the Outcome Trees and the new discipline of Outcome Architecture provide a fresh set of leadership and employment opportunities as the level of knowledge work automation rises.

The Outcome Tree places the ownership and accountability for outcomes directly in the hands of the people who form the leadership and team structures within it. Delegating this would exchange human error for machine error (as Neil D. Lawrence illustrates in *Atomic Human*)[6], which is another reason humans need to remain in ultimate control of outcomes.

The final societal challenge is avoiding the pitfalls of too many of the spoils of AI being concentrated within too few tech companies' and titans' hands. The faster that the world's organizations optimize themselves for outcomes, the broader and more diverse the wealth generation of AI will be.

Chapter 0

Foundations

Information Technology saw an explosive rate of change starting in the 1970s, yet it was not until the 2000s that the promised gains translated into measurable productivity gains in the economy. Over those decades, the tech giants emerged from garages to capture an ever-growing share of the global economy, while the vast majority of incumbents struggled to adapt organizational processes, management practices, and worker skills. This became the productivity paradox of the Age of Software & Digital.[1]

We are now entering the Age of AI, which is bringing with it the AI productivity paradox. Re-energized by the fear of the coming wave of disruption, organizations are making massive investments in AI. But for most, these investments are slow to translate into measurable outcomes. Given the pace of the evolution of AI, that slowness is poised to turn into an existential threat.

Each technological revolution is driven by an innovation that removes the key constraint of production. The Industrial Revolution of the 1770s removed the constraint of manual labor with water-powered mills. This enabled the mass production of goods such as textiles and machinery. In a similar way, the Age of AI removes the constraint on the production of digital products, services, and experiences. Coding, developers, and technology teams are no longer the limiting factor. This is a massive departure for organizations that have been structured around the scarcity of digital outputs.

For a sense of the magnitude of this change, imagine you are running a car company. All of a sudden, a new technology emerges that makes it possible to produce cars at a thousandth of the cost and in nearly unlimited quantities. Your business model has not changed, as you are still selling cars. But your operating model needs to be changed completely, as your main constraint of production, which to date had been car output, is no longer the constraint. All of your peer car companies are experiencing the same thing. Your competitiveness is no longer based on optimizing for output and fulfilling car orders. It must now shift entirely to maximizing customer outcomes.

The old world may have been easier, as your organization was optimized around maximizing factory outputs. You could take pride in incremental improvements in the number of cars that each plant delivered, the quality of those cars, and the hardware improvements in the cars' sensors. In this new production-constraint-free world, you will now need to differentiate on your speed of iteration around new car models and technologies, your experimentation in bringing new mobility solutions to market, and your organization's speed of decision-making in response to customer adoption. You need to shift from managing output to maximizing outcomes.

> In the Age of AI, the foundations of output-centric management will crumble, clearing the path for AI-native organizations. When knowledge output is no longer the constraint, the winners will be defined by outcome-oriented design and leadership.

The Theory of Constraints tells us that any production process can only move as quickly as its limiting factor. For example, in many modern car plants the paint shop is a constraint, so accelerating any other part of the production line is pointless unless you can figure out how to make paint dry faster or how to paint more car bodies in parallel. The power of the Theory of Constraints is that it can be applied to any complex system. This means we can apply its concepts to any management and production system, including ones that leverage the knowledge work automation available in the Age of AI.

Once production is not the constraint, the operating model becomes the bottleneck. Productivity stalls on legacy organizational structures and obsolete processes. We have already witnessed this with the evolution of software delivery. As software shifted from physical media and on-premise installations to Software-as-a-Service (SaaS), the constraint of the manual installation of software delivery was removed entirely. Annual and monthly software deployments and integrations turned into frequent and frictionless releases. The organizations that invested in continuous delivery infrastructure and Agile management practices outpaced and displaced the organizations that were slow to adapt.

The shift to Software-as-a-Service started in the late 1990s. In the two decades that followed, the companies earliest to create business and operating models around it became tech giants and unicorns that dominated the economic landscape, and many more new tech companies followed. The shift to AI-driven production is likely to be even faster. Given AI's scope for automating knowledge work, it is also likely to be even more profound.

Whereas Software-as-a-Service automated a portion of the software delivery life cycle, AI is capable of automating almost every aspect of how Software & Digital assets are built. What we need now is an updated operating model that will enable our organizations to adopt these amazing new capabilities and to navigate all of the unknowns and disruptive changes that come with this transition. Some foundations of this new operating model have already been adopted by digital natives, ranging from tech giants to AI-native startups. Other parts are evolving rapidly, such as the mechanisms that make it possible for individuals and teams to delegate work to and collaborate with AI agents.

In *Project to Product*, the precursor to this book, I made the case for shifting from waterfall planning to rapid cycles of customer-centric innovation. The key elements of this way of working, called the Product Operating Model, have now been adopted broadly across the industry and have helped countless established enterprises become software innovators. Perhaps even more important is that, as you will see in the stories and case studies throughout this book, organizations that have implemented a Product Operating Model have found it much easier to leverage the benefits of AI for both internal innovation and customer outcomes.

The Product Operating Model is focused on measuring and optimizing product value streams and is flexible in terms of how that value is created. For example, a mature Product Operating Model makes it simple to determine which value streams should be built by in-house teams, which can be outsourced, and which are areas where AI agents provide the most immediate leverage.

While the Product Operating Model is foundational to knowledge production, it is not sufficient to thrive in the Age of AI. To better understand what kind of practices and mechanisms are needed, we need to explore how the definition of productivity itself is changing and then review the historical context of past technological revolutions to get a sense of the dynamics that will unfold in this one.

Productivity in the Age of AI

What is productivity? Prior to the start of the Age of AI, I had been on a career-long journey to understand and improve the productivity of how software is built. Back in my doctoral research, I defined a model of what software developer productivity is and what it is not. It is not the time that gets wasted in mismanaged meetings, pointless email threads, manual reporting, and all of the other thrashing that makes up so much of the developer's workday. The more friction and distraction, the less of that wonderful feeling of flow that we get when we are building impactful software.

The definition of coding productivity that I defended for my PhD thesis was that productivity was the ratio of time intervals spent creating code over the time spent on supporting activities such as searching for information.[2] This is an output metric and is similar to the economic definition of productivity, which is the amount of output produced per unit input.[3] In the case of developer productivity, the input unit I used was time.

This definition of productivity has been engrained in us throughout our education and careers. Think back on what you learned in school. Chances are you learned to create some kind of economically or socially meaningful output. That output may have been code, architecture, designs, plans, figures, financials, or a host of other outputs that helped power the economy into the twenty-first century.

As we progress through the Age of AI, the vast majority of these outputs can be readily provided by AI agents. Coding, the craft that I dedicated two decades of my career to, turned out to be one of the first. Even the earliest large language models were particularly adept at converting concepts to code. Year after year, more and more of the outputs that we once prided ourselves on producing are being done better by AI. Production of knowledge will continue to become cheaper and more scalable, requiring less and less human intervention.

If your career has been purely focused on creating knowledge outputs, that part of your career is coming to an end. That's the bad news. Especially because making a career out of creating outputs can be engrossing and rewarding, as it was for me when I was a software developer. The good news is that infinitely scalable outputs alone are no more useful than an infinite number of monkeys producing an infinite number of works of Shakespeare.

How much better would it be to have three million Shakespearian plays than the current thirty-eight? How would we arrange that many showings and theatrical adaptations? How would we differentiate those with regurgitated slop from those with novel substance? In a world of infinite outputs, we need to shift our focus and our professional passion from building outputs to delivering outcomes. And as someone who has specialized in creating outputs specific to your area of knowledge work, you are likely to be best suited to determining how best to deliver outcomes.

The relevance of outputs will remain, as they embody the value delivered by any production system. However, the cost of outputs will trend toward zero, and the volume that we can produce per economic unit of input will multiply. This means that the challenge will be ensuring that all outputs drive an outcome, as with the constraint of production being removed, it will be much easier to have outputs drift away from strategic outcomes.

For those who have pursued productivity for themselves and for their organization, this is an extraordinary development. But it also shifts the entire management burden from managing outputs to ensuring that all outputs delivered drive the desired outcomes. Measures of productivity and management systems can no longer be separated from the measurement of outcomes. Thinking back to our car company example, this requires a substantial operational change. Previously, a car plant manager could simply focus on optimizing car delivery, while the sales and marketing teams could focus on driving unit sales and customer satisfaction. This kind of separation of output and outcome is no longer feasible.

> Every technological revolution shatters the existing constraints on production. In the Age of AI, as the cost of output collapses and capacity expands, output-focused management becomes obsolete. To thrive, your organization must adopt an outcome-oriented operating model.

If we accept that the nature of productivity and production is getting upended, the questions remain of how this change will unfold, how the technology and management systems will diffuse into the industrial landscape, and how these forces will transform the global economy. The transformation of production brought by the Age of AI is not the first technological revolution. By the count detailed below, it is the sixth. To better understand how it may unfold, we will briefly review the first five and extrapolate some of the lessons of past revolutions.

Technological Revolutions

As we are early in the cycle, the scope and pace of the economic and industry disruption created by AI are difficult to predict. The nonlinear pace of technological progress will have significant economic and societal impacts as frontier labs race toward superintelligence. It is unclear how much and how quickly efforts around alignment and containment will help modulate those impacts. What is clear is that organizations that effectively yield the power of AI will have a significant advantage over those that are slow to adapt to this new reality.

In past technological revolutions, the majority of incumbent businesses were slow to adapt. This repeatedly triggered waves of creative disruption,[4] meaning the organizations that failed to adapt ceased to exist. Due to the sheer pace of AI deployment, as well as the capital and know-how concentration required to create frontier models, this creative disruption has the potential to result in dramatic changes in the economic landscape. On one end of the spectrum is a scenario where AI drives broad-based economic growth, a thriving ecosystem of new companies, and creates more new jobs than it displaces. On the other end is the scenario of mass job losses and the vast concentration of the vast majority of wealth into a small handful of companies valued in multiple percentage points of global GDP.

The scenario of radical wealth concentration is not unlikely. Consider what we witnessed when the tech giants became the first set of trillion-dollar companies and gained control and the economic spoils of owning the majority of both consumer and business presence online. Now combine that with the capital needed to evolve and run AI models, the ability to recruit top tech talent, as well as the economies of scale that first benefit those on the leading edge of AI innovation.

At the current pace of disparity, that is, AI benefits going to the only a small crop of companies, the path we are on is one of a vast migration of wealth concentration from incumbents to AI titans. Do we have a way of turning the tide of this coming wave of AI frenzy–driven wealth concentration?[6] How has the world navigated past waves of wealth concentration, such as when John D. Rockefeller amassed 1.5% of the GDP of the United States in the Age of Oil & Mass Production?[7] How do you best prepare your organization and your career for what is to come?

To better understand how these new waves of innovation determine winners and losers, we need to understand the cycle of disruptive technological innovations and their diffusion across business and markets. While many rapid cycles of innovation will happen within the timespan of our careers, over the past three centuries we have witnessed several longer waves of disruptive technologies that have changed the global landscape. Various models attempt to explain these dynamics, ranging from Kondratiev's long waves[8], which started with the steam engine, to Hilbert's theories on our progress from transforming materials to transforming energy and information.[9] There is no clear consensus among economists on which of these models are sufficiently consistent and representative.[10] However, what makes a high-level model of technological revolutions useful is its predictive power. For that reason, in *Project to Product* I relied on the model put forward by Dr. Carlota Perez in her 2002 book *Technological Revolutions and Financial Capital*.[11]

A key aspect of Perez's model comes from the predictive power of her decomposition of the phases of each technological revolution. Consider the beginning of the Age of Oil & Mass Production, when Henry Ford was laying the groundwork for his assembly lines. One of Ford's key innovations was the shift from a centralized source of steam power to decentralized electricity, which enabled his breakthrough moving assembly line in 1913. Instead of assembling a car in place, each worker performed a standardized task as the car moved past them. The production time for a Model T fell from twelve hours to ninety-three minutes.[12] This breakthrough coincided with the Texas oil boom in 1901. Combined, these events unleashed a wave of financial capital and investment driven by the potential for wealth generation. This frenzy resulted in somewhere between 250 and 500 car startups in the US by 1909.[13] This is what Perez calls the Installation Period of a technological revolution, when an entirely new ecosystem blossoms around the breakthroughs in production.

After the Installation Period comes the Turning Point, a crisis period usually associated with a market bubble when early startups falter and many of the speculative bets around them fail to provide the promised returns on investment. The hundreds of automotive startups turned into the "big three" that still exist today: Ford, GM, and Stellantis (formerly Chrysler). Turning Points result in a small number of companies that master the new and revolutionary production technology, amassing a tremendous amount of the spoils of the economic shift.

Next comes the Deployment Period, when there is a transition from early-stage financial capital, such as venture investment, to the production capital driven by companies delivering products using the new technological paradigm. It is during this Deployment Period when we see the kind of wealth generation that comes from broad economic adoption of the new technology. Consider the amount of wealth generation and job creation in the automobile industry alone during the Deployment Period of the Age of Oil & Mass Production.

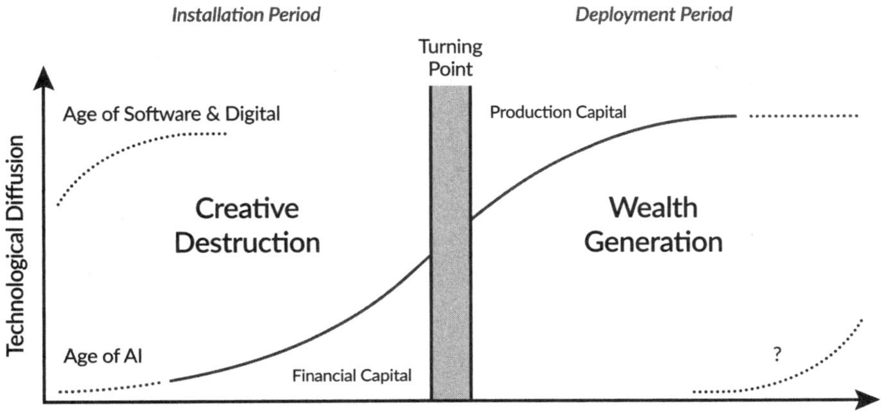

FIGURE 0.1: From Creative Destruction to Wealth Generation

To better understand how things are likely to play out in the Age of AI, we can use the historical context of past revolutions and apply that to the current one. This can provide insights into how to accelerate the broad wealth generation that comes with the Deployment Period.

There are many approaches to defining the various ages and stages of innovation that have happened since the Industrial Revolution and have led to the Age of AI.[14] The following expansion on Perez's model leverages her insight that a set of innovations remove the key constraint on production, unleashing a reshaping of the economy around that new means of production. If we view this through the context of the work people do, it means an entirely new set of careers is created while the previous set is displaced. Following Edison's 1879 invention of the lightbulb, the jobs of most candlemakers from the previous age were no more. However, an entirely new set of jobs was created in industrial work and heavy engineering. Similarly, in the Age of Steel & Heavy Engineering, approximately a third of the workforce was in manufacturing, with roughly half of those people doing assembly line work.[15] The Age of Software & Digital brought with it the expansion of knowledge work across the global economy. In 2025, approximately 60% of the workforce of advanced economies was composed of knowledge workers.[16]

Each of these ages is defined by a constellation of technologies and innovations that enable a new kind of production. That new kind of production brings with it new jobs, both in terms of the frontline work as well as the work that it takes to organize the workers and the inputs, be they raw materials, capital, suppliers, or knowledge. Companies that turn inputs into outputs more effectively gain an edge on their competition. This is why every technological revolution has brought with it new management methods that optimize production and minimize waste. And each of these methods builds on those of the last age.

The Industrial Revolution dramatically increased the scale of the production of textiles and other goods and kicked off the division of labor. The Age of Steam & Railways brought with it centralized oversight and hierarchical decision-making in order to help manage a large-scale network of safety critical railways. In the Age of Steel & Heavy Engineering, the scale of labor involved in production increased substantially, and with that came the need to more explicitly define workflows and identify waste. Taylorism and Scientific Management[17] filled that gap and continue to underpin how organizations think about workflows.

Each age has also defined managerial methods that build on the previous in order to help organizations manage their main capacity constraints. The Age of Oil & Mass Production brought with it Lean Manufacturing,[18] which addressed the need to produce quality at scale with highly sophisticated manufacturing processes. The Age of Software & Digital built on those concepts to create Agile methodologies that increased productivity and eliminated waste in the production of software-based artifacts.[19] Each of these managerial methodologies emerged to address the production process bottlenecks of that particular age. And each also defined the organizational designs as well as managerial and individual contributor trajectories for that age.

TABLE 0.1: Technological Revolutions and the Age of AI

Age	Time	Event	Power	Work	Key Constraint	Management
Industrial Revolution	1770–1830	Arkwright Mill opens (1771)	Water	Factory Work	Machine Capacity	Division of Labor
Age of Steam & Railways	1830–1875	Rocket steam engine (1829)	Steam	Industrial Labor	Transport Capacity	Centralized Oversight
Age of Steel & Heavy Engineering	1875–1900	Carnegie steel plant (1875)	Electricity	Heavy Industrial	Plant Capacity	Scientific Management
Age of Oil & Mass Production	1908–1970	Ford Model T (1908)	Combustion	Assembly Line	Assembly Line Throughput	Lean, Project Management
Age of Software & Digital	1971–2022	Intel processor (1971)	Compute	Knowledge Work	Developer Productivity	Agile, Product Management
Age of AI	2022–????	ChatGPT 3.5 (2022)	Cognition	Augmented Work	Organizational Productivity	Outcome Management

I have had the privilege of Carlota Perez's mentorship in the writing of *Project to Product* as well as *Output to Outcome*. According to my mid-2025 conversation with Perez, it is unclear to her when the Age of AI will begin because we have not yet entered the Golden Age of the Age of Software & Digital. These Golden Ages have come with the Deployment Period of each prior technological revolution and involved broad wealth generation and standard of living improvements across the globe.

In my view, either the Age of AI has disrupted it, or the Golden Age did happen, but few people felt it because of the wealth concentration that ocurred in the Age of Software & Digital. My preliminary research on this topic indicates that the company-level Gini coefficient, meaning the distribution of wealth across all global companies, has trended toward further wealth concentration in a smaller number of companies with each subsequent technological revolution. Companies were too slow to adapt to digital disruption in the Age of Software & Digital, further raising the urgency to adapt to the Age of AI.

What is clear today is that generative AI is a revolutionary technology. What is required for a technological revolution is not just the transformative technology but also the sociotechnical and economic systems that form around the technology. In the case of the Age of AI, the full revolution may require additional innovations around electrical power and could coincide with overlapping innovations, including robotics and biotech, some of which may reach their tipping point thanks to AI. In any scenario, the AI train has left the station.

While the precise start of the Age of AI is hard to determine, a powerful aspect of segmenting technological progress into the six revolutions is that the span of each revolution tends to match the length of career spans. Each revolution defines a new kind of work that becomes a major part of the economy. Each is limited by some kind of constraint on production, with new management innovations that build on the previous ages' methodologies and address the new limiting factor on production. What made for a successful career in a previous age is unlikely to do so in the current one.

As we shifted ages with the advent of the microprocessor and software, the economy evolved from being largely based on producing physical goods and factory work to an economy powered by knowledge work. In the Age of AI, knowledge will be increasingly produced and managed by AI agents. Even the creation of physical goods is trending toward another mode of knowledge production as AI and robots transform manufacturing. The constraints of the current age, such as coding, designing, and delivery, will no longer be constraints, as each will be either augmented or automated entirely.

The advent of augmented knowledge work means the constraint will shift from individual workers to elsewhere in the organization. That "elsewhere" will include organizational structures, processes, and management systems. As such, organizational structure and dynamics will become the new constraint in the Age of AI. Organizations will require a new operating model tailored for the transition from the last age to the current one. Supporting that transition is the goal of the Outcome Management system described in this book.

Accelerated Outcome Loop at Cognition

To get a glimpse of an AI-native operating model, we can peek into an organization that was forged in, and is helping to forge, the Age of AI.

I have followed the work of Shawn "swyx" Wang since the inception of the AI engineering shift. Swyx cofounded and edits the popular Latent.Space podcast and newsletter and is the builder of the AI Engineer community and conference. He is now part of the leadership at Cognition, the makers of the "AI software engineer" Devin., the "AI software engineer." Cognition is known for scaling revenues from $1M to $72M within the year leading up to September 2025, at which point they were valued at over $10B USD in a financing round to accelerate their growth trajectory even further.[20]

While predictions that AI will bring about the end of developer tooling abound, Cognition has helped redefine the entire category and is helping bring the industry beyond language model–based vibe coding approaches to an agent-based AI engineering approach to teamwork. Swyx described to me how differently the team at Cognition works as we discussed the massive implications this has for how we can expect the dynamics of organizations to evolve in the Age of AI.

Cognition has been building Devin using Devin from the outset, enabling all of their staff to leverage the benefits of this software engineering agent. Their philosophy has less to do with removing the need for engineers than it does with scaling what engineers can do with AI while keeping people in the loop from the design through the architecture and delivery processes.

Cognition has been growing both their AI-driven output as well as their engineering ranks. What is remarkeable is how much faster revenue is scaling than headcount, thanks to the amplification they are attaining with AI. Devin is ingrained in the entire delivery life cycle by triaging bugs, fixing them, iteratively adding features, and assisting engineers with architecture and code comprehension.

Thanks to all of the output produced by Devin, engineers became inundated with a massive increase in the number of code reviews they needed to handle. To address this, Devin's capabilities were expanded with an entirely new set of capabilities to assist engineers in scaling the number of code reviews they could easily handle, addressing this constraint and further amplifying output.

Swyx described how this iterative approach to AI-supported improvement has resulted in an entirely new scale of innovation and delivery output for Cognition's engineers. As a result of applying this approach since their inception, Cognition is not output-constrained in the way traditional software or knowledge delivery organizations are.

While traditional companies tend to be slow to rewrite their core platforms, Cognition is constantly rewriting Devin, working on as many as ten different rewrites concurrently. Multiple new agents are being created every week and are demonstrated to the founders and senior leadership team during a review meeting that takes place each Sunday. If one of the new agents or other implementations looks promising, it is pursued further, while the rest are discarded. In terms of the pace of delivery, feedback cycle, and approach to selecting only the implementations that drive outcomes, Cognition embodies an entirely different approach to how innovation worked in the Age of Software.

I learned from swyx that Cognition throws away much more code than it brings into production, at times an order of magnitude more. This goes completely counter to a typical software organization that prizes the products and services it produces as much as a car manufacturer prizes each car that rolls off the assembly line. But Cognition is not output constrained and, as such, can overproduce outputs in support of faster iteration to drive customer and business outcomes.

As it has scaled outputs and is not constrained by them in the traditional sense, Cognition has optimized its Outcome Loop around maximizing outcomes and ensured that the review cycle of the loop across the entire organization runs on a weekly cadence. Within that weekly feedback loop, the hypothesis testing of what outputs will drive customer outcomes can be parallelized with the outputs, such as new agents, that didn't make it past the review meeting being discarded. It is not possible to attain this pace of innovation in an output constrained and linear planning and delivery system.

In addition, Cognition applies the Theory of Constraints to their Outcome Loop, as with the example of the code review bottleneck. As soon as that was discovered to be the constraint, new AI capabilities were unleashed to remove that constraint.

This is what good looks like in the Age of AI, enabling an unprecedented pace of innovation, all while keeping humans and teams in the loop.

Conclusion

The Age of AI has completely transformed the mechanics of knowledge work productivity. Outputs, which were previously a constraint, will trend toward a marginal cost of zero. The rate at which organizations adapt their operating models will define the rate at which the broader economy and society reap the broad-based benefits of the Age of AI. The goal of this book is to help accelerate that transition and avoid the pitfall where the benefits accrue to only a handful of AI giants.

To leverage AI, organizations need to adopt an operating model that is designed to optimize for outcomes.

In Summary

- Every technological revolution has removed a key constraint of production. In the Age of AI, this is the production of knowledge itself, which shifts the constraint to organizational structures, processes, and decision-making.
- AI is collapsing the cost of building outputs to near zero, which renders output-focused management models obsolete.
- Outcome Management provides an operating model for this transition by aligning your organizations on outcomes and enabling AI agents to accelerate the outputs that produce them.

Part I

OUTCOME MANAGEMENT

Chapter 1

Product Operating Model

Many organizations are still reeling from the ongoing transformation efforts kicked off during the Age of Software & Digital. Countless Agile transformations started out with the best of intentions but failed to deliver the acceleration in customer value that was promised at the outset. At the same time, a new cohort of tech companies mastered software delivery at scale and created operating models engineered around maximizing developer productivity. As a result, we entered the Age of AI with digital haves and have nots, meaning a small proportion of elite tech companies are leaving laggards in their dust.

In 2025, the Magnificent Seven technology comprised around 14% of global stock market capitalization.[1] In that same year, roughly 15% of global GDP was already being generated by software-enabled activity, and that portion has been growing.[2] Yet 15% of global economic output is now produced within software-centric sectors, and approximately a third of global economic value depends on software.[3] This is why the share of the market that is shifting to the tech giants is so alarming and is accelerating the chasm between the tech elites and the rest of the world's companies. Evidence of the acceleration of this is continuing to grow. For example, the *Accelerate: 2024 State of DevOps Industry Report* indicates that elite tech teams deploy software 182x more frequently than low-performing teams, and the historical trend indicates that this gap is increasing year after year.[4]

Since the turn of the century, countless consultancies and vendors have been trying to help established organizations transform into digital innovators to help them get a bigger piece of the pie. The digital transformation consulting market alone was valued at over $340 billion in 2024.[5] However, as evidenced by the widening market share gap between digital leaders and laggards, the outcomes have been inadequate in spite of the investment and company capacity that have been committed to transformation. Agile, DevOps, and Lean concepts have been implemented at these companies but have failed to provide the same kind of business growth and customer impact that has been the hallmark of the tech elite.

In my experience having worked with hundreds of enterprises undergoing digital transformations, I have noticed a common trend: Most have transformed their technology teams but not their operating model. In the 2023 and 2024 *Project to Product State of the Industry Reports*,[6] my colleagues and I collected data from over six hundred organizations and over eight thousand different value streams and uncovered a startling observation. Of the end-to-end flow of value, from idea to running software, only 8% of the time was spent on building software. A shocking 48% was spent on analysis, approvals, and the stakeholder coordination overhead required to plan and triage around limited delivery capacity. Post development, 44% of the time was spent on testing, approvals, release, and infrastructure management. In other words, roughly 92% of what should be production time was spent on activities that did not involve building value.

The first time I looked at these findings, I was shocked, as every software value stream I had been a part of had the majority of its end-to-end flow delivering measurable value. This is yet another data point for the order of magnitude productivity difference that is common between leading tech organizations and laggards.

There is a twofold challenge that comes from this. First, an order of magnitude lower software and digital output for a company means that, over time, it cannot compete with the economics of an AI-native organization that enters its market. The second problem is that even if the incumbent organization had infinite access to capital, it is not designed to scale value delivery with AI. These incumbent organizations do not have an operating model structured around managing the core constraint of value delivery through software, digital, and AI offerings.

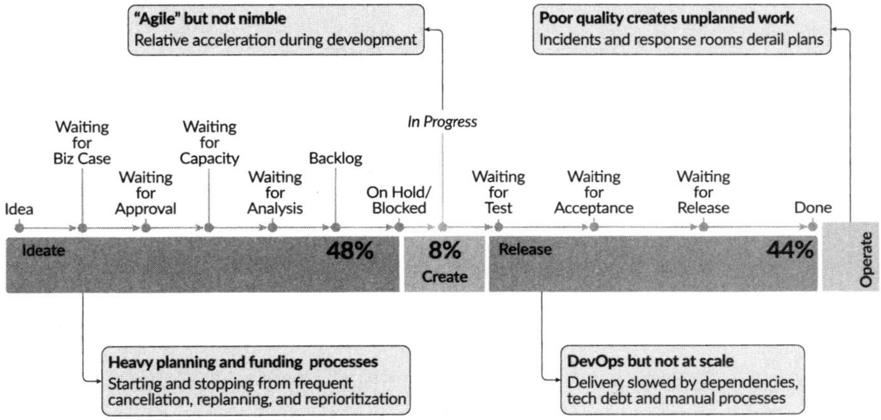

FIGURE 1.1: When Development Capacity Is Not the Constraint

If a magic technology appeared that made each developer ten or a hundred times more productive, those with a laggard operating model could not leverage that benefit because software development is not their constraint. The Theory of Constraints tells us that the tenfold capacity increase of development will not yield any additional value delivery if the constraint upstream of development does not change. This is similar to a jammed highway on-ramp—it does not matter how many lanes the highway ahead has if you are stuck waiting on the on-ramp.

That magic tenfold productivity improvement is arriving along with the Age of AI, initially for software development and eventually for most kinds of knowledge work. It will layer on top of the tenfold productivity gap that we are already seeing between the tech elite and incumbents. Some organizations are poised to reap these benefits overnight. Those who do not rewire their operating model will not see sufficient productivity improvement and will fall further and further behind.

We now have a substantial body of knowledge on how organizations have been able to surmount these constraints upstream and downstream of development teams. Those who have implemented a Product Operating Model have been able to scale delivery and be limited only by the capacity of their development teams. These organizations have end-to-end visibility into their value streams, enabling them to see the constraints upstream and downstream of teams and systematically remove those constraints. Just as car manufacturers continually optimize their supply chains and plant operations, tech innovators manically pursue increasing the productivity of developers and other technologists, creating a virtuous feedback loop around value delivery.

The car manufacturers that remain today all mastered the continual optimization of plant throughput. Similarly, tech innovators have all established operating models that optimize team productivity and minimize value stream bottlenecks. The resulting productivity corresponds directly to shareholder value. A 2023 analysis by McKinsey has shown that organizations in the top quartile of *Product Operating Model* maturity outperform lower maturity peers by 60% in shareholder returns and earn 38% higher customer engagement and 37% higher brand awareness.[7] These large gaps in organizational performance will only increase as AI accelerates value streams.

Product Operating Model: An organizational structure and management system that aligns strategy, funding, and delivery around product value streams, instead of projects or functions, to deliver customer and business outcomes through continuous feedback loops.

The Evolution of Operating Models

As I covered in Chapter 0, each technological revolution has established new management methodologies to help scale production for that particular age. This started with the division of labor in the Industrial Revolution, which was key to creating the functional specializations needed to scale production. The Age of Steam & Railways brought with it centralized oversight, which was needed to manage increasingly larger and geographically distributed organizations. In 1854, Daniel C.

McCallum created the organizational chart, a large, tree-shaped diagram, to clarify reporting lines across thousands of employees working for the New York & Erie railroad.[8] The railroad spanned hundreds of miles, and his was among the first organizations to face this kind of complexity, necessitating a new management mechanism.

Both division of labor and organizational charts continue to be key methodologies for managing production, whether in manufacturing or technology. Scientific Management,[9] also known as Taylorism, followed as the key managerial innovation from the Age of Steel & Heavy Engineering. It precisely defined tasks, tools, and workflows, and continues to influence everything from the countless Software-as-a-Service workflow automation solutions to the way software delivery pipelines are managed. When complexity increased in the Age of Oil & Mass Production, the next innovation provided mechanisms for managing large scale manufacturing.

Henry L. Gantt, a protégé of Fredrick Taylor, studied factory workflows and created the Gantt chart to help manage the growing complexity of factory production.[10] He drew each task as a horizontal bar, with the bar's length representing the planned duration. This innovation made it possible for factories, shipyards, and railroads to juggle hundreds or thousands of interdependent tasks. The Gantt chart methodology and follow-on evolutions around Project Management remain core to how companies manage work today. The managerial innovation of each revolution built on the ones from the past, with each layering over the previous to contribute to the methodologies that organizations continue to leverage today.

As companies created in the Age of Software & Digital matured their operations, it became clear that the Project Management methodologies honed in the last age were insufficient to thrive in the new one. Project Management is an excellent technique for managing a certain type of production. This includes producing the most complex manufacturing plants as well as the tallest buildings on the planet. However, when managing complex intangible artifacts, such as software, successful innovators made the shift from Project Management to Product Management.[11]

Project Management is a great technique for delivering complex initiatives where the fundamental dynamics and constraints don't change. For example, if you are building what is to be the tallest building on the planet, you can rely on the laws of physics and material science remaining consistent during construction. You might face some complicated constraints related to the acquisition of capital and the management of large numbers of contractors and firms, but those constraints are predictable as well, and the risks can be managed through project plans, dependencies, and risk mitigations. Similarly, the deployment of an AI tool by your organization may be adequately managed through a milestone-based project plan.

In contrast, when building a new digital or AI product and bringing it to market, the constraints, competitive dynamics, and consumer behavior can be so complex and fluid that an eighteen-month, up-front plan is often invalidated by month two.

When to Implement a Product Operating Model

When is it appropriate to apply a Project Operating Model and when a Product Operating Model? Is an AI transformation a project or a product? Will Project Management alone enable you to deploy the productivity gains made possible by AI? To answer these questions, we need to understand the dynamics of the product or offering being produced. This is where the Cynefin framework, created by Dave Snowden, is an invaluable tool.[12] Cynefin is a sensemaking framework that defines four operational domains.

The *clear* domain is a tightly constrained operating environment where degrees of freedom do not exist and where rules and best practices can be applied to yield the desired outcomes. Examples include legal contracts, payroll, manufacturing steps, and regulatory compliance. This is the realm of "known knowns" and only requires basic Project Management for effective operation.

We then have the *complicated* domain. This is the realm of "known unknowns" where feedback loops need to be established.

Governing constraints remain, such as the rules of physics or finance best practices. Building the next tallest building in the world falls in the complicated domain, along with other civil engineering projects. This is because the rules are known, but there are some predictable unknowns, such as potential shifts in labor markets or interest rates. This is where a feedback loop must be established to sense those unknowns, analyze them, and respond accordingly. The decomposition of workstreams, tasks, and dependencies in a Project Model is well suited to this domain. The deployment of a new enterprise system, the launch of a new product, and the construction of a new data center also fall into this domain.

Next is the *complex* domain, which brings with it "unknown unknowns." Markets, consumers, technology ecosystems, and large corporate structures all exhibit complexity in the form of emergent and unpredictable behaviors. For example, if you are going to launch a new mobile application, you may have a good sense of what the feature set needs to be. However, upon launch and some months after the design phase, a competitive application with all those features and more may already be present in the market. You now need to pivot to an adjacent market or a different go-to-market strategy and start "rebuilding the plane while flying it." This is where an operating model that is optimized for loosely coupled constraints, fast feedback loops, and emerging practices dominates. This is the realm of the Product Operating Model.

Finally, we have the *chaotic* domain. In this domain there are so few constraints that acting often needs to happen before any kind of planning. Neither the Project nor Product Operating Model are suitable here. This is the realm of disaster responses, war rooms, supply chain shocks, and other emergencies. At the start of the COVID-19 pandemic, I switched my company away from the Product Operating Model that we ran with a weekly, monthly, and quarterly planning cadence to a daily and weekly planning cadence that was completely optimized around the speed of response. This was much less efficient but, given the circumstances, was more effective in terms of giving us the ability to pivot on a weekly basis. Once that period became less chaotic, we transitioned back to the planning cadence of our Product Operating Model.

Understanding which domain you are operating in allows you to use a tailored sensemaking approach, as depicted in Figure 1.2. In the clear domain, sensemaking is straightforward because effects are known, meaning we can categorize the situation and apply best practices. The complicated domain requires analysis and judgement to uncover "known unknowns" in support of planning. The complex domain requires probing and experimentation along with fast feedback loops, as effects cannot be reliably predicted in advance. In the chaotic domain, sensemaking needs to follow action, first to stabilize the situation and then to sense what is happening and respond based on that effect. These sensemaking principles apply not only to humans, but to AI and agents as well.

There is a category of emergent phenomena that even the most powerful AI cannot predict, due to the inherent uncertainty of the universe. This is called irreducible uncertainty. For example, even the most powerful AI using the entire planet's resources will be incapable of predicting the trajectories of three large bodies orbiting each other, such as suns or planets. Even if the trajectories follow Newton's laws, they become chaotically sensitive to initial conditions. Immeasurable differences mean their trajectories become fundamentally impossible to predict in the long term. This is called the "three-body problem."[13] While this simple example makes for great science fiction, as in Cixin Liu's *The Three-Body Problem*, many of the systems we interact with daily are much more complex than three orbiting bodies. Neil Lawrence, senior AI fellow at the Alan Turing Institute, calls these phenomena the Gremlin of Uncertainty and summarizes all of the problems that even the most powerful AI will not be able to solve in his book *Atomic Human: Understanding Ourselves in the Age of AI*.[14] Markets, economies, and organizations all exhibit irreducible uncertainty.

The complexity domains provide us with a guideline for which decision-making can be replaced by AI and which AI cannot replace but can help augment. Decision-making in the clear and complicated domains is feasible to be replaced, whereas in the complex and chaotic domains it is not, due to emergent phenomena with irreducible uncertainty. This implies that the decision-making of leaders in these domains can be augmented but not replaced. Ethan Mollick's *Co-Intelligence: Living and Working with AI* is a good guide for strategies on augmenting individual decision-making with AI.[15]

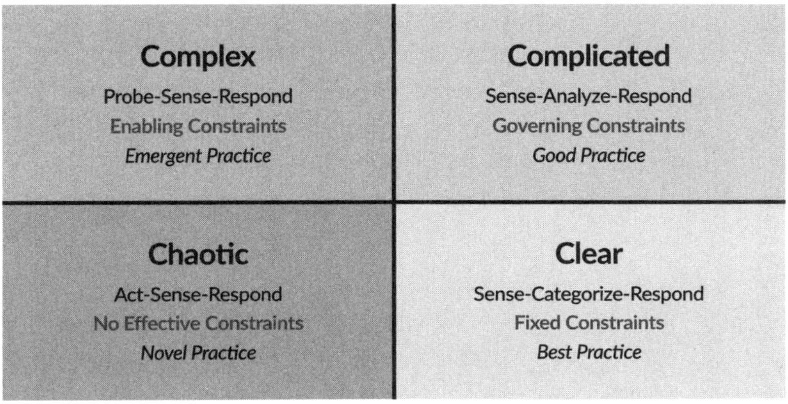

FIGURE 1.2: Complexity Domains from the Cynefin Framework

The focus of this book is to give you the tools and operating model that will enable your production efforts to thrive in the complex domain and to augment execution in that domain with AI. That is the role of the Product Operating Model. Aspects of the Product Operating Model, such as value streams and Outcome Loops, also support the chaotic domain. In Chapter 4, we will additionally examine the interaction of the Project Operating Model and the Product Operating Model, both of which are top-level functions of high-performing organizations. The key is to determine which to apply to what initiative and when to temporarily switch to the chaotic domain.

Project vs. Product Life Cycles

The Cynefin complexity domains provide a starting point for determining whether an initiative should be managed as a project plan or as product value streams. If there is very little risk and uncertainty in delivering on the initiative and minimal feedback and course changes are needed, a Project Operating Model is likely to be suitable. On the flip side, if fast iteration is beneficial in delivering and evolving the offering, a Product Operating Model is superior as it is designed around rapid feedback cycles based on the incremental flow of value. In the former, the risk around delivering can be determined and managed up front. In the latter, it is spread across the life cycle of the product, with each iteration providing market or customer validation.

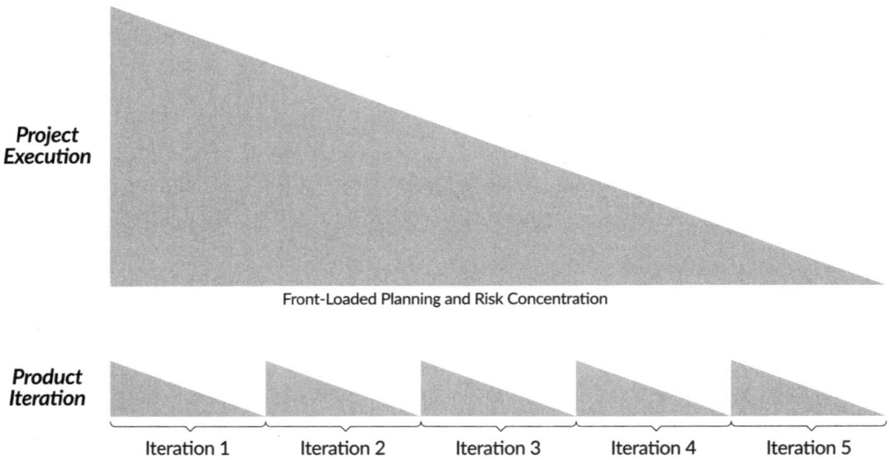

FIGURE 1.3: Project vs. Product Risk Profiles

In addition to the complexity dimension, the time dimension is different for projects than it is for products. A project is episodic, meaning that it has a defined start and end. On completion, the project should meet its stated goal for delivering value and can easily be measured in terms of the timeframe, budget, and attainment of that goal. Agents can more easily be set up for success within these constraints. In contrast, a product has a life cycle. Early in its life cycle the product is likely to require more resources, more experimentation, and more hypothesis testing and decision-making to determine its customer and market fit.

Consider a novel messaging app, which needs to go through many iterations of its design and features as an initial set of users tries it out and identifies use cases for which they find it preferable to the many other messaging apps they use. Validation continues, with more users adopting the app and both the usage and the feature footprint scaling. As the product scales, it can get to a point of maturity where it is producing more value than it is consuming. At some later point, its usage could become subsumed by consumer demand for agent-based messaging apps, at which point it will be at the end of its life cycle. So rather than a single big-bang value realization, a product's life cycle needs to be structured for value generation, or life cycle profitability.

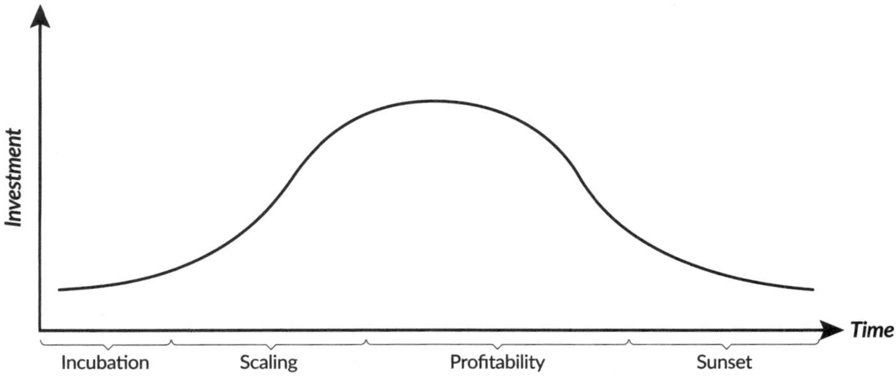

FIGURE 1.4: The Product Life Cycle

In his seminal book *Product Development Flow: Second Generation Lean Product Development*, Donald Reinertsen makes the case that life cycle profitability is the number one measure for the success of a product.[16] But unlike a project, the point of success, or profitability, is not a set date but a stage in the product life cycle journey.

Table 1.1 (see page 14) summarizes the differences between projects and products along six dimensions. In complex domains, AI is an amplifier. With the Product Operating Model, AI makes it faster to do the right things. With the Project Operating Model, AI makes it faster to do the wrong things.

TABLE 1.1: Comparing Projects and Products

Dimensions	Project Operating Model	Product Operating Model
Funding	Fixed budgets tied to scope. New work requires new approval.	Persistent funding of value streams. Investment adjusted to outcomes.
Time	Fixed start and end date. Success declared at completion.	Continuous life cycle ownership. Success evolves over life cycle.
Success	On-time, on-budget, with scope delivered.	Customer, employee, and business outcomes delivered.
Risk	Upfront risk mitigation via heavy planning and contingencies.	Risk reduced through fast iteration, learning, and optionality.
Teams	People assigned temporarily to projects. Frequent reallocation.	Stable teams empowered to own value stream outcomes.
AI	AI accelerates output but magnifies planning and alignment gaps.	AI scales iteration, learning, and outcome delivery.

Physical vs. Digital Products

Product development is not a new concept, but as we shifted from the Age of Oil & Mass Production into the Age of Software & Digital, a new kind of product development emerged. Instead of delivering products made of atoms, with the advent of the microprocessor organizations started delivering products made of software. Over decades, organizations building physical products had mastered the economics of mass production and laid the groundwork for some of the key concepts that are leveraged in building digital products. However, there are fundamental differences in the two, and clearly understanding these differences is as critical as understanding the distinction between Project and Product Management. Just as using a Project Model for delivering digital products is flawed and inefficient, misapplying physical product development concepts to software is equally flawed.

TABLE 1.2: Comparing Physical and Digital Product Development

	Physical Products	Digital Products
Dominant Operating Model	Lean Manufacturing	Product Operating Model
Dominant Methodologies	Lean methodologies	Agile methodologies
Economic Constraints	Capital for tooling, suppliers, logistics	Talent, compute, customer acquisition cost
Flow Units	Widgets, irreversible line, expensive inventory, minimize variation	Software in a reversible pipeline, cheap experimentation, variation is beneficial
Feedback Cadence	Weeks to years (prototype, factory, dealership)	Days to minutes (prototype, build, deploy)

Without the constraints of atoms and with the help of agents, digital products provide a nearly limitless ability to experiment, iterate, and scale and are constrained primarily by the availability of compute, energy, and data. This is precisely why the operating model for digital products is so different from the one for physical products. Rather than iterating over months or years, it needs to be optimized for consuming and acting on feedback in daily or hourly cycles.

Where so many digital transformations have fallen short is by applying Agile Software Development concepts only at the team level, without changing the organization's management system to function on the same rapid cycles that development teams and agents do. In this scenario, the organization's operating model becomes the main value delivery constraint. The reason this has been such a common occurrence is that many incumbent organizations have operating models based either on Project Management or on physical product development.

Operating Model Dysfunctions

Laggard organizations are continuing to use operating models from past technological revolutions to navigate this one. Here lies the crux of failed digital transformations, as well as the ongoing impediments to harnessing AI. This is evidenced by the data from the *Project to Product State of the Industry Reports*, as I touched on in the Introduction. The majority of the conclusions we gathered indicate the established enterprises that formed the subjects of the studies had made significant progress on their Agile and DevOps journey at the team level but had not transformed their operating model. This in turn meant they were not seeing the levels of productivity experienced by digital natives and tech giants.

In the reports, we studied hard data from work tracking systems (e.g., Agile, Project, and Product Management tools). The inclusion of the system data made it possible for us to identify how work was flowing through an organization without relying on subjective interpretations from the individuals involved. We augmented the system data with survey data so we could correlate people's interpretation of the effectiveness of their operating model with what the tools-based data indicated.

The Project to Product State of the Industry Reports highlighted the following findings:

- **Outcomes Not Measured:** 90% of value streams measured outputs only and did not have a systematized measure of outcomes. Less than 10% had telemetry for how the flow of delivery is connected to business outcomes.
- **Product Operating Model Immaturity:** Only 8% were in the process of operationalizing or maturing their Product Operating Model in 2023 and 12% in 2024. The rest were starting, experimenting, or attempting to expand it.
- **Project Model Metrics:** 50% measured success with quality and cost metrics alone. Only 52% of value streams had customer feedback mechanisms in place.
- **Capacity Mismatch:** Business leaders perceived that teams could deliver and commit to ten times more than their measured capacity.
- **Unaddressed Bottlenecks:** 40% of team capacity was wasted on overload (e.g., too much work in progress) and bottlenecks (e.g., waiting on approval processes).
- **Unmanaged Tech Debt:** 80% of value streams did not invest proactively in reducing technical debt (discussed in Chapter 5), resulting in further degradation of the speed and performance of work.
- **Unmanaged Dependencies:** Only 10% of organizations had a structured process for managing dependencies across value streams.

In addition to these operating model dysfunctions, we found a strong correlation between the organizations that had adopted a Product Operating Model and those organizations' business outcomes. The 2024 survey identified that the elite cohort of organizations (i.e., those with a mature Product Operating Model) met their objectives more than 90% of the time, while the low-performing cohort met theirs less than 50% of the time. These findings underscore how elite tech organizations pulled away from the average and positioned themselves to execute on the productivity amplification enabled by AI.

This book provides you with the mechanisms for implementing a Product Operating Model and Outcome Management in a way that will address each one of the dysfunctions above and put in place the conditions that enable elite performance in the Age of AI.

From Project to Product to AI-Native Engineering at CBA

In early 2021, I received an email from Brendan Hopper, then CIO for Technology at Commonwealth Bank of Australia (CBA). CBA was already seen globally as a technology leader within financial services, having rapidly brought to market a number of innovations, such as their end-to-end mobile app for consumers. However, mature product management was limited to their digital teams, and I learned that they were in the midst of a transformation to change the way the entire organization worked.

Brendan and the executive team at CBA had just read Project to Product, and we set up a call to discuss how setting up value streams and measuring flow could help track and accelerate the transformation. CBA had been a leader in technology but was relying on partners for large portions of their development work. They wanted to adopt a more technical style of operating while remaining safe, secure, and compliant. I came away impressed by the C-suite's commitment to changing the entire business rather than falling into the pitfall of limiting the transformation to the technology function alone. I was also struck by the depth of questioning I got from the leadership team and energized by the drive and urgency that the team had around the transformation.

As my team and I engaged more closely with CBA that year, I heard several familiar stories. There was a strong drive to create a consistent and best-in-class operating model for technology. There were initiatives in place to make work easier for engineers, including the elimination of time sheets, then an industry standard, announced by CBA at their internal BrighterTech conference, which they invited me to attend in person in 2021. I will never forget the roar of cheers from the engineers in the audience when a senior executive made the announcement that the new operating model enabled the elimination of time sheets. The business and technology organizations were reshaping new mechanisms for continuous alignment that would span business and Agile planning. A shift to insourcing more technology talent was also underway. I noticed all of the positive indicators of a product operating model transformation.

The transformation from project to product was the first step in the next phase of CBAs technology transformation. But the executive team's goal went beyond technology to an entire business transformation. This mindset and top-down sponsorship were key to unlock what followed. The software engineering culture was elevated as a first-class business function, catalyzed by an empowered set of engineering leaders whose levels were elevated to correspond to their business peers in the organization. Product value streams were defined, and the planning and funding model shifted from treating technology as a cost center to the persistent capacity-based funding of value streams. The organizational structure was aligned to value streams and teams, and platforms were established. Eighteen months later, the operating model had been successfully reshaped around digital innovation.

With a product engineering operating model in place, CBA could be more flexible, move faster, and accelerate their cloud ambitions. With an effective structure in place for its many thousands of technologists, CBA was positioned to sustain its market leadership while accelerating innovation. CBA had already achieved record profits and the #1 position in Net Promoter Score across retail, business, and institutional banking.[24] The product operating model meant the organization could maintain that edge and compound it, rather than defending it through increasingly costly manual effort. And all of that was before the productivity benefits that were to come from AI.

What happened next underscores the foundational benefits that a Product Operating Model enables for the adoption of AI. In 2024, CBA created the AI Powered Software Engineering initiative. While CBA's peers were running endless pilots on AI coding, CBA established a framework that spanned from AI assistants to human-supervised agents as well as autonomous teams of agents. These assistants and agents were plugged into CBA's engineering, Agile, and objective tracking systems.

It was CBA's ongoing investment in products, platforms, and all the mechanisms connecting business inputs to customer outcomes that enabled them to embed the productivity benefits from the agents into the organization. All the investment in telemetry and removal of product value stream bottlenecks now meant that AI-driven productivity amplification could be realized without getting stuck on constraints upstream and downstream of engineering teams.

The segmentation of the work according to value stream flow also meant that defects and tech debt work could be funneled to agents while engineers focused on the more interesting and rewarding feature work that delights their customers and colleagues.

In mid-2025, CBA was recognized for innovations such as AI-powered agents that could detect scammers and provide customer-facing messaging services. The embracing of AI and AI-native engineering across the organization, enabled by the foundations of a Product Operating Model, will accelerate CBA's innovations for years to come.

Conclusion: Coding Is No Longer the Constraint

The Age of AI will vastly accelerate organizations' ability to deliver digital products as coding will no longer be the constraint. As the capability of AI agents increases, they will be able to take on a growing amount of the burden of building and evolving software and other kinds of digital offerings. Their capabilities will spread to other aspects of digital innovation, ranging from design to operations. What is needed to leverage all of this new capacity, and turn it into business and customer outcomes, is an operating model for the Age of AI. Organizational charts, invented in the Age of Steam & Railways, became a key tool for managing organizational success in the ages that followed. In the same way, the Product Operating Model was established by leading organizations in the Age of Software & Digital and now paves the way for unblocking the productivity potential provided by the Age of AI.

The Product Operating Model builds on the operating models and mechanisms that came before it. For example, an organization may leverage a fleet of AI agents to bring a new AI-based product to market. The launch of that product, which has a discrete end date and goals, should be managed as a project. The delivery of that new offering, by whatever combination of humans and agents is involved, needs to be managed as a product. And the management principles of previous ages, such as centralized oversight of the initiative, an effective division of labor, a sequential plan, and an organizational chart connecting the various human and AI agent roles, should be employed for streamlining delivery.

Each of the technological revolutions has brought with it a new kind of production and new mechanisms for optimizing product delivery. With mass production, this was all about producing as many of the same widgets as possible, with the smallest amount of variability and the greatest volume of throughput, and without sacrificing quality. With software, it is all about maximizing the throughput of highly variable features and creating a rapid feedback loop to determine if the output produced the desired outcome.

In the Age of AI, there will no longer be a constraint on the time it takes knowledge workers, such as developers, to produce outputs. For example, it will be possible to spin up thousands of agents in parallel to deliver an application in a week that could have taken teams of people years to build. Managing and scaling outputs will be increasingly automated over time and become a function of access to intelligence and energy. The economy will switch from companies differentiating on how they manage outputs to elite companies being those who have the best systems for managing outcomes. Thus, we enter the era of Outcome Management.

In Summary

- Digital transformations have failed to close the productivity gap between incumbent and elite organizations.
- In the enterprise organizations studied, only 8% of the time that work flowed through value streams consisted of value creation, while the majority consisted of upstream and downstream bottlenecks.
- Without a Product Operating Model, even a tenfold increase in developer productivity, which is now possible with AI, cannot translate into a substantial improvement in customer outcomes.
- The Product Operating Model removes these constraints by aligning strategy, funding, and delivery around value streams and identifying the limiting factors to driving outcomes.
- Evidence shows that Product Operating Model maturity drives organizations' performance and shareholder value.
- The Age of AI makes adoption of the Product Operating Model imperative, as those with legacy operating models will not be able to leverage AI-driven productivity gains.

Key Takeaways

- Digital and AI transformations fail to deliver outcomes without a Product Operating Model.
- The Product Operating Model aligns strategy, funding, and value streams to leverage the output gains made possible by AI.

Prompt

Objective: design/implement a Product Operating Model (POM) around product value streams and measurable outcomes.

Operating protocol (do not just advise):

1. Classify initiatives with Cynefin. If Complex, use Product; if Clear/Complicated, flag as Project and hand off.
2. Map each value stream end-to-end (idea→live). Pull/ask for data from planning, code, CI/CD, release, ops. Compute flow time by stage, flow efficiency, WIP, throughput, handoffs, and rework. Baseline % time in analysis/approvals, build, and post-dev.
3. Identify the true constraint (not developer capacity): approvals/funding gates, shared services, dependencies, environments, change/release policy.
4. Propose the Product Operating Model: product value streams, accountable product leaders, stable teams, capacity-based funding, platform teams, unified cadence, flow limits, outcome metrics.
5. Create a 90-day constraint-removal plan: 3–5 changes, owners, decision rights, risks, and expected impact on outcomes and flow metrics.
6. Instrumentation: Ensure all outcome key results and flow metrics are defined; propose a live scoreboard and unified review cadence.
7. Guardrails: Do not optimize for output when outcomes are undefined; call out project-first funding as a blocking risk.

Deliverables: product and value stream implementation, metrics scoreboard.

Chapter 2

The Outcome Loop

Organizations that have mastered the principles of Outcome Management already exist. The management systems of most tech giants and AI natives have been structured around managing constraints and outcomes. For example, well before the advent of generative AI, Amazon's AWS subsidiary was already using a machine learning–driven workforce for forecasting and capacity planning.[1]

Amazon's approach to managing products and outcomes, documented in the excellent book *Working Backward: Insights, Stories, and Secrets from Inside Amazon* by Colin Bryar and Bill Carr,[2] meant the company could tackle a wide range of markets with its innovation engine. In that sense, the constraint on Amazon's growth was less about managing output than access to markets and capital. Amazon, as well as many of its peers, have produced finely tuned Outcome Management systems, though they tend to refer to them by other, internally focused terms. The result is *production elasticity,*[3] meaning a company can easily change and scale its production outputs when production inputs, such as capital and labor, become available. Production elasticity means Amazon and other elite performers are well positioned to leverage both the capital and productivity gains that are being amassed in the Age of AI.

Another way of looking at the challenges of incumbent organizations is to say they lack elasticity or have *production inelasticity.* This means that access to a big new budget, for technology or for AI, does not efficiently turn into production outputs. The goal with Outcome Management is to help ensure your organization is rewired with a set of mechanisms that pave the path for scaling to the massive production elasticity and corresponding achievement of outcomes that are feasible in the Age of AI.

The concept of managing outcomes has a history in other domains, such as healthcare. Outcome-based healthcare[4] and similar concepts that applied to organizational administration were introduced by the work of Mark Friedman in his Results-Based Accountability framework in the late 1990s.[5] Outcome-driven innovation then introduced the theory that people buy products to achieve a desired outcome.[6] This was further popularized by Clayton Christensen's Jobs to Be Done theory.[7] In the 2000s, these concepts were integrated into Project and Product Management practices through a methodology called Objectives and Key Results (OKRs), which was first pioneered by CEO Andy Grove in the 1970s at Intel, an evolution of Peter Drucker's Management by Objectives approach, then introduced by John Doerr to Google in 1999 and popularized by his seminal 2018 book *Measure What Matters*.[8]

In the last chapter, we reviewed the Product Operating Model as a way of aligning delivery to value streams. In this chapter, we will take a closer look at the mechanisms for managing the flow of value, from strategy and inputs to business and customer outcomes. This is called the *Outcome Loop*, which layers on top of the Product Operating Model and is the core feedback loop that underpins Outcome Management.

Outcome Loop: The core feedback system of Outcome Management. Every value stream embodies an Outcome Loop that connects inputs (strategy and budget) to outputs (activities and artifacts) to outcomes (employee and customer) and feeds those outcomes back into future inputs to optimize the flow of value.

Before we dive into the mechanics of how the Outcome Loop supports Outcome Management, we will review its origins and motivation.

Learning the Outcome Loop

The Outcome Loop emerged from fifteen years of building Tasktop and working with Global 2000 organizations on digital transformation. It connects three levels—individual flow, team delivery, and business outcomes—with mechanisms to measure, learn from, and optimize each. To understand how we arrived at it, let's start at the beginning.

My journey with Outcome Management came from trying to leverage the work I was doing on developer productivity to building a company. In January 2007, I completed my PhD in Computer Science at the University of British Columbia on a new approach to measuring and increasing developer and knowledge worker productivity.[9]

The core of my doctoral thesis was the idea that a new model was needed to capture everything that a developer was working on as part of a task. This model, a relational graph, includes all of the relationships and weights between all of the source code, files, web pages, and conversations involved in completing that task. It was built not from the documents themselves, but from the activities of the people and teams working on those documents. Capturing this graph made it possible to store it, recall it, and share it within tools and across individuals and organizations.

We defined a new measure of productivity related to how much time a developer spent in the flow of work and then proved that this new approach had a statistically significant impact on developer productivity. It was the removal of the wasteful friction and distraction from the flow of work that resulted in the productivity increase. We then realized that this approach could scale to other types of knowledge work. I made the implementation of the experiment an open-source project,[10] which became popular with developers and grew to over a million monthly downloads.

Three days after the thesis defense, my supervisor, Gail Murphy, and I founded Tasktop to explore and further validate these concepts in a commercial context. We bootstrapped the company to bring this concept of structuring around the flow of value to not just individual developers but also entire organizations. We then expanded on the concept of flow to go beyond individual developers and into the bigger challenge of organizational value streams. Instead of time wasted thrashing at the individual level, waste in value streams came from the various wait states that blocked the flow of work across people and teams. These included the various approvals, dependencies, manual security reviews, and other steps that slow or block progress. We built a software platform that allowed enterprise organizations to measure the flow of value streams. We then set out to define a new market category, which we called Value Stream Management, and a new management approach called the Flow Framework®.[11]

Over the course of fifteen years, we grew Tasktop from a university lab to a successful company with over two hundred employees that came to dominate the category we created. On that journey, I served as Tasktop's CEO, which provided me with more management system learning opportunities than I could have ever wished for. We sold Tasktop to Planview in 2022, where I served as CTO for four years. It was on this journey that we built and implemented a new approach that connected value streams to Outcome Management.

We had the benefit of founding the company on breakthrough developer productivity research. As we grew, we needed to connect the productivity of our teams to a management system that could keep pace. We also wanted to validate our solution in very large, complex organizations. Our startup's product development focus became connecting developer productivity to very large-scale organizational operating models. And here we found a nearly insurmountable gap. Based on the data we were collecting, large organizations were somewhere between ten and a hundred times slower at delivering than our own teams.

The mismatch between highly productive teams and highly ossified operating models, and the corresponding waste I witnessed in enterprise software delivery, is what motivated me to introduce the Flow Framework in *Project to Product*. However, in the years following, I learned that flow was only one component of the solution.

On my journey of going from the very early days of a Lean startup to a rapidly scaling company, I drew on the mentorship of countless industry experts to help me create a scalable operating model for Tasktop. As integrating value streams was part of our business model, we also had the unique experience of partnering closely with dozens of leading technology vendors. This gave me the opportunity to work with their CEOs and CTOs and learn how they operated their business. Finally, over nearly two decades of working with transformations

Global 2000 companies, I had the opportunity to learn from thousands of meetings with executives who shared with me their operating models and, in recent years, how they are adapting those models for AI.

Key aspects of Tasktop's journey shaped how we discovered and implemented Outcome Management mechanisms. We were bootstrapped for the first seven years, meaning that we had no institutional funding and grew to seventy staff through sales. "Lean thinking; less is more" was one of the core values that got us there. We then realized the scope of the market opportunity and, for the following ten-year period, shifted into a much faster growth mode. This required scaling up our product development, which we supported through three rounds of venture capital and one round of growth equity financing. But we kept our bootstrapping roots reflected in our operating model, which was focused on capital efficiency and removing waste from our production processes.

As we grew the company in Vancouver, Canada, we created a team model that was optimized for getting new grads to highly productive output as quickly as possible. Our measured growth and limited ecosystem were in stark contrast to some of the rapid scale ups and Blitzscaling[12] that my colleagues in the Bay Area experienced, where the management system needs to optimize for efficiency taking a backseat to supporting rapid growth. But that drive for efficiency in our operating model helped shape a manic focus on turning scarcity in inputs to maximized outcomes. While we actively managed to maintain a high-performance culture, this operating model enabled us to successfully navigate two recessions and the pandemic without laying off more than a handful of people over the fifteen-year existence of the company. Our operating model made it much easier for us to pivot as the market and opportunity evolved.

Throughout our journey, we knew our operating model worked and had the continual confidence to know that we could quickly adapt the organization to whatever the market and macro conditions threw at us. And in the process of seeing how our customers implemented this model, it allowed us to learn how to scale it to organizations that were orders of magnitude larger than ours. The experiences of others who implemented the Flow Framework and Outcome Management, along with examples of companies that leveraged these approaches for AI-driven transformation, are summarized in the case studies in this book.

In addition to the large set of qualitative experiences with the successes and failures of various operating models, Outcome Management is based on studies and multiple years of data modeling and analysis of Tasktop's and, more recently, Planview's customers' value streams. The value stream management product offerings provide enterprise organizations with work management tool visibility and integration. As discussed in Chapter 1, we have been able to leverage that tooling to collect the data from over eight thousand value streams to study the ground truth of software delivery. That data includes all of the artifacts that flow through Agile, Project, Product, Portfolio, and Customer Service Management tools. This allowed us to mine for patterns of both functions and dysfunctions of operating models and was foundational to informing the model and practices presented here.

Outcome Management does not prescribe a particular planning methodology and is instead designed to be compatible with a broad range of methodologies. For example, at Tasktop we used the Plan/Build/Run methodology in use at many tech companies and hyperscalers.[13] Planview employs SAFe® methodology[14] across the organization. Methodologies continue to evolve, and as such, Outcome Management is compatible with any planning methodology that supports the very short iterations needed for the combination of human and agentic delivery. With this context, we can define the next Outcome Management model: the Outcome Loop.

Starting with Inputs

Outcome Management begins with the end in mind. The goal for an organization is delivering outcomes for customers, stakeholders, and shareholders. In Outcome Management, we need a simple way of expressing how we manage outputs, how those outputs drive measurable outcomes, and then connect those outcomes back to inputs that come from the strategy and budget. While the terminology of various implementations of Outcome Management can vary, this approach opts for simple, top-level terminology that can then be extended with precise business context–specific implementations.

For example, in a software company context, customer outcomes can be measured through a retention metric, whereas in a government context, they can be measured as a citizen satisfaction metric. Outcome Management only provides these high-level buckets, and each bucket can be decomposed further to meet the needs of your organization. For example, for customer outcomes, a software company may track gross retention, net retention, or customer Net Promoter Score.

At the core of the Outcome Management is the input to output to outcome feedback loop, or Outcome Loop for short. It provides two top-level input categories: strategy and budget. The *strategy* category is where the high-level vision, direction, and organizational focus are defined. This can include market segments, differentiation approaches, and competitive positioning. For example, a new financial services institution might have a strategy of: "Establish ourselves as the leading AI-first banking solution for Generation Alpha." The strategy is accompanied by a *budget*, which is the financial means by which the strategy will be implemented as a series of outputs whose outcomes should drive attainment of the strategy as supported by the budget.

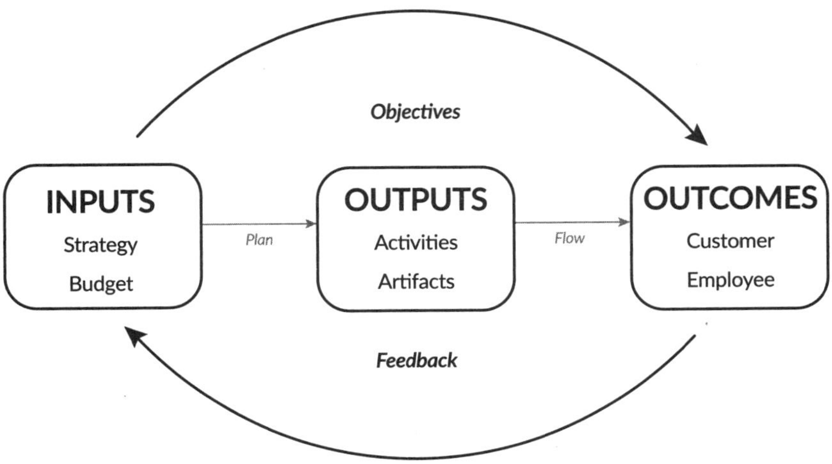

FIGURE 2.1: The Outcome Loop

Established organizations tend to have mature strategy and budgeting processes. The mechanics and best practices of planning and finance have evolved over the course of multiple technological revolutions. This is not to say that strategic planning and budgeting processes are always smooth, as our survey data shows how common frustration with it is. The challenges reported come from a lack of connectivity of strategy and budgets to output capacity and outcome feedback, resulting in overly long and misguided planning and budgeting processes.

For example, a lack of measurable outcome gains provided by AI agents makes it difficult to know how much to budget for agent costs and how much for additional staff. Strategic planning and budgeting best practices are well documented, and it is in their lack of direct connectivity to outputs and outcomes that these processes break down.

Connecting to Outputs

Best practices for managing and tracking outputs are also generally well understood and documented in the many Agile and DevOps frameworks. In Outcome Management, outputs fall into two top level categories: activities and artifacts.

Activities comprise all of the work that is done. For a software value stream, activities include designs, features implemented for customers, defect fixes, and documentation improvements. These activities, done by a person or an agent, produce *artifacts*, such as the widget for the feature that appears on a mobile application or new documentation on how to use the widget. As they are created, those artifacts then flow to end users. At a high level, this Outcome Loop is what defines the flow of value through a product value stream.

When planning, we assume that the faster the flow through the value stream, and the more activities and artifacts produced, the better the outcomes should be. However, without a feedback loop, this assumption can easily go astray. For example, developers could be delivering many new features for a mobile application, but if the entire user experience (UX) design team is on holiday and the features are poorly designed, end users' adoption may suffer. Or agents could be producing AI slop that is of low value due to inadequate guidance. To ensure outputs connect to planned outcomes, we need a closed feedback loop between the inputs, outputs, and outcomes.

The top part of the Outcome Loop is connected through objectives, which we use to map inputs to outcomes. We then create a plan to connect the inputs to the activities and artifacts that will be produced and sequence the activities via an *Outcome Roadmap* (a term popularized by the Silicon Value Product Group.)[15] The activities supporting the delivery of the outputs are done by the team supporting the value stream, who are responsible for ensuring that the rate of flow to the customer and business meets the needs determined by the feedback cycle for the objective. For example, if we want to increase active users by 10% next month, the flow of outputs has to be delivered quickly enough to drive the desired changes in customer behavior. Once customers are using the new features, we can measure progress against this objective and close the feedback loop back to the strategic plan item.

> **Outcome Roadmap:** A planning tool that connects strategic inputs, defined as objectives, to a set of activities and outputs, defined by a sequential roadmap that specifies all of the activities that will deliver on each key result.

Just as the planning portions of the Outcome Loop can be implemented with various methodologies, such as Agile planning, the objectives portion of the loop can be implemented with various goal tracking and measurement methodologies. *Objectives and Key Results* are a popular methodology adopted by technology companies and will be used throughout this book, but numerous other methodologies exist.

> **Objectives and Key Results (OKRs):** A goal-setting framework that pairs objectives with a small set of measurable key results to track progress toward desired outcomes.

To implement the Outcome Loop, we need to ensure both clearly defined objectives and a quantifiable measurement for each objective, referred to throughout as the key result, regardless of which measurement methodology is used. The key results should not be confused with Key Performance Indicators (KPIs) for the Outcome Loop. Each key result is connected to an objective and must represent an improvement target. In contrast, Key Performance Indicators are tracked regardless of whether they are connected to an objective or not. For example, it's common to track customer retention for a product, but unless there is an objective to improve retention, this metric will not be included as a key result. As such, the set of key results is usually a subset of the full set of Key Performance Indicators for the Outcome Loop.

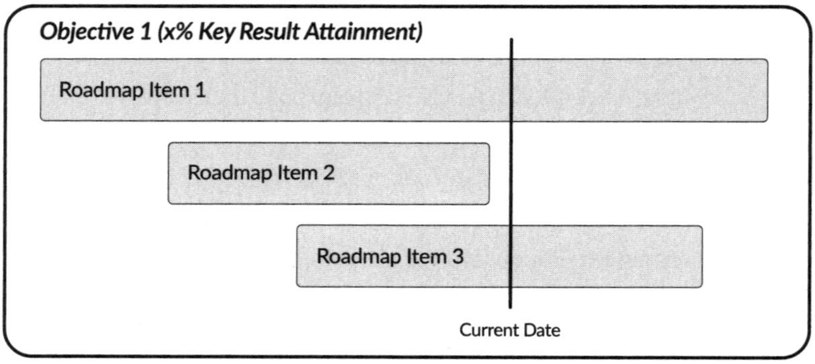

FIGURE 2.2: The Outcome Roadmap

Example Outcome Loop

We can unpack this with a simple but concrete example that we will refer back to throughout this book. While company strategies and plans often contain thousands of elements, the example here is kept as simple as possible for the purpose of illustrating common elements and their interactions.

Consider an organization with a vision of transforming healthcare, which produces a TeenWellness app. An effective strategy for a new product often relies on market segmentation and key differentiators, so this organization's strategy is to leverage AI and focus uniquely on an initial market beachhead of teenagers. In this simplistic example, the strategy portion of the inputs can be summarized as: "Help a generation of teens build healthier lives, one habit at a time."

The other key input is the budget. Let's assume there is an initial $10 million budget to deliver on the first phase of this strategy. This budget includes the staffing, agent, hosting, and AI inference costs of supporting the development and operations of the application.

We now need to create a set of objectives to connect the strategy and budget to the outcomes that will be the measure of success for this strategy. High-level strategic and budget inputs of this sort tend to focus on longer timeframes, such as a fiscal year. Since outcomes are lagging indicators, a key role of objectives is to decompose those lagging indicators into incremental feedback and leading outcome indicators. Note that at this phase we focus entirely on the outcomes, not the outputs. Using the Objectives and Key Results format, objectives might include:

Objective (O1): "Become the #1 daily wellness app for teens."
Key Results:

- (KR1) "Increase monthly active users from 10K to 20K."
- (KR2) "Improve app store star rating from 3.5 to 4.5."
- (KR3) "Grow # of teens reporting improvements from 0% to 25%."
- (KR4) "Grow pediatric expert endorsements from 1 to 5."

The exact nature of the objectives will differ by the life cycle stage of the product. For example, with a new app the outcomes are likely to focus on driving adoption and validation, whereas for an established app they may focus on driving scale and profitability.

As we will explore further in Chapter 6, the time scale also shapes the outcomes we define. For example, the above could be suitable for quarterly objectives, whereas annual objectives are likely to roll up a considerably larger amount of activity. Whatever the timeframe, each key result should be structured as a quantitative outcome that is directly connected to our strategy.[16] For this example, let's assume the time box is a calendar quarter.

Guidance: Every Key Result Must Be Quantitative: Each measure of an objective's attainment needs to define an outcome as a number, not an activity, so that progress toward objectives can be precisely and directly measured.

The objectives are then broken down into a plan. The planning methodology that underpins Outcome Management is the Outcome Roadmap, which includes all of the activities and artifacts that will be produced in support of each outcome. Thus, each roadmap item is directly connected to the objectives it supports. Note that this kind of bidirectional connectivity is prevalent through the entire Outcome Loop as our goal is establishing a completely closed-loop feedback system. The Outcome Roadmap in our example can then specify how we will deliver on each of the objectives.

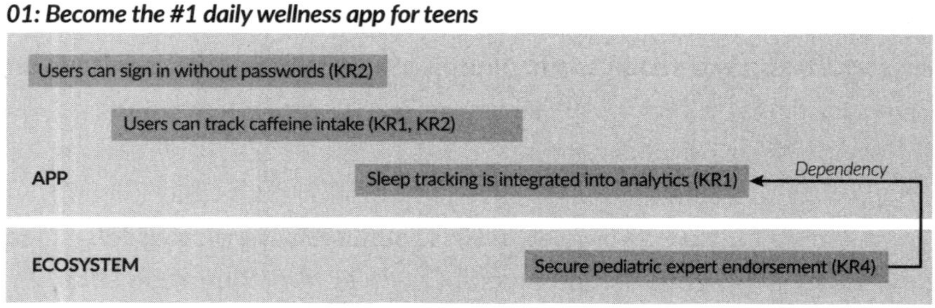

FIGURE 2.3: Outcome Roadmap for TeenWellness Example

The Outcome Roadmap creates the sequencing and makes explicit any dependencies between the activities and artifacts that will be delivered. For example, it makes it clear that if the two features are not delivered on time, we can expect that securing endorsements will be affected.

Dysfunction: Order Taker Model: Value stream leaders and teams act as passive executors of roadmaps and other requests rather than as owners of outcomes.

Each of these roadmap items is decomposed into a series of work items, such as backlog items planned for the set of iterations, or sprints, supporting the span of the roadmap and objectives. We then need to determine whether there will be enough capacity in the product value stream to deliver on the outputs specified on the roadmap and to do so in a timeframe that achieves the outcomes specified by the objective.

This is where the *flow* portion of the Outcome Loop comes in. *Flow metrics* provide us with the end-to-end output delivery capacity of the value stream. As we will explore in Chapter 5, the best practice is to leverage the value stream's historical capacity. For this example, let us assume we see enough flow from the value stream to deliver three of the four features that we planned. We can now feed this information back into the objectives and determine whether that is sufficient to meet the "pediatric endorsements" key result or if we should push that objective to next quarter. As part of that planning feedback loop, we can then determine whether the lack of capacity affects our strategy and determine whether we want to allocate more capacity, for example, by increasing the budget to grow the delivery team and agents.

Flow Metrics: Metrics that track the end-to-end flow of value through a value stream, providing visibility into the speed, efficiency, and capacity of delivery.

This example involved a single pass through the Outcome Loop that was done in support of a planning cycle. In practice, the Outcome Loop should be running continuously and responding to events that correspond to the state changes of the items in the loop. For example, as soon as the "caffeine tracking" feature is delivered, we can start tracking the customer adoption of that feature and determine how much it is increasing the usage key result. If we see that it is not increasing usage, there may be a problem with the output. For example, the feature may have been delivered in a state that was not sufficiently compelling to drive usage due to issues such as insufficient focus on design, performance problems, or user sentiment shifting.

For each input, output, and outcome, we need to define a set of metrics, which will be described in detail in Chapter 5. At a high level, for the inputs we have budget numbers, such as headcount and agent costs, and strategic plan targets, such as customer retention and revenue growth. For the outputs, we have activity metrics, such as the number of features delivered, as well as artifact metrics, such as the number of services deployed. For the outcomes, we have business metrics, such as revenue; customer metrics, such as customer satisfaction; as well as employee metrics, such as employee satisfaction. Optimizing outputs is about increasing efficiency, or doing things right, whereas optimizing outcomes is about increasing effectiveness, or doing the right things. In the Age of AI, effectiveness becomes the primary constraint.

These metrics give us a static snapshot of a value stream. The goal for each value stream is to affect change that drives the outcomes as specified by the strategy. We then specify the changes we want to deliver through outcomes as objectives. We then need to turn those objectives into the roadmap items that will drive the attainment of the key results.

Connecting Objectives to Outcome Roadmaps

Objectives specify the outcomes that we plan to achieve (i.e., the "what"). Roadmaps and flow specify the "how" of achieving the outcomes. The organization's mission, vision, and values specify the "why." The "why" should be connected to the overall vision of the organization and then cascaded to each value stream through the strategy input. We will examine that cascading structure in the next chapter. Before we do that, let's break down how to connect objectives to the Outcome Roadmap for the value stream. To do this, we define and sequence the activities that will drive the outcomes defined by the objectives.

Since a significant portion of product development resides in the complex domain, as described in Chapter 1, in most cases we will not have a direct cause-and-effect line between a specific output and the outcome. For example, the sample objective of becoming the #1 daily wellness app for teens will be a function of a large number of activities and artifacts that are undertaken as part of that objective. As such, the relationship between an objective and the outcomes is a correlation, not a direct causal relationship. This means that the set of outputs done in support of the objectives is correlated to the outcome.

The implication of this is that the Outcome Loop is a hypothesis testing loop. We hypothesize that a set of features, such as caffeine and sleep tracking, will drive adoption. We then plan to deliver those features via a roadmap. We then build the features resulting in a flow of value to the customer. And then we test whether those features met the outcome we were after, for example, driving increased adoption.

If the usage key result is met, our hypothesis was correct. If it is not met, we return to the objective to determine why the outputs failed to meet the outcome. It could be that the features were poorly designed. Or that they were not discoverable enough. Or that we were losing users to a competitor. The faster we can iterate through the Outcome Loop, the faster we can align and realign our activities in support of the stated outcomes.

Guidance: Optimize the Outcome Loop for Fast Feedback: The faster the flow and feedback through the Outcome Loop, the higher the speed of decision-making.

The speed of Outcome Loop feedback needs to support not only the speed of feedback to the team of people on the loop but also the faster feedback that can be leveraged by agents. For example, agents can enable parallelized hypothesis testing, create multiple variants of an application, and deploy it to different user cohorts. We will discuss this parallelization in detail in Chapter 7. Whether running sequentially or in parallel, the mechanics of the Outcome Loop are the same.

To ensure the feedback is connected, we need to align the outputs we will produce to the inputs. We do this by creating a roadmap where each roadmap item is connected to a specific outcome as captured by an objective. The Outcome Roadmap is based on the concept of a product roadmap, which is a sequence of high-level deliverables and their dependencies. A common representation is with the columns or x-axis representing timeboxes, such as months or years, and the rows or y-axis representing a categorization of those deliverables.

We will explore Outcome Roadmap categorization further in Chapters 5 and 9. The key features in the Outcome Roadmap are that every roadmap item is connected directly to the objective that it supports, and attainment is measured by the key results supporting that objective. This ensures clear connectivity to the hypothesis testing validation part of the loop. A team may have numerous backlog items not linked to an objective, but once these are planned for implementation and land on the roadmap, they need to be linked to an objective to ensure connectivity of the Outcome Roadmap.

Guidance: Outcome Roadmap Items Must Tie to Objectives: For every roadmap item, define the hypothesis for how it will help achieve the objective that it supports. In aggregate, the completion of all the roadmap items should result in the achievement of the objective.

Roadmaps are not the only approach to planning product development. However, other approaches are similar enough in how they represent sequences of work to be done at a high level that the Product Operating Model uses this term and concept. The role of Outcome Roadmaps is to connect high-level strategic plans to detailed implementation work while being directly connected to the objectives. As agents scale the amount of output that can be produced, this ensures that all of the output is directly tied to the objective and outcome.

Flow and Feedback

The front end of the Outcome Loop, which we just covered, supports planning with iterative feedback in a way that is connected to outputs produced by a team of people and agents. This is the *planning loop* portion (or inner loop) of the larger Outcome Loop. What we now need to examine in detail is the delivery and feedback loop portions.

> **Planning Loop:** Connects strategy and budget inputs to a sequenced roadmap that defines the activities and artifacts that will deliver on the corresponding value stream's objectives.

Once roadmap items are defined, they create work on the backlogs of the corresponding value stream's team or sets of teams. The work is then done, for example, with a combination of humans and agents creating the compelling caffeine tracking features in our example app. These activities produce artifacts that flow to the end user of the app through a delivery pipeline. *Flow* is what connects the outputs to the delivery needed to drive employee and customer outcomes. Once this and other features are delivered, we can close the feedback loop. In our TeenWellness app example, this would be done by monitoring how the caffeine tracking feature helped with a key result, such as adoption. Flow connects this *delivery loop*, and feedback takes the next hop to complete the Outcome Loop.

> **Delivery Loop:** The portion of the Outcome Loop where planned work is executed, producing activities and artifacts that drive the value stream's outcomes.

In the Age of Software & Digital, the main constraint on knowledge work, such as software development, was the delivery of outputs. The end-to-end throughput at which outputs are created is tracked by measuring the flow of the corresponding activities and artifacts. Flow metrics, described in detail in Chapter 5, are designed for this end-to-end measurement of the flow of value through a value stream. With highly scalable agents delivering outputs, measuring the flow of value delivery is even more critical to ensure that the outputs are driving the desired outcomes.

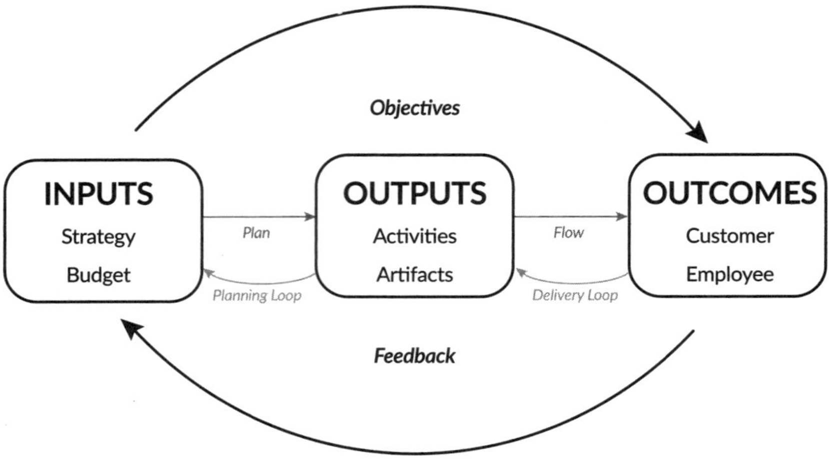

FIGURE 2.4: The Planning and Delivery Loops

The challenge is that the majority of the organizations studied in the *Project to Product State of the Industry Report* had only invested in telemetry for measuring outputs and lacked telemetry for measuring flow and outcomes. Relying on output metrics alone to manage an Outcome Loop is akin to running a hospital by tracking the number of procedures performed while ignoring the length of patient stays and clinical outcomes.

Measuring how many times per week or day teams deploy software says nothing about whether that deployed software helped or hindered a customer's experience. Measuring how many user stories were closed by a team is not the same as measuring whether features were used. Assuming that activity metrics automatically correspond to outcome metrics is problematic and error prone as it results in optimization around an output, not an outcome metric.

Artifact-centric metrics can be just as misleading. For example, many organizations use lines of code delivered by AI coding and agents as a proxy for the value provided. But unless there is clear evidence that this code flows into the application as a useful and performant solution, no assumption should be made about whether value was delivered. Without this correlation, we may be building things right, but we do not know if we are building the right things.

Just as we need to connect outputs to outcomes with flow, we need to connect the outcomes back to the inputs to close the full feedback cycle of the Outcome Loop. For example, if we flow many features into the application that delight users, without a feedback mechanism to understand which are the most useful and which are the least, we cannot connect outputs to outcomes and thus have a broken Outcome Loop. We may even see customer or business metrics improve, such as a customer retention figure. Unless we can attribute that retention improvement to what was delivered to the customer, we are running a disconnected Outcome Loop. In this context, celebrating the retention improvement can be just as misleading, as the improvement could have come from a pricing change rather than from the product features delivered.

To ensure that our Outcome Loop is connected, the feedback mechanism must trace back to the inputs and objectives. For example, if we are tracking how a set of features helped delight customers, we need to implement telemetry for measuring the usage of the roadmap features that were delivered, to monitor their rate of adoption, and then to connect that adoption to progress on key results, such as improved star ratings in the app store. In some domains, gathering real customer feedback can become the constraint. Agents can be leveraged to accelerate feedback through the simulation of users or environments. For example, Salesforce's Agentforce AI agents can simulate marketing campaign scenarios,[17] similar to how manufacturers create digital twins of new models to support faster iteration.[18]

Applying the Theory of Constraints to the Outcome Loop

The goal of implementing an Outcome Loop is to enable us to shift from optimizing for outputs to optimizing for outcomes. The Outcome Loop is a feedback system that is designed to function as a learning loop. With each iteration through the loop, we learn whether our assumptions were correct, whether we surmounted the risks associated with those assumptions, and whether the desired outcome was delivered.

We then feed that back into the objectives and strategy for planning the next iteration. Whether this optimization is done by humans or by agents, in order to optimize for outcomes, we need to ensure that the Outcome Loop itself is connected so that it can be optimized iteratively. Once connected with telemetry for each stage, we can apply the Theory of Constraints to the Outcome Loop.

Constraints can appear at every stage of the Outcome Loop. For example, turning a strategy and budget into a roadmap can be constrained by the many conversations and negotiations that happen in an organization's overloaded matrix structure, as discussed in Chapter 7. Constraints can occur during delivery activities, for example, if a team needs to wait for capacity approval before implementing a new set of features. Flow can be constrained by under-resourced teams, by overloading people with the need to review the work of agents, or by dependencies between value streams. Feedback can be constrained by a lack of telemetry or ability to attribute employee or customer outcomes to outputs and objectives.

The Theory of Constraints states that for any complex system, to optimize flow we want to identify and address the weakest link in the system and then repeat this process until we achieve the desired performance of the system or hit on a fundamental limitation that is no longer feasible to optimize. Once we hit that fundamental limitation, we then shift to managing around the constraint. For example, given the constraint of waiting for paint to dry, car plants tend to create buffers for storing painted car bodies and make the paint shop a station that continues to run over the weekend. In practice, for complex systems with dependencies and networks, such as value streams, this can involve concurrently managing multiple constraints.

Our first step is to make sure that every part of the Outcome Loop is connected, meaning we have created a closed loop system. If we are missing feedback telemetry, we do not have a closed loop. If we are missing the ability to connect marketing, sales, and revenue metrics to a product or value stream, we do not have end-to-end connectivity supporting the Outcome Loop's value stream.

If we are missing feedback telemetry, we cannot connect customer activity and need to address this broken link before optimizing further. If we are missing flow metrics that provide us with the historical capacity of a value stream, then we cannot accurately create a roadmap based on existing capacity, creating another broken link in our loop. If we rely on third parties to create some of the value stream's artifacts, but those artifacts are not connected back to the roadmap, then another gap is created in our loop. The foundational step on the journey to Outcome Management must be connecting every disconnected part of the loop.

Once the Outcome Loop is connected (i.e., each stage is visible and there are no broken links), we then need to identify the main constraint, or the bottleneck, of the flow and feedback through the loop. In my experience, too often executives' reaction to challenges in attaining strategic outcomes is to blame the slowness of the teams producing the outputs. This is common as so much organizational focus and investment is allocated to producing those outputs. However, the *Project to Product State of the Industry Report* demonstrates that output being the constraint is the exception, not the norm. And the adoption of AI agents delivering output will continue a shift away from scarcity of output to a surplus. For this reason, identifying the constraint in your Outcome Loop by applying the Theory of Constraints is the critical first step in optimizing for outcomes. It also provides a data-driven approach to improvement, helping avoid misdirected blame.

Once you have identified and addressed the constraint, it will shift to another part of the Outcome Loop. For example, if overly onerous planning and coordination meetings to finalize the roadmap are the constraint, you can remove that constraint by following the principles outlined in Chapter 6. At that point, wait states in planning will be replaced by productive flow. With that constraint removed, wait states or other bottlenecks will appear elsewhere in the Outcome Loop. For example, wait states may indicate that there is more development capacity than design capacity. We can then address this by growing the design capacity. Once that is done, we can move onto the next constraint.

Eventually, we hope to accelerate flow and feedback to the point where the only constraints are external to the Outcome Loop. This includes the customer, the market, and the budget. At this point, we have achieved a level of productivity and efficiency where we are only limited by our market dynamics and access to budget. We can now be confident that applying more budget will drive the additional outcomes, assuming sufficient market demand. Similar dynamics hold for internal products and platforms as well, where success is defined by internal, not external, adoption.

For a single value stream that is delivered in isolation, defining inputs, building outputs, and delivering outcomes can be an exhilarating experience. Continually optimizing the Outcome Loop further invigorates the team to do great work. For anyone who has experienced the momentum of working on a high-performing and self-sufficient team, achieving this point is when you start feeling like you and your team can move mountains.

As a software developer, I have experienced the joy of this epitome of team productivity twice in my career. The first instance occurred when I was on a highly cohesive open-source team building a new programming language, and the second instance happened in the early days of my startup when we were small enough to function as a single team.

The challenge is that, whether managing humans or AI agents, we need more than a single team and value stream to deliver. And this is where things can get much, much more complicated. As Tasktop grew, I realized my goal was to scale this feeling to our entire organization. In the next chapter, we will tackle the scaling of Outcome Loops.

Optimizing the Outcome Loop at VS Code

While working on my PhD thesis, I needed to change how code editors worked so I could do user testing on the integration of tasks and value streams into developer workflow. I submitted countless requests to change the core functions of Eclipse, the most popular developer environment at the time. In the process, I formed a close relationship with Kai Maetzel, one of the leaders of that open-source product, partly by tackling him at conferences to prioritize my changes. Kai went on to create and colead Visual Studio Code (VS Code) at the beginning of 2016.

As of 2025, VS Code had over 44 million monthly users[19] and more than twice the traction of any runner up.[20] VS Code is also the home of GitHub Copilot, which, as of July 2025, is the most used with 20 million all-time users.[21]

What underpins the past three years of growth at VS Code is a case study in how to adopt AI-native engineering on a large, existing codebase with a relentless focus on optimizing the Outcome Loop.

In the very early years of building VS Code, Kai explained to me that he had focused all of his engineers on objectives that to some seemed out of the scope of engineering. The objectives were focused on the outcome metric of growing the number of engaged users. That outcome was supported by all of the feature and quality work that delighted and engaged developers using VS Code. The faster, more productive, and more fun VS Code was to use, the more developers would come to the platform. That outcome orientation guided the VS Code team's journey to the 44 million monthly users that they are at today.

The VS Code team has embedded AI in its delivery loop since mid-2021. Most recently, they have applied AI-native engineering practices to their large existing codebase that supports tens of millions of users, a considerably harder problem than leveraging AI for building new applications. Their journey illustrates how to apply the Theory of Constraints to the Outcome Loop as AI capabilities increase and how to put engineers in the driver's seat on that journey.

At the start of their journey, the VS Code team started using AI code completions, then chat-based assistance. This provided a modest productivity boost. In 2024, the teams built and adopted Edit Mode, which enabled GitHub Copilot to update multiple files in one shot. This further increased output. Three months later, Agent Mode and Next Edit Suggestions were rolled out internally, driving another uptick in productivity. At this point, the team needed a way to measure the additional velocity of outputs to understand where they were getting the biggest benefit.

Kai knew that simply measuring output was not sufficient. While he tracked how much of the codebase was AI generated, he did not manage to this metric as it could easily mistake slop for substance. The team instead leveraged both tracking of the flow of pull requests over time as well as live output generation via the number of characters written by AI versus by humans in each code editing session.[22]

For some developers, an impressive one-third of their code output was being written by AI. Pull requests increased substantially, but not only thanks to GitHub Copilot assisting directly. The ability for developers to discuss and understand the codebase by chatting with GitHub Copilot amplified the developers' ability to work on this highly complex system in a way that was clearly connected to outcomes. Kai's teams were already structured around all of the best practices associated with the Outcome Management and were able to leverage these capacity gains without reorganizing.

Things evolved further with the team adopting GitHub Copilot's Agent Mode. Agents were able to produce entire applications. This proved useful not only for prototyping but also for automating key aspects of development. Kai has long recognized that a hallmark of great development teams is that they automate everything they can. Now, every constraint that the team found in the Outcome Loop, from onboarding to monitoring, could easily be automated by apps created by agents. Any internal apps that turned into slop and were no longer relevant to outcomes could easily be deleted and recreated. This enabled much faster resolution of constraints in the Outcome Loop.

With most delivery constraints gone, the bottleneck shifted to developer onboarding. Between the complexity of the system itself and the added complexity of an ever-growing codebase accelerated by AI, onboarding was becoming more, not less, difficult. Chat-based interrogation and agent-based experimentation with the codebase helped dramatically with this constraint as Kai's teams continued to onboard more and more developers to keep up with the demand for VS Code.

They did not stop there. The next big opportunity was applying agentic coding to the production codebase itself. For small codebases, this was easy. But even with the most capable AI agents available, initially the team struggled to gain meaningful improvements in velocity when handing work off to agents. Kai and team realized the challenge was that the codebase itself had to be modularized and updated in a way that would make it easier to effectively onboard AI agents to contribute in meaningful ways. That meant writing instructions and context to guide the agents for each folder of their codebase and structuring the codebase in a way that allowed the modules to be worked on more independently by the agents.

The journey of applying the Theory of Constraints to the Outcome Loop continues for Kai and his teams. With agents now able to contribute more to the production codebase, the bottleneck is becoming code review for those contributions. Code review tends to be a less fulfilling task for developers than creating new features, so Kai and team are now envisioning an amplified Outcome Loop that has a hundred or thousand times more contributions that need to be reviewed, and they are creating ways of leveraging AI to help engineers handle that massive increase in code reviews in a more fun and productive way.

With outputs being amplified, they are also realizing that traditional collaboration and source configuration management may become the next bottleneck, as they were created for the pace at which humans build, not the pace at which AI can build. Their journey of trailblazing innovation and iterative Outcome Loop optimization continues. As they solve these problems, the solutions continue to be shared through open-source products so that other teams can adopt them and accelerate their own Outcome Loops.

Conclusion: Mental Models

In our professional lives, we navigate complex systems on a daily basis. This includes the evolution of markets and industries, the dynamics of product development, the complexities of organizational design, and the tidal wave of AI. Through our education, we have been taught a set of mental models that help us navigate complex systems. For example, the common concept of "opportunity cost" is a mental model that allows us to frame an objective in terms of what we give up by not pursuing a different objective. In a series of profound and practical books, Shane Parrish has documented the Great Mental Models that many of us use daily, sometimes without realizing it.[23] These range from simple concepts, like inversion, to the more complex feedback loops, bottlenecks, and network effects models that are core to the operating model described in this book.

A key goal of *Output to Outcome* is to provide you with a new set of mental models to help you create, evolve, and optimize an Outcome Management practice that will enable your organization thrive in the Age of AI. For example, a highly complex Outcome Roadmap could contain hundreds of items, a scenario where agents can help dramatically with data-driven sequencing. Without a connected and optimized Outcome Loop underpinning your value streams, it is impossible to effectively leverage the amplification made possible by AI.

The Outcome Loop is the core model that each of the Seven Shifts explored in Part II builds on. It is an expansion of the feedback loop mental model. When working in large or complex environments, the goal is always to return to the simplicity of the Outcome Loop and to optimize the entire management system around it. The additional mental models introduced act to support the dynamics that originate outside of the core Outcome Loop that we are trying to optimize.

Consider our simple TeenWellness app example. The app is going to need to store user data. That means it will be dependent on a storage services platform that we will need to build for this particular domain. That platform will be a separate value stream, with its own Outcome Loop, Outcome Roadmap, team, and agents supporting its development. Our app value stream will now depend on the platform value stream. Adding an AI chat interface to the app will create a third value stream. While our top-level objectives may remain the same, our roadmap becomes much more complicated due to the dependencies between these value streams and must consider the capacity and Outcome Loop for each. To simplify the interactions between these multiple Outcome Loops, we will leverage the Outcome Tree introduced in the next chapter.

In Summary

- The Outcome Loop is the feedback system that connects inputs (strategy and budget) to outputs (activities and artifacts) to outcomes (employee and customer).
- Objectives and Key Results and Outcome Roadmaps operationalize the planning loop portion of the Outcome Loop, translating strategy into measurable outcomes that value streams deliver on via hypothesis testing and iteration.
- Flow and feedback close the Outcome Loop by measuring the capacity and throughput of outputs that are correlated to outcomes.
- Optimizing the Outcome Loop requires telemetry that applies the Theory of Constraints to continually identify and address end-to-end bottlenecks in planning and delivery.

Key Takeaways

- The Outcome Loop connects strategy to business outcomes.
- Objectives and Outcome Roadmaps connect strategy and budgets to coordinated execution.

- Flow and feedback and Outcome Loop optimization drive learning and speed of decision-making.

Prompt

Objective: Help humans implement a closed Outcome Loop (inputs → outputs → outcomes → inputs) for each value stream. Humans own intentions, decisions, and accountability.

Operating protocol (assist, don't act unilaterally):

- Identify a single value stream and clearly capture Inputs: strategy, budget, and 3–5 Objectives with quantitative Key Results.
- Map the Outcome Loop: connect inputs → Outcome Roadmap (activities and artifacts) → outcomes (customer, employee, business), and back to inputs.
- For each roadmap item, ask: "What hypothesis are we testing, and what outcome metric will move if this works?"
- Propose simple telemetry linking work items → features → usage/adoption → outcome metrics; highlight missing data or broken links.
- Apply Theory of Constraints: Surface where the loop is stuck (planning, delivery, feedback, attribution), and propose 2–3 options.

Guardrails: Do not optimize for output metrics; always push to reconnect work to outcomes and a closed Outcome Loop.

Chapter 3

The Outcome Tree

To achieve large-scale outcomes, people form organizations. The sizes and shapes of organizations have evolved over the course of technological revolutions. Management methodologies, organizational designs, and processes are as varied as the leaders and consultancies that put them in place. The most successful companies often credit their organizational design for their success. On the flip side, failed transformations often fail due to flawed organizational designs and operating models, as we will review at the start of this chapter.

With the advent of AI and agents becoming a core part of how knowledge work is done, we are in the process of the most disruptive change to organizational design since the emergence of knowledge work. Organizations now need to adapt to enable coordination and collaboration with AI agents, as well as create structures that can manage and direct agents that can vastly outnumber people. In the previous chapter, we defined the Outcome Loop, which supports the controlled scaling of value stream outputs. A single Outcome Loop supports one value stream. However, today's large organizations can have hundreds or thousands of value streams. To support this, we need a scaling structure for Outcome Loops. That structure is the *Outcome Tree*.

Outcome Tree: The hierarchical structure of Outcome Loops across an organization, with individual teams forming the leaves of the tree. Provides the scaling model that enables the strategy and objectives to cascade across all of the teams delivering outcomes for the organization.

Agents and Teams Caught in a Waterfall

Agile, DevOps, and ways of working transformations have taken a tremendous amount of organizational energy and investment. They are now being augmented by AI and agentic transformations. Yet they have typically yielded so few tangible business results that for many the word *transformation* has negative connotations. Now, in the midst of AI transformations, early signs indicate that the vast majority of AI projects fail.[1] We are blaming "transformation failures" all over again for our lack of success with AI, all while AI natives accelerate and outperform incumbents.

The most common theme I have seen in these transformations is that the operating model at the team level is changed in a positive way, but the organizational wiring is ineffective at the team of teams level and above. Organizations have well-functioning Agile teams that apply practices such as plan/build/run, SAFe®, and Scrum Nexus. They deploy AI or agentic coding to help a team become more productive. The principles of Agile and Lean practices are highly aligned to cross-organizational Outcome Management. However, if they are only implemented at the team level, the organization ends up with Agile teams augmented by agents, but still no meaningful business agility.

The organizational wiring mismatch is the most common state that I have seen as the unintended result of large-scale Agile transformations and is reflected in the initial crop of AI transformations. The common symptoms of this are leaders voicing concerns that the technology organization has transformed, but the business as a whole has not. In this scenario, funding and work management remain waterfall and project based, while teams operate in an Agile mode. History is now repeating itself for AI transformations, where teams adopt AI-native practices, but the organizational operating model has not adapted and becomes the main impediment.

ⓧ **Dysfunction: AI Deployed in Waterfall:** Teams adopt AI-native practices, but outcomes do not improve due to the broader operating model remaining rooted in project and waterfall methodology.

The goal of the Project to Product movement is to address this dysfunction and to help rewire the organization around end-to-end value streams. While the principles of this organization are clear and described in books such as *Team Topologies: Organizing Business and Technology Teams for Fast Flow,*[3] the structure of an end-to-end operating model has been less clear. We can apply the Outcome Loop to better understand this dysfunction and to derive a structure that results in an organization that embodies agility at every level of leadership, not only at that of teams.

The Water-Scrum-Fall dysfunctions are easy to model using the Outcome Loop. The input and outcome portions of the loop remain the purview of "the business." The business defines strategy and tracks employee and customer outcomes. The output portion of the loop is the purview of the technology organization, which is typically composed of numerous teams organized in a hierarchical structure. The deeper and more complex the team structure, the more disconnected it becomes from the strategy and budget inputs, as well as the business and customer outcomes.

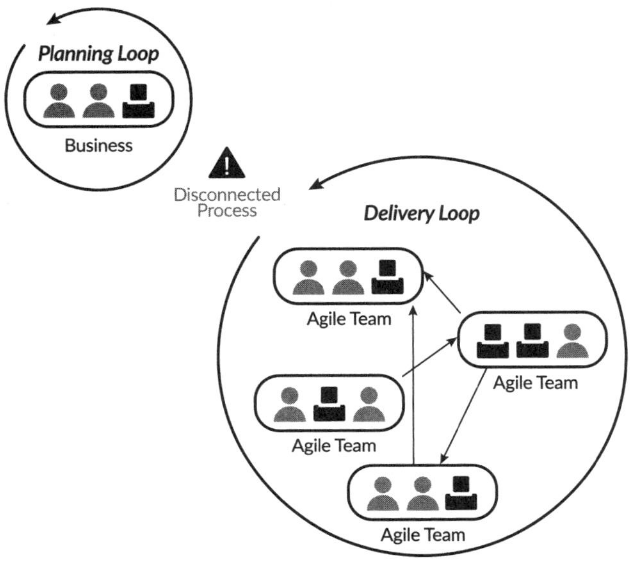

FIGURE 3.1: Agile Teams Disconnected from Inputs and Outcomes

In this scenario, the organization has scaled the output portion of the loop without scaling outcomes. The more the organization invests in this structure, the more disconnected the outputs become from outcomes. In this mode, organizations fall into a destructive feedback loop of further investing in outputs by hiring more staff and deploying more agents in the hope that this will eventually drive the desired outcomes. The core of this problem is that the organization is scaling the wrong thing. The output delivery teams and agents should not be the sole scaling unit. In order to achieve Outcome Management, the Outcome Loop itself needs to be the scaling unit.

Crippling Coordination Costs

With the scaling unit of the Outcome Loop established, we need to understand how to wire the scaling itself. A thorough summary of how to connect organizational dynamics of this sort is covered in Gene Kim and Steven Spear's profound book *Wiring the Winning Organization: Liberating Our Collective Greatness Through Slowification, Simplification, and Amplification.*[4] As they describe, organizations are sociotechnical systems built to create value. Kim and Spear define a model that can be used to determine the coordination cost of different types of organizational wiring. For example, if a doctor wants to urgently perform surgery, but the procedure is delayed for days because radiology, bed management, and medical histories need to be consulted, the health outcome is affected by coordination cost.

If we have a large organization where a person needs to talk to every other person to perform some work, even at small scales value delivery will grind to a halt. A similar thing will happen if every manager or team leader has to talk to every other team leader. This can easily be explained by looking at the complexity of a connected network that forms when an organization is fully connected. That complexity is written $n^*(n\text{-}1)$, where n is the number of people and the result is a fast-growing exponential. That means that if we have an organization with one thousand people, those people can have one million connections between them.

To address this problem, most organizations form teams and then ensure that the work done by teams encapsulates some kind of functional unit. If this encapsulation is done effectively, the complexity of communication can be reduced tenfold if teams of ten people become the units that are connected.[5]

However, with a thousand-person organization that has one hundred teams, we still have ten thousand connections. This means that even if we apply an optimized Outcome Loop to each team, the coordination cost of connecting the organization's strategy to teams' delivery becomes unmanageable. While many organizations prize open communication and collaboration, without a model to constrain and focus the communication, the coordination cost becomes prohibitive.

> ⊗ **Dysfunction: Saturated Communication Networks:** When leaders must coordinate with multiple other leaders to get work done, complexity and coordination cost rise exponentially. Over-collaboration consumes capacity and impedes flow.

There is no lack of business literature on different approaches to wiring organizational networks and communication paths. Many of these have been in response to the challenges of the hierarchical organizational charts that we discussed earlier. These include creating overlays on top of the hierarchical organization, as is the case with Matrix Management. In this mode, the organizational chart is set up to support functional priorities, and "dotted" or matrix lines are set up as overlays to support project priorities.

The overlay structure can also be more dynamic, such as in John Kotter's "second operating system" approach,[6] where there is a dual system of a formal hierarchy that is combined with an "agile network" overlaid on that hierarchy. The network exists to enable innovation and strategic change by crosscutting functional silos.

There are also approaches that do away with the hierarchy altogether, such as Holacracy.[7] With Holacracy, the hierarchy is abolished entirely, and a distributed authority model is put in place where teams form so-called circles intended to provide increased autonomy and push decision-making to the edges so that it is closest to where the work happens.

While well-intentioned, the hierarchy-minimizing Holacracy model has not succeeded at scale. This is in large part because the amount of coordination that is needed can saturate teams and organizations. The ambiguity that comes from the lack of a decision-making hierarchy results in the explosion of political structures and bureaucracy, as was witnessed by the large-scale failure of Holacracy at Zappos.[8]

More recent approaches, such as the RenDanHeYi Model developed by Haier, seek to minimize the traditional managerial hierarchy by replacing it with autonomous, market-facing microenterprises focused on customer outcomes.[9] Such systems encode a different kind of hierarchy through clear ownership and escalation mechanisms, reinforcing the patterns of hierarchy and encapsulation as scaling mechanisms.

This implies that for effective Outcome Management we need a hierarchical structure. While adding a Kotter-style second operating system is tempting, the matrix lines that result mean there are now two structures introducing coordination cost: the hierarchy and the network. As such, for Outcome Management we want to make this "second operating" system the first operating system and ensure that it is organized into an effective hierarchy. The question is what defines the hierarchy, as the remaining relationships that we need to capture in our model will cut across that structure. In other words, what are we scaling?

Superlinear Scaling of Outcomes

For organizations delivering products to customers, whether those products are physical or intangible, such as software and knowledge, what we need to scale is our ability to deliver those products. That is at the core of Outcome Management. To scale product development, we need to scale the Outcome Loop.

There is no shortage of evidence and grounded theoretical guidance on how scaling works in complex systems ranging from organisms to cities. A thorough and mind-expanding documentation of this is in Geoff West's book *Scale: The Universal Growth, Innovation, Sustainability, and the Pace of Life in Organisms, Cities, Economies, and Companies*, which describes how power laws govern scaling and explains that most complex systems do not scale linearly.[10] For example, if you double the size of an animal, its metabolic rate does not double. Instead, it scales sublinearly, meaning that larger animals are more efficient per unit of mass than smaller ones. In sublinear scaling, as we add more input, we get less output per unit input. This effect is also called diminishing returns.

Sublinear scaling is not necessarily undesirable. For example, as cities grow, they tend to show sublinear scaling of energy use and carbon footprint per person. In other words, the bigger the city where population is the input, the less carbon it produces per person.

In contrast, cities show a superlinear scaling of income, patents filed, wages, and crime, meaning these tend to grow faster than population growth (roughly 1.15x faster). Superlinear scaling means we get more output per unit of input, or accelerating returns.

West also discusses how companies scale sublinearly, with innovation and revenue growth slowing due to inefficiencies. However, we now have examples of firms, such as the elite technology and AI-native companies, that have avoided this trend. They have done so because they have created organizational structures and management systems that are optimized for the superlinear scaling of outcomes.

The goal of Outcome Management is to create organizations that scale superlinearly in the outcomes they deliver. This means that growing the organization will result in proportionally more outcomes delivered to the market, the customer, or the citizen. But it is important that this increase in outcomes is not accompanied by an exponential increase in costs, such as additional coordination and overhead costs. As such, we also want a structure that scales sublinearly in terms of resources. As the organization grows, and as we add value streams and teams, it should become cheaper, not more expensive, for the growth to add to value delivery.

The effect of efficiently scaled organizations is already visible in the market today. As of 2025, the top seven tech giants represent around 14% of global stock market capitalization.[11] Without some kind of monopolistic or captive market dynamic, it is impossible for an organization that has scaled outcome delivery sublinearly to compete with one that scales it superlinearly. This effect was amplified during the Age of Software & Digital as production cycles accelerated with the loss of physical constraints. It is going to be magnified further in the Age of AI, where we will shift from the weeks or months it takes to hire and onboard a new team of ten people, to the ability to instantly provision thousands of AI agents.

Scaling Inspirations from Natural Systems

To help guide approaches to organizational scaling, we can look to nature for inspiration. Plants have scaled to grow into massive trees that deliver nutrients to their leaves. The same system that delivers nutrients to ten leaves on a houseplant scales to delivering nutrients to the over 100 million needle-like leaves that a Coast redwood can support.[12] Similar scaling principles are employed in your body, where your circulatory system manages to deliver nutrients to the roughly 100 billion neurons in your brain.

We are familiar with the shapes of such scaling structures when we see them. The way that a large trunk splits into branches, then into smaller branches, then into twigs, and then into the stems of leaves forms a compelling, self-similar hierarchy.

Self-similarity, or fractal geometry, brings with it "scale invariance," where the same hierarchical pattern repeats at different scales. Think zooming into a fern, examining the hierarchical branching of a circulatory system, or magnifying a fractal. The same structural pattern repeats itself at different levels of magnification. West's Scaling Law tells us that hierarchical branching structures have sublinear scaling, making larger systems more efficient per unit of mass.[13]

This is exactly the dynamic that we want to emulate in our organizations. The more we grow the organization, the more efficient we want it to become at outcomes delivered per unit of input.

But resource consumption is only half of the equation. Our organizations could become more and more efficient at consuming resources but less and less efficient at delivering outcomes. According to West's analysis, this is the unfortunate fate that most organizations fall prey to as they grow large and bureaucratic.[14] No matter how well structured, the deeper the hierarchy, the harder it is for signals to get from the leaves to the trunk due to the growing distance they need to travel. The same goes for organizations.

So, how do highly complex systems in nature solve this scaling problem? To exhibit superlinear effects, West's analysis tells us that, in addition to the self-similar hierarchy, complex systems must have feedback signals that can act faster than the propagation through the hierarchical structure.[15]

Consider your vascular network. The very intricate self-similar hierarchy of blood vessels delivers oxygen and nutrients to your body. On top of this hierarchy, we have other feedback loops, such as hormonal signaling. For example, the insulin feedback loop ensures that when blood sugar rises, the pancreas releases insulin to help cells take up glucose. This is the kind of self-correcting feedback loop in nature that is present as a structure that overlays the self-similar hierarchy.

These kinds of feedback loops are critical for complex systems to function at scale. If the Coast redwood experiences water stress, the roots rapidly synthesize and release abscisic acid into the vascular system. This signal reaches the leaves and tells the stomata, which control respiration and water loss, to close rapidly. Once water availability improves, the acid levels drop and the stomata reopen.

This is exactly the kind of signaling we need our organizations to exhibit in order to respond to times of stress, for example, to changing macroeconomic conditions. Yet, as we saw with Holacracy, we cannot scale with feedback loops alone. We need a connected, resilient, and self-similar hierarchical structure that such signals can traverse. Regardless of how many of the leaves are populated by people and how many by agents, the structure of the tree is critical for effective scaling.

With these principles of self-similar hierarchies and feedback loops, we are ready to define the core scaling model for Outcome Management: the Outcome Tree.

Outcome Tree Structure

The smaller the organization, the easier it is to communicate, coordinate, and collaborate. For example, if there are only three teams in an organization, it is possible for each of those teams to have a tacit understanding of both inputs and outcomes without needing to codify these in the mechanisms of an operating model. It is also possible for those three teams to manage dependencies effectively through good collaboration and clear communication.

These dynamics change entirely when the organization grows from three teams to thirty or three thousand. The resulting disconnects mean teams at the bottom of the organizational chart, where the majority of the work is done, may be unable to impact any change on the inputs passed to them, and they may have no feedback loop at all with the outcomes they are attempting to deliver. In addition, without a clear scaling structure in the operating model, the complexity of the connectivity between teams grows exponentially.

The solution to this is the Outcome Tree.* The leaves of the Outcome Tree are the teams that deliver the value that drives outcomes, each of which is a value stream. Each value stream is an Outcome Loop within the organization. The value streams can be composed entirely of humans, a mix of humans and agents, or entirely of agents.

The size of value streams is governed by the nature of the work. For example, in delivering software, "two-pizza" sized teams, where two pizzas can feed the entire team, are a common size limit that ensures team cohesion and productivity when working with entirely human teams. A value stream composed of a mix of humans and agents may

* I first encountered the OKR-specific term of Outcome Tree from Felipe Castro and our collaboration on connecting OKRs to flow. The idea extends from concepts such as the "opportunity solution tree," popularized earlier by Teresa Torres. While the Outcome Tree described here has mechanisms specific to Outcome Management, the high-level motivations are similar.

have a "one-pizza" sized team or have just a single human. Smaller team sizes tend to work better for the complex domain, while teams in the complicated domain, such as manufacturing, can grow much larger. For example, a manufacturing plant can have a team of a hundred employees who perform standardized tasks. Regardless of the size, the atomic unit we are scaling in the Outcome Tree is the value stream, supported by a team and defined by its Outcome Loop.

The value stream and its team being the atomic unit has very specific implications. The value stream needs inputs in the form of strategy and budget. For those inputs to be effective, the value stream's team must participate in the setting of strategy and how that strategy turns into an actionable budget. This step is key as the point of the Outcome Loop is that the leadership of the team is fully responsible for turning the inputs into outputs and outcomes. As we will discuss further in Chapter 8, the managerial structure and empowerment of the team are critical for establishing a functional Outcome Loop.

Using a natural tree structure as a metaphor for the Outcome Tree, we can envision every value stream and its team as a leaf of the tree. These leaves have the most important function in our organization as they are what delivers the value. A natural tree leaf takes signals and nutrients as its inputs, but it is autonomous in photosynthesizing light into energy for the tree. Each of our value streams must be similarly autonomous in delivering and optimizing their own Outcome Loop.

Most organizations have achieved some level of organizational maturity for establishing teams. What tends to vary between elite and average organizations is the level of autonomy, empowerment, and support provided to the teams. These challenges arise less from a lack of understanding of the benefit of empowered teams and more from the failures in the structure and mechanisms that connect the leaves to the trunk. In order to match the familiarity of organizational charts and conventional tree diagrams, the Outcome Tree figures in this book depict the branches expanding as we go down the tree. However, the same structure can be visualized with the tree growing upward as trees do in nature, which has the positive metaphor of the trunk supporting the branches and teams. And the function of the trunk, branches, and twigs is to provide those leaves with both the support they need as well as the pathways providing the signals that enable them to adapt to changing conditions.

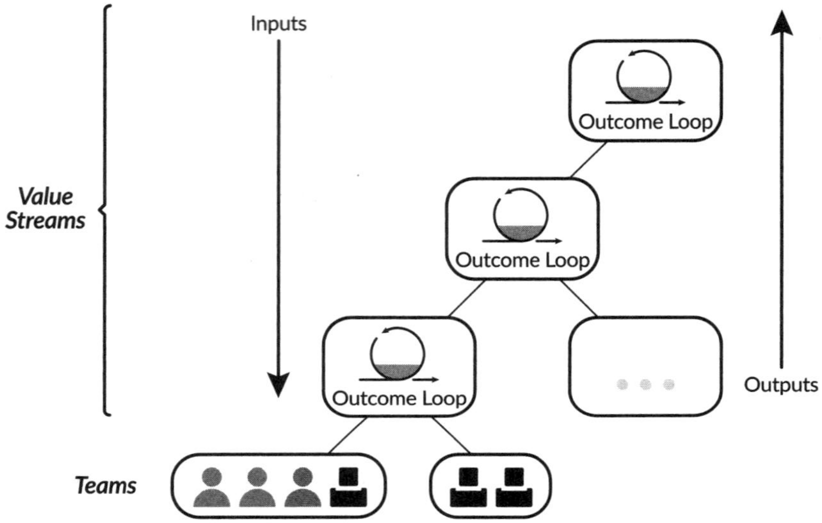

FIGURE 3.2: The Outcome Tree
Hierarchy of Outcome Loops that scales strategy into outcomes across all teams.

In the Outcome Tree, the layer above the value stream is the team-of-teams layer, which is just another value stream composed of multiple value streams. This higher-level value stream combines two or more value streams in the way that a twig connects multiple leaves. That aggregate value stream forms its own Outcome Loop.

Each node in the tree is dependent on a set of inputs. This is similar to how a natural tree is dependent on water and nutrients coming from the soil. In the case of an organization, those inputs are the strategy and budget. In the Outcome Tree, each node is a value stream that delivers outcomes to its customers. Each value stream can be decomposed into child value streams, which can then be further decomposed until we reach the leaves of the organization, represented by the teams.

Similar to a tree in nature, the leaves, or teams, can attach to any one branch in the Outcome Tree. For example, the CEO can have a value stream reporting directly to them just as a tree can have leaves attached to the main trunk or one of its main branches. An example of this is the CEO directly managing a frontier AI skunkworks value stream, as we will review in Chapter 9.

Thus, the structure of our Outcome Tree has each node represent a value stream that delivers an Outcome Loop and cascades up the outcomes of value streams that are its children in the tree. Each value stream has dedicated leadership in the form of one or more managers, as we will discuss in Chapter 8, and each value stream can have a direct team. The team can be humans, a mix of humans and agents, or purely agents in the case of autonomous value streams (discussed in Chapter 10).

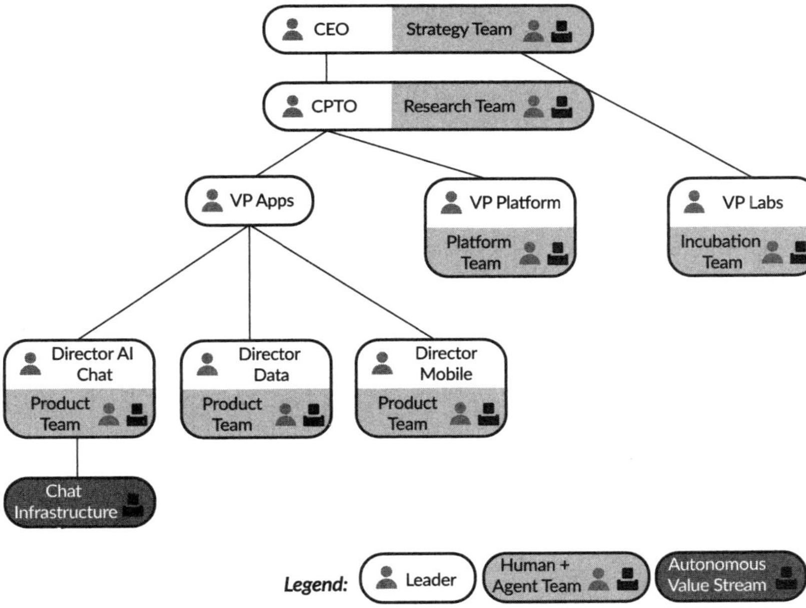

FIGURE 3.3: Example Outcome Tree Leadership Structure

If the value stream does not have a team supporting it, it is instead composed of other value streams rolling up to it as its children in the tree. These are like the thicker branches that do not directly support any leaves in a natural tree. In this scenario, the leaders of those value streams form the team for the higher-level value stream. For example, in our TeenWellness example, the vice president of apps will own the Outcome Loop for all customer-facing value streams. In that scenario, each app, as well as the corresponding data layer, should have a leader who supports that value stream and is responsible for its Outcome Loop. The vice president's team is that set of leaders. Those leaders can then have multiple leaders who report to them and are responsible for various teams and functions. A team can also have an autonomous value stream (see Chapter 10) supporting it, such as Chat Infrastructure in Figure 3.3. The chief product and technology officer (CPTO) is responsible for all of the product, platform, and incubation value streams. Together, this hierarchy defines the ownership structure of value streams and teams that collectively deliver all organizational outcomes.

Outcome Tree Partitioning

To enable effective scaling and avoid the pitfalls of coordination costs, the allocation of leaders and teams to the Outcome Tree must be mutually exclusive and collectively exhaustive (MECE).* Such a structure has no overlaps, so it is a clean partitioning of the entire organization. This means that the Outcome Tree functions like a standard organizational chart, with each team member and leader having one place in the chart. In other words, a person cannot appear more than once in the chart or be part of more than one value stream.

The decomposition of the Outcome Loops is a clean partitioning as well. Recall that in the Outcome Loop we connect inputs to outcomes via objectives. The top Outcome Loop, which encompasses the entire organization, has a set of objectives. These are then decomposed into child objectives, all the way down the Outcome Tree hierarchy. For example, if there is a growth objective with a key result of achieving

* Barbara Minto developed the MECE principle while at McKinsey & Company in the 1960s and incorporated it into her renowned Pyramid Principle communication framework.[16]

$100 million of revenue this fiscal year, and that revenue is to be provided by five different products, the key results for each product's value stream must add up to $100 million. Each key result must be a quantifiable number to enable this precise partitioning. This enables scalable decomposition, whether the numbers add up as they do with revenue or whether they are combined in another way, for example, by weighted averages of per-product retention rates.

Each value stream can add additional objectives to its Outcome Loop. For example, to experiment with launching a pre-revenue product. However, they cannot remove the objectives that flow down from above in the cascade. This empowers each value stream to drive additional activities and create artifacts specific to their role in the organization. For example, a team building a brand-new product may decide to experiment with a new kind of AI automation that has not been employed by the rest of the organization. This will be manifested in objectives that are specific to that value stream. However, while allocating some capacity to that experimentation, that value stream is still responsible for delivering on its stated outcomes.

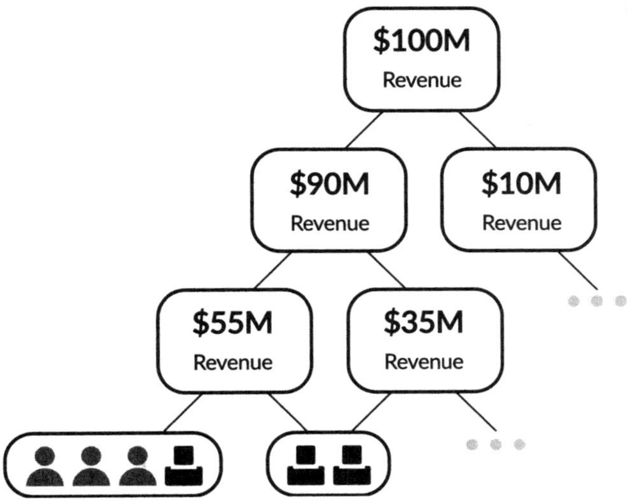

FIGURE 3.4: Objective Cascade Through the Outcome Tree

This structure will be familiar to those who have worked in other kinds of outcome-oriented management systems. For example, sales organizations often use the same type of decomposition structure to go from a global revenue target, break that into regional targets (e.g., per continent), then break that down into country targets, and then team or vertical targets. This makes outcome ownership clear and ensures a clean rollup of both sales forecasts and sales outcomes. This translates into clear sales quotas and a direct attribution of sales outcomes to compensation.

In some cases, sales organizations introduce "overlay" roles, for example, when an expert in a particular product supports multiple regions. These matrix lines overlay the Outcome Tree and dramatically increase the complexity of the structure, forecasting, and compensation due to the additional coordination costs. The closer the sales structure can be to the Outcome Tree, the easier it is to manage.

The clean partitioning of the Outcome Tree also provides the structure for implementing access control mechanisms. In some scenarios, we may want to give agents read access to all of the documents and code supporting the entire Outcome Tree. However, at large scales, or in scenarios where sensitive information is involved, we may want to contain agents' ability to modify documents and code to just the value streams they operate in. The modular boundaries between value streams enable this kind of partitioning. We will explore both modular boundaries and matrix lines further in Chapter 7.

Branching Factors

So far, we have defined what each node in the tree is, and we will explore details on how to approach the creation and evolution of these value streams in the next chapter. For example, how every product value stream is responsible for the end-to-end delivery of a product and has the persistent capacity and funding to deliver on the outcomes set on that product through its objectives. That capacity comes from inputs (i.e., the budget that funds headcount, agents, and hosting and that is decomposed as we move down the tree). If the budget for the "Mobile Apps" value stream in our TeenWellness example is $10 million, then each of the mobile apps will have a portion of that budget, with all portions adding up to $10 million. In this way, the inputs cascade all the way down the tree to the leaves, or teams, that deliver on the outcomes, and the outcomes cascade back up the tree. We thus have a scalable, self-similar, and closed loop system for turning inputs into outcomes.

The next step is to determine which Outcome Tree shape is suitable for your organization. In nature, some trees are tall with a small number of thick branches, while others are broader with countless twigs. These are called branching factors, which define how many child nodes a parent tree node supports. When growing a new organization, we can utilize the team size heuristics discussed above. As AI agent capabilities evolve, we can also adjust these branching factors accordingly.

For example, an organization could define a best practice for the maximum branching factor, which determines how many child value streams a value stream can break up into, to be limited to ten. This implies that if a vice president were responsible for more than ten mobile applications and supporting services, they would end up with more than ten direct reports, at which point it would make sense to segment the mobile applications into two separate value streams.

There are no hard rules on what this branching factor should be. For example, Jensen Huang, the CEO of Nvidia, had sixty direct reports in 2025.[17] In contrast, managers at Amazon's AWS division have historically targeted six to ten reports.[18] What is critical is that the branching factor of the tree is optimized for your organization's context. If the Outcome Loop is indicating bottlenecks at a particular level of the Outcome Tree, the number of value streams being managed by that level should be examined. We will dive deep into measuring the flow of value through the Outcome Tree in Chapter 5. In Chapter 10, we will dive deeper into the mechanisms and roles involved with architecting the Outcome Tree.

Building the Outcome Tree at Tasktop

Two key aspects of my early career have been instrumental in helping me navigate the Age of AI. The first had to do with the way our team worked at Xerox PARC. We automated everything. We were releasing and consuming user feedback on a continuous basis. We were a team of five people, led by Gregor Kiczales, one of the pioneers of Object-Oriented Programming.[19] Our pace of innovation was constrained largely by our ability to digest and design for the feedback we were getting from our users.

It is that same feeling of fast flow and feedback that I made a point of emulating and scaling at every step of my career. This was my first time experiencing just how energizing an optimized Outcome Loop is for its team's members. While we worked in a research lab that did not have any of the monetary incentives enjoyed by my friends at dot-com startups, our value stream was energizing enough that it had me periodically sleeping in my office so as not to miss the opportunity to push more changes out early the next day.

Many others I know who have felt this think back on those times as some of the best experiences of their careers. The global CIO of one of the top international banks once fondly reminisced with me about his days as a programmer on the trading floor, where he worked with an Outcome Loop that was creating algorithmic trading changes in minutes. Many are now reliving that feeling through the productivity rush that comes from vibe coding.

The second lesson applies to how programming languages have influenced the evolution and applications of AI. My team and I were creating a new programming language intended to make it easy to express "crosscutting concerns" in complex software systems. Popular programming languages like Java were good at making hierarchical modules, so we built an open-source crosscutting modularity mechanism over top of Java called

AspectJ.[20] We had the opportunity to collaborate with Carliss Baldwin from Harvard Business School, whose work demonstrated the economic value of modularity via option theory.[21] These same principles underpin the structure and scaling mechanisms of the Outcome Tree.

Understanding the mechanics of programming languages provides some insight into the effectiveness of large language models. To turn a programming language into running software, there is an intermediate representation tree structure of the program.[20] I spent the bulk of my four years at PARC, and then the next four years of my PhD research, working on the tree structures that underpin programming languages and tools before applying the same concepts to organizational structures. AI research is now discovering that these language models create structures that approximate such trees, in part because they are trained on billions of lines of code and language examples and end up encoding grammatical and hierarchical patterns as a result.[23] The result is that large language models are extremely good at programming in addition to performing other linguistic tasks. These modular, tree-based structures help traditional computers, AI, and humans work with complexity, whether the structures organize programs or people. The human brain works similarly through linguistic mechanisms reinforced by prediction and feedback.[24] While we cannot handle complexity in the same way that the massive tree structures of software and AI can, we can leverage their ability to handle that complexity as long as we connect it to control structures that match our objectives.

Fast forward a decade, and I found myself working on a seemingly unrelated problem. My PhD supervisor Gail Murphy and I founded Tasktop based on my dissertation work on applying the concepts of syntax trees for code to value streams. Once the company had grown to over fifty people, the informal team and communication structure started failing us. Meetings and coordination costs were rising, and far too many decisions were coming up to me as CEO. Gail pointed out that the teams did not have enough autonomy and had became disconnected from our strategy. We had been trying to avoid creating a hierarchy, yet it was the lack of a hierarchy that was preventing the decomposition of responsibilities that enabled ownership and autonomy. How did we end up with such a clean, modular, and hierarchical structure for our codebase, yet nothing of the sort for our organization?

At that time, I read Ben Horowitz' book *The Hard Thing About Hard Things*, which makes the case that the communication architecture is the most important operational responsibility for the CEO to establish in an organization. According to Horowitz, communication architecture includes organizational design, meetings, processes, and feedback loops that enable the effective flow of information and ideas.[25]

That was when the epiphany struck. We should apply the same modularity mechanisms that we applied to our code to our organization and use that to reshape our communication architecture.

Many popular programming languages allow the programmer to specify a "static structure." Imagine you are building a mobile app for chat. The structure will include the hierarchy of all the widgets, such as the search box and buttons, that render on a mobile screen. That static structure is deployed to the cloud and then can be interacted with dynamically as you use the app, where each object exhibits the various behaviors it was programmed for. Programmers think of this as "instantiating" the objects in the static structure.

I realized that these exact same mechanisms apply to organizations. We create a static structure through an organizational chart, specify the mechanisms through processes, and then instantiate it by announcing the changes and watching the dynamics unfold. These are the concepts of organizational structure and dynamics summarized in *Wiring the Winning Organization*.

The Outcome Tree is a structure and set of mechanisms that helps organizations optimize for outcomes. My initial goal was to make a structure was easy for our leadership team to reason about and optimize in a way that helped Tasktop scale effectively. The hierarchical and ownership-based team structure supported the doubling of the company to one hundred employees. However, after that doubling in size, we experienced another scaling problem as the planning and goal-setting processes of the company diverged from the team structure.

John Doer's book on OKRs, *Measure What Matters*, was released in 2017 and provided the mechanisms I needed to connect a planning framework directly to the team ownership structure that same year. That became our first instance of a management system that exhibited the alignment, empowerment, and control mechanisms as it enabled a clean partition of objectives to cascade through our entire Outcome Tree. It allowed us to double in size gracefully to two hundred staff. And then yet another set of disconnects and drifts appeared.

This time, the problem was a misalignment between the Outcome Tree and all of the new roles and staff that had been added to the company. We had started Tasktop as a team of software engineers, and over half of the staff were still in engineering. However, we now had product managers, designers, and data scientists, not to mention all of the other sales, marketing, finance, and operational roles. Each function was connected to the strategy via objectives, but the ownership of value streams was diluted and confused by all the new roles. Did product managers own the outcomes or did the engineering leaders? Who owned the outcomes of the data science and machine learning work we were doing? Who should set sales targets for our various products, the sales leaders or the product leaders? We fumbled our way through planning, but the coordination costs were unnecessarily high and impeded ownership and the speed of decision-making.

The breakthrough came when I sat down with Adrian Cockcroft, then VP of Cloud Architecture Strategy at AWS and known for having created Netflix's cloud architecture. Adrian was a master of making planet-scale modular architectures and helped Netflix implement the Reverse Conway Maneuver, an organizational design strategy where teams and collaboration lines are reshaped to produce the desired software architecture. (Conway's Law states that organizations tend to produce the architecture that mirrors the organization's internal communication patterns. We will discuss this further in Chapter 7.) He told me to do the same thing he had done—to align the organizational design with the planning structure and the software architecture. The key was to make this a single, self-similar scaling structure.

Adrian pointed me to the work that Geoffrey West from the Santa Fe Institute had done on how complex systems scale. We implemented this newly unified and self-similar Outcome Tree structure at Tasktop, and it was a critical factor in our success as our business scaled and as the number of our products, platforms, and teams grew.

Since then, I have had the chance to leverage AI and apply these concepts to large and complex organizations. When a hierarchical organizational structure is clearly defined, AI models are able to provide insights and operate on the Outcome Tree much the way they are on code. The goals of the Outcome Tree are ownership and empowerment of humans who leverage AI to scale outputs that then drive outcomes for other humans. Having this modular architecture enables that ownership, and the leverage of AI optimizes the Outcome Tree in a way that empowers the staff in the organization and maximizes the value that the organization provides to the people it serves. Just as we shifted to infrastructure as code in the Age of Software, we can enable the organization as code in the Age of AI.

Conclusion: Foundations for Outcome Management

The Outcome Tree is the new organizational design needed to harness the capacity gains provided by AI. It draws inspiration from scaling structure in nature to enable value streams and Outcome Loops to be deployed in arbitrarily large configurations.

At its core, the Outcome Tree provides a single organizational structure to enable scaling while minimizing coordination cost. The combination of the Product Operating Model, the Outcome Loop, and the Outcome Tree provide us with the foundations needed to implement Outcome Management.

In Summary

- Agile and AI transformations fail without scaling the full Outcome Loop, as organizations may improve team-level output without the alignment or visibility necessary for improving outcomes.
- Coordination costs explode without a scalable structure due to unmanaged communication networks and matrix overlays that impede flow and decision-making.
- Scaling outcomes in the Age of AI requires creating organizational structures and mechanisms that scale outcomes superlinearly while keeping resource and coordination costs sublinear.
- Natural systems provide valuable guidance on how to scale with self-similar hierarchical branching structures that provide both efficient scaling and feedback loops.
- In Outcome Management, the Outcome Tree makes the Outcome Loop the unit of scale, with each team acting like a leaf that is connected upward through a hierarchical and cleanly partitioned Outcome Tree.

Key Takeaways

- The Outcome Tree is the scaling model for outcomes as it cascades strategy and budgets down, while outcomes cascade back up through a clean hierarchy of value streams.
- Teams alone cannot be the unit of scale when they are not directly connected to inputs and outcomes and embedded in an Outcome Loop.
- Efficient scaling combines a value stream hierarchy with feedback loops.
- Inputs cascade all the way down the tree to the teams that deliver on outcomes, while outcomes cascade back up the tree. This provides a scalable, self-similar, and closed-loop system for turning inputs into outcomes.

Prompt

Objective: Help humans design, refine, and operate an Outcome Tree that scales Outcome Loops across their organization.

Operating protocol (assist, don't act unilaterally):

- Identify current value streams and existing teams; help implement the Value Stream Management definition and telemetry.
- Propose a candidate Outcome Tree: a MECE hierarchy where each node is a value stream with its own Outcome Loop and leader(s), identifying any gaps or overlaps.
- For each node, clarify its inputs (strategy and budget slice), outcomes, and how child value streams roll up to parent objectives and metrics.
- Surface over-saturated communication networks: matrix overlays, leaders with too many connections, or teams not tied to clear inputs and outcomes.
- Suggest alternative branching (span of control) and resolve overlaps/gaps in outcome ownership.
- Ensure strategy and budgets cascade down the tree, while outcomes and feedback cascade up; propose simple visualizations and review cadences.

Guardrails: Do not change reporting lines or targets yourself. Always present options, trade-offs, and risks so human leaders can decide how to evolve their Outcome Tree.

Conclusion to Part I

As knowledge work outputs are increasingly automated and scaled by AI, traditional output-oriented management is no longer sufficient. Without a new operating model, organizations risk investing in outputs that do not translate into business and customer outcomes.

In Part I, we reviewed the three core Outcome Management models that are needed to operate effectively with AI. The Product Operating Model is the overarching structure that aligns strategy, funding, and delivery around value streams. The Outcome Loop is the core feedback mechanism that connects inputs to outputs and outcomes. The Outcome Tree is the hierarchical structure that scales value streams and their Outcome Loops across the organization, ensuring cascaded alignment from the top down and feedback of outcomes from the bottom up.

In an era where knowledge work output is no longer the constraint, productivity depends on organizational wiring that can effectively convert AI-amplified capacity into outcomes. Flow becomes the primary unit of analysis, as it enables measuring how value streams deliver strategic outcomes. Scaling value streams requires both a hierarchical structure and feedback mechanisms to avoid complexity and coordination costs growing exponentially. Elite organizations already embody these principles, and incumbents must make them explicit and systematic to compete in the Age of AI.

With these foundations in place, we can now tackle the seven shifts required to move from legacy structures to the scalable practices provided by Outcome Management. In Part II, each chapter summarizes an operational shift from legacy ways of working to an AI-native operating model. Each chapter also introduces a new mental model whose intent is to guide and support that transition. When combined, these ten models provide all of the structure and mechanisms needed to implement Outcome Management.

The following chapters will take you through each shift and model sequentially and provide you with both the conceptual and the implementation guidelines that you need to shift your organization from output to outcome. The models and shifts are presented in a logical sequence that is suitable for a comprehensive rollout of Outcome Management, though each can be applied independently. While CEO-sponsored deployments of Outcome Management may have the fastest time to impact, Outcome Management can be rolled out incrementally to portions of the organization or by implementing one shift at a time. Each chapter in Part II will guide you on how to implement one shift and conclude with a case study on that shift.

The first shift is from *Functions to Flow*, where we will examine the organizational and leadership structures needed to support the Outcome Tree. The shift from *Slop to Substance* digs deeper into value streams and measuring flow to ensure that amplified outcomes are delivering value and not noise. To shift from meeting and reporting *Chaos to Cadence*, we will apply the Unified Cadence Model. We will then examine the detailed mechanics of how to effectively structure value streams and organizations by shifting from *Matrix to Modularity*. Next, we will dig into more detailed practices around connecting strategy to outcomes by moving beyond basic objective tracking via the shift from *Objectives to Ownership*. To facilitate larger Outcome Trees that need to manage value streams ranging from incubation to maturity, we will review the shift from *Divisions to Domains*. The final chapter in Part II will summarize the shift leaders need to undertake from *Managers to Makers*, as the lines between those functions increasingly blur.

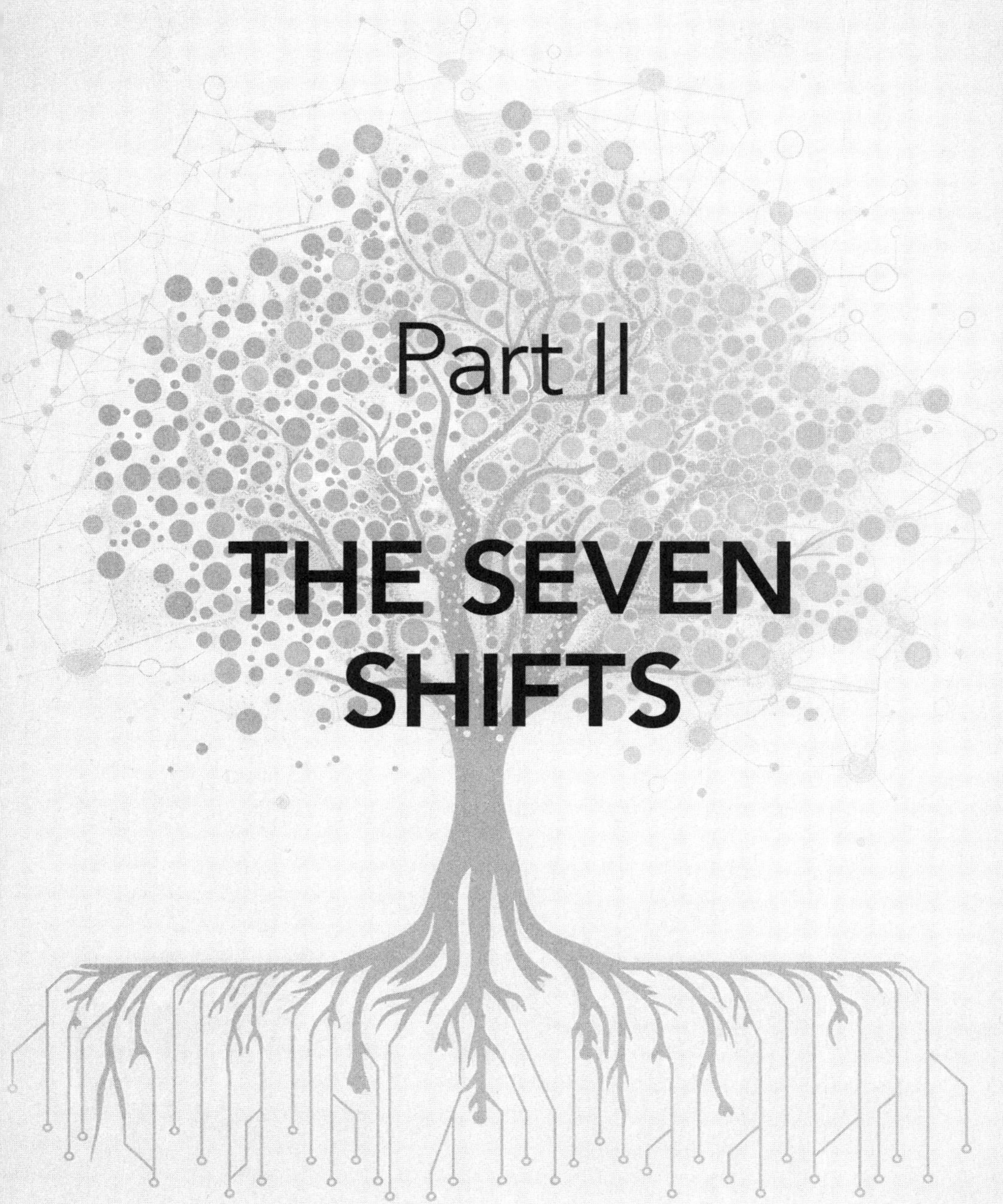

Part II

THE SEVEN SHIFTS

Chapter 4

First Shift: Functions to Flow

With AI amplification of cross-functional expertise, organizing around functional silos will cease to be a viable model. In this chapter, we explore how organizations need to shift from functions to flow by replacing silos with value streams structured into an Outcome Tree. We then discuss how leadership needs to be dedicated to each value stream, providing empowerment and clear outcome ownership for each team supporting the value stream. The chapter concludes with strategies for making value stream flow measurable and connected to strategy, enabling people and agents to scale output delivery in ways that are directly connected to driving outcomes.

In Part I, we established the Outcome Loop as the mechanism for connecting inputs through to the production of outputs and the delivery of outcomes. We now need to define how to align organizational structures and processes in a way that enables the implementation of an Outcome Loop.

In traditional output-oriented management, the dominant organizational construct is the organizational function. These functions include core business specializations, such as sales, marketing, finance, and technology. Those functions break into sub-functions. For example, the sub-functions for technology might include design, business analysis, product management, engineering, data science, quality assurance, security, and operations. The sub-functions can further be specialized by domain, such as cloud-native engineering, AI-native engineering, web development, and mobile development. As the complexity of organizations and technology has grown, so have the number of specializations. However, the DevOps movement has demonstrated that cross-functional teams and value streams are more effective.[1] In addition, AI is enabling an entirely new level of cross-functional work by extending people's reach and expertise across domains.

Shift: Functions to Flow: The dominant hierarchical structure of the organization moves from functional specialization to value streams accountable for end-to-end outcomes, organized into an Outcome Tree. Other organizational structures, such as reporting and matrix lines, exist solely to support the flow of value through this structure.

With Outcome Management, instead of organizing around functions, the organization is structured around value streams. The Product Operating Model prioritizes the flow of value to the customer over functional specialization. Organizing around functions leads to handing off work from one function to another. For example, from design to development and then from development to testing. This kind of handoff can work in less complex domains where iterations are slower and where efficiency can be gained by decomposing work into independent disciplines. This breaks down as work gets more complex. Even in the simpler case of assembly lines, the concepts of Lean Manufacturing were introduced to optimize lines for flow over functional handoffs.[2]

As we discussed in Chapter 1, the Outcome Management relies on even faster end-to-end iteration. As such, the operating model needs to remove functional handoffs and optimize for flow along the Outcome Loop. To do this, we need to create an organizational and leadership structure where the primary construct is the value stream and where functions and other kinds of specializations are secondary.

The acceleration of flow that comes from switching from a functional and project-oriented structure to a value stream structure can be nearly instantaneous. As we will review more closely in the case study in Chapter 7, when Priceline implemented the Product Operating Model, they instantly moved from needing fifteen handoffs to ship product features to needing only five. Not only did this dramatically accelerate delivery, AI then enabled a scaline of delivery that would not have been possible if all of those functional handoffs were still in place.

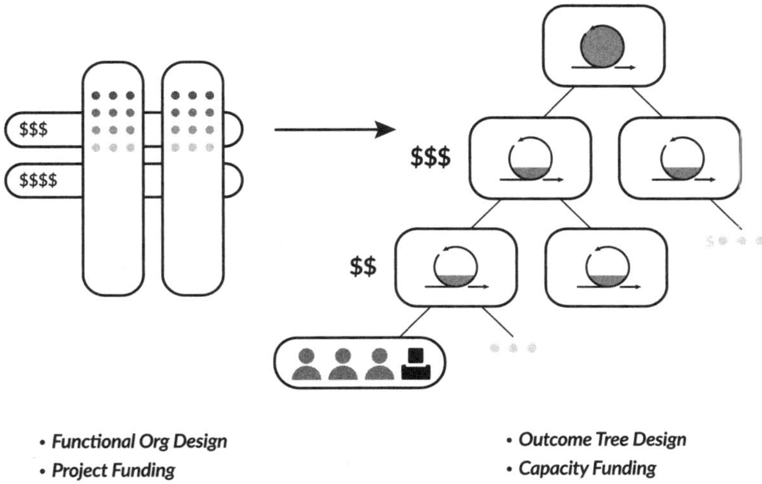

FIGURE 4.1: Functions to Flow

Dedicated Leadership Model

A product value stream is composed of all of the activities, artifacts, people, agents, and processes required to turn inputs into outcomes. As with other organizational structures, it is intrinsically tied to the leadership structures that support it. The leadership structure that supports the Outcome Tree is the *Dedicated Leadership Model*. In this approach, each value stream has dedicated leadership whose entire focus is driving outcomes for that value stream. This leadership structure mirrors Amazon's Single-Threaded Ownership Model, documented in *Working Backwards* by Colin Bryar and Bill Carr.[3] What started as the leadership structure for "two-pizza teams," with leaders who had a singular focus on the success of that team, evolved into the Single-Threaded Ownership structure that scaled regardless of the team size and number of sub-teams under the team. *Working Backwards* details how this structure creates clarity, cohesion, and autonomy.

In this chapter, we will detail how the Dedicated Leadership Model supports hybrid human and AI teams, how agents are evolving team sizes down to "one-pizza" sized, and in some cases to a single person, and how human-centric leadership is the core managerial structure needed to support value streams and the Outcome Tree.

> **Dedicated Leadership Model:** Ensures that each product value stream has leadership whose sole managerial focus is driving outcomes for that value stream.

There is an often-overlooked nuance in Amazon's Single-Threaded Model, as Amazon distinguishes between Single-Threaded Owners, who have teams and delivery responsibility reporting directly to them, and Single-Threaded Leaders, who are accountable for strategic outcomes without direct reporting lines. As Amazon scaled, it became clear that finding one person with the necessary technical, product, and business expertise was difficult. For this reason, many organizations adopt the "Dual-Leader" Model, also referred to as Two-in-a-Box Leadership Model,[4] where an engineering leader and a product leader are paired to provide Single-Threaded Ownership.

The Dedicated Leadership Model focuses on the reporting and ownership structure for the Outcome Tree. As such, it is most closely related to the Single-Threaded Ownership Model and generalized to support "dual-leader" and on occasion "triple-leader" structures. We will explore the title leveling for these multi-leader structures in Chapter 8.

Consider the potential leadership structure for the TeenWellness example. The leadership of Mobile Apps for TeenWellness can be a single person with product and engineering management responsibility with the title of vice president of mobile. In this case, we have the Dedicated Leadership Model with a single leader structure.

In some contexts, having a single person lead a value stream is not feasible. For example, deep business expertise may be required for a product domain, such as clinical aspects of wellness, as well as deep engineering leadership, for example, in AI engineering. The organization's talent pool may not have a person who has sufficient expertise in both domains. In this case the dual-leader approach can be used to implement the Dedicated Leadership Model, where a product and engineering leader are partnered and are both entirely dedicated to leading the TeenWellness apps value stream. The engineering leader is likely to have all engineers reporting to them, while the product leader typically oversees product managers.

If AI expertise is just as relevant as product domain and engineering expertise, this could turn into a triple-leadership structure. However, the more people in the leadership box, the more leadership complexity can arise due to the additional alignment that is needed between the individuals filling the roles.

The key is that the Dedicated Leadership Model provides fully committed leadership for the value stream, and the outcomes for that value stream are entirely owned by its single or multiple leader(s). Given that the Outcome Tree is partitioned so value streams fully cover all work, it also follows that each leader must be entirely dedicated to that value stream and not lead any other value streams.

The simplest structure for the Outcome Tree is the single-leader structure, with dual-leader structures applied as needed. With this approach, the reporting structure in the organizational chart and the structure of the Outcome Tree have a one-to-one mapping. Digital native organizations are commonly built with this as the dominant structure and have been able to leverage its simplicity to deliver industry-leading economies of scale and rapid adoption of AI. In other words, to deliver superlinear outcomes with sublinear resource consumption. For example, this means that Amazon has increased its pace of revenue growth, innovation, and customer value faster than it has increased its headcount and cost base. In my experience, this approach works effectively at any scale and is what we employed at Tasktop right from being a single-team startup to a scaled-up leader in our market.

The single-leader approach may not be feasible for larger organizations and those making the shift from older ways of working. In this case, it is possible to apply the dual-leader approach to the entire product and engineering organization, as we will explore below. Even at Amazon, the dual-leader model is not uncommon due to the challenges of finding individuals with sufficient breadth of expertise.

> **Guidance: Clarify Ownership by Streamlining Leadership Structure:** Default to a single-leader structure where possible, using dual-leader models when necessary. Leverage AI to amplify the expertise of existing leaders to help them span functional domains.

The amplification of leaders through AI helps fill experience gaps. For example, an engineering leader who may not have expertise in our example TeenWellness domain can rely on AI to augment their domain understanding. Similarly, a leader with a business background can leverage AI to amplify their competence in engineering. This AI amplification means the single-leader model will be suitable in more cases than it was previously. However, there will still be cases where deeper domain expertise and hands-on experience are required, resulting in the dual-leader model. We will discuss this amplification of leadership roles in more detail in Chapter 10.

The invariant of Outcome Management is that the product development organization has a dedicated leadership structure where the leader or leaders own the end-to-end Outcome Loop for each value stream. This implies owning the entire set of objectives for that value stream, as well as the cascade of objectives down the Outcome Tree. If a dual-leader structure is used, then this same part of the Outcome Tree is implemented in two areas of the organizational chart.

For example, some technology organizations have a chief product officer and a chief technology officer who both report to the CEO. In this case, the leadership structure of each executive needs to be aligned into the Outcome Tree to ensure the cascade of dedicated leadership. If the chief product officer has three vice presidents for three product areas, the chief technology officer should have three corresponding engineering vice presidents, creating a matching dual-leader structure across their two teams.

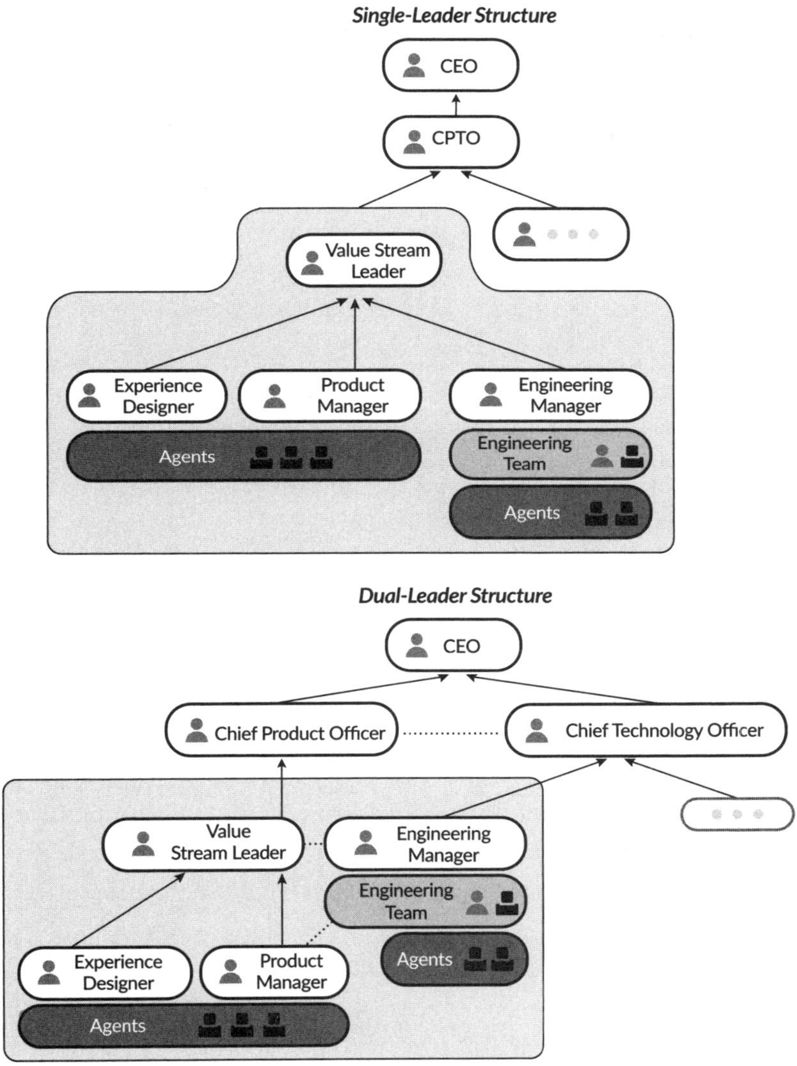

FIGURE 4.2: Single-Leader vs. Dual-Leader Model

In some enterprise organizations, this dual leader might be a combination of a business leader and a technology leader. In other circumstances, a triple-leader structure may be needed. The structure depends on both the available talent and the product and life cycle context. For example, six months into creating an agentic AI solution, I realized that my teams needed to switch to the triple-leader model for a year to ensure that AI, product, and engineering leadership were on equal footing as we built out the core AI platform. Once built out, it became feasible to switch back to a dual-leader model. This journey is described in the case study in Chapter 8.

The single leader is optimal from a simplicity perspective. However, what is more important is that the right leadership is in place for each value stream. How you staff the leadership role or roles for each value stream is a function of your talent pool and organizational context. There are other talent-related factors that need to be considered, such as management and mentorship. For example, some organizations may determine that for training and mentoring purposes, engineers should report to engineers. Or they may determine that a scarce role, such as an AI engineer or specialized data scientist, is easiest to recruit if they report to a known expert in that same specialization.

All of these options can be supported as long as the formal reporting structures mirror the structure of the Outcome Tree and adhere to the Dedicated Leadership Model. If they do not mirror the structure, objectives and outcomes cannot cascade effectively. This is where matrix management can create major misalignments with the Outcome Tree, such as when a product leader and the corresponding engineering leader are accountable for different objectives or have different incentive structures. We will discuss the problems with matrixed leadership in Chapter 7.

If the organization uses dual or triple leadership, ensuring outcome ownership and alignment requires making the Outcome Tree and its cascade the primary organizational structure. If it is not, the cascade of objectives will differ in the different parts of the organization. In that mode, the product organization will define their own objectives as will engineering. Following that, multiple alignment mappings, communication, and collaboration cadences will result in complexity and coordination cost, with the additional overhead leading to further misalignment. Ensuring that the reporting structure mirrors the Outcome Tree ensures that ownership is aligned to outcomes in every function of the organization.

Dysfunction: Multiple Misaligned Objectives: When Objectives and Key Results are defined by function rather than by the Outcome Tree, product and engineering leaders are inadvertently driven by conflicting and misaligned objectives.

Guidance: Align Leadership Structures to Value Streams: Leadership structures must mirror the Outcome Tree, forming a single hierarchy of ownership, even if they are implemented across multiple functions.

The Outcome Tree is the primary organizational structure supporting Outcome Management. Functional structures, such as specializations, are secondary. This is a significant shift for organizations that may be accustomed to functional decomposition being the dominant organizational paradigm. In the Age of Software & Digital, this kind of functional decomposition lost ground in elite organizations that were structured around outcomes. In the Age of AI, functional organizational structures will become even less relevant as the scope of each leader's knowledge is amplified by AI.

Value Stream Scope

We have defined the structure of the Outcome Tree and how it maps onto the organizational chart in terms of both the leadership (which corresponds to the nodes in the tree) and the teams (which correspond to the leaves). To complete the shift from organizational chart to Outcome Tree, we must also identify the scope of value streams. To determine the scope of each value stream, we must return to the goal of the value stream. The goal of each value stream is to maximize the flow of value in support of that value stream's Outcome Loop.

As we discussed briefly in Part I and will explore further in Chapter 7, dependencies that fall outside the value stream introduce wait states. These wait states occur when teams on one value stream are waiting for another value stream to complete work that they require to progress their own roadmap. As with manufacturing processes, wait states derail productivity. Wait states commonly result from dependencies or from process problems, such as overly long approvals or reviews. Consider the scenario where a team built amazing new mobile app functionality but must wait for a business review before it can be released. If that review takes a week to complete, that entire wait is time wasted from the point of view of how quickly the Outcome Loop can go through its feedback cycle. As such, we want to ensure that value streams are as self-contained as possible in terms of their ability to deliver flow and track feedback.

To use a concept from *Wiring the Winning Organization*, we want "independence of action" for each value stream.[5] We will explore this concept in detail in Chapter 7. Independence of action requires the structuring of processes and teams in a way that enables autonomous work without the need for constant coordination or approval from other parts of the organization. We want each value stream to take its input of strategy and budget and deliver outcomes as quickly and autonomously as possible. The alignment of the value stream to the strategy starts in the planning process, which helps enable the empowerment of the value stream even when working on highly mission-critical initiatives.

The scope of a value stream is defined by the scope of its Outcome Loop. The leadership of the value stream must work with the value stream's team to iterate on the strategy and budget and turn that into roadmaps that define the output of activities and artifacts. This means the team that supports the value stream must include leadership as well as everyone involved with the production of that value stream's outputs. The value stream "ends" with the customer receiving the artifacts that provide the value that drives both customer and business outcomes. This means that the team or teams supporting the value stream include all of the people and agents that manage inputs, deliver outputs, and track outcomes for that value stream.

In parent value streams higher up the Outcome Tree, the output may be entirely delivered by child value streams, but the principle remains. For example, for the TeenWellness app, this could include all of the staff and agents that provide the design, analysis, development, operations, and telemetry instrumentation for that particular application. In this case, the parent value stream includes all applications, with outputs delivered by each of the individual app value streams.

Organizations can have numerous functions that support value streams. For example, the Legal team can provide contract negotiation for suppliers. The Revenue Operations team may provide Outcome Loop metrics used by the leadership of the value stream. While these supporting functions are a form of dependencies, if they do not block the flow of the outputs of the value stream, they can be managed effectively outside of the value stream.

It is possible for dependencies of this sort to block flow, for example, if legal support is needed to leverage a new web service or open-source library for the value stream. However, these dependencies can be handled via straightforward service level agreements (SLAs). SLAs ensure that simpler dependencies, such as legal or reliance on web services, have well-scoped and acceptable wait states to prevent the blocking of flow. Other functions, such as product marketing, can belong within or outside the value stream depending on the organizational context and size. We will further discuss value stream scope and dependencies in Chapter 7.

What is key for maximizing flow is clearly setting the scope of the value stream to ensure autonomy, to minimize external dependencies, to include all of the people and agents to support delivery, and to provide the dedicated leadership to support and manage the Outcome Loop.

As long as an organization is evolving, the process of refining value stream scope does not stop. For continuous, data-driven improvement of managing scope and dependencies, Outcome Loop telemetry is critical. At other times, a more substantial reorganization and rewiring of the Outcome Tree may be necessary. For example, as Tasktop went through its phases of growth, we had to undergo several cross-company reorganizations. The ones that were most complex were those that involved moving between single- and dual-leader models. In addition to relying on existing telemetry, I worked with Geordie Henderson,[6] an organizational design consultant, on a data-centric analysis of the entire Outcome Tree to get an external holistic view of rewiring opportunities and pitfalls. Geordie is a seasoned engineering leader and former general manager at AWS, and our iterative work on this data, and the reorganizations that followed, inspired and informed the mechanisms of the Dedicated Leadership Model.

Value Stream Management

Value streams are the organizational structure that underpin the shift from functional organizational design to a design that optimizes flow to drive outcomes. *Value Stream Management* is the methodology and practice that provides the organizational underpinnings for Outcome Management. It captures key operational practices, including the shift from funding projects to the capacity-based funding that is key to the Product Operating Model.

Because value streams function with a self-contained set of inputs, such as their budget, headcount, hosting, inference, and agent costs, funding the capacity of value streams becomes a straightforward process at each level of the Outcome Tree. The cost of the value stream is simply the total cost of that node and its children in the Outcome Tree. This is in stark contrast to the Project Management and funding process, which involves the mapping of resources across various functional siloes to a multitude of projects.

As we will see in Chapter 7, product and value stream funding avoids the complex mappings of matrix management, where Agile teams and other costs need to be mapped into various investment initiatives to capture the cost of those initiatives. These mappings are often inaccurate due to teams, services, and agents providing shared capabilities. In Chapter 9, we will examine how to partition the Outcome Tree into product, platform, and other supporting value streams, which enables another level of granularity for tracking of cost and investment. Value streams provide a simple and clear organizational structure where every leader and every individual knows exactly which part of the Outcome Tree they support. This is not to say that each value stream only works on a single product or platform service. For example, a value stream can take on a mix of new and legacy apps, resulting in a single team needing to build a new app while concurrently supporting several legacy apps. This makes the value stream's roadmap much more complex and will likely result in multiple conflicting priorities on that roadmap. But this does not complicate the structure of the value stream itself, as it is the team and its outputs that define the capacity of the value stream. If there are too many apps to support, the team can make this clear during the planning process and triage accordingly. And as we will see in the next chapter, connecting the flow-based capacity of the value stream to the roadmapping process makes planning straightforward even in cases of complex product portfolios.

Value Stream Management: The practice of measuring, managing, and improving the flow of work through a value stream to accelerate the delivery of outputs that drive customer and business outcomes.

The concepts of value streams originate with physical production and value stream mapping, which is the practice of supporting both materials and information flows in manufacturing.[7] In *Project to Product*, I introduced Value Stream Management as a new practice, inspired by value stream mapping but specific to software development. Whereas value stream mapping creates a static picture of the flow of information and materials, Value Stream Management leverages software to enable organizations to continually measure and manage the flow of knowledge work. Similar to how supply chain management software provides real-time telemetry of the flow of value through highly complex flows of materials, Value Stream Management software provides real-time views of workflows and bottlenecks. Outcome Management incorporates Value Stream Management to optimize the flow of value from outputs to outcomes by identifying constraints in the broader delivery process. While value streams are defined at the Outcome Tree level as the nodes of the tree, Value Stream Management optimizes the delivery loop portion of each Outcome Loop.

This is only half the equation, as we also need to optimize the planning loop. For each value stream, we need to take the discovery work and inputs and ensure the sequence of work that is defined by the resulting roadmap maximizes the outcomes as specified by the objectives. This is where many organizations leverage Agile frameworks and similar planning methodologies. For example, Weighted Shortest Job First[8] is a heuristic for determining which backlog items should be prioritized on the next iteration of the roadmap. This approach considers the cost of delay[10] of not delivering a particular item in terms of the opportunity cost of the missed outcomes and prioritizes the items on the roadmap that minimize the cost of delay. Regardless of the methodology used, to leverage AI the planning process must keep pace with dramatically accelerated delivery.

Throughout my entire career, I have leveraged flow-based prioritization models for product development because they map clearly onto outcomes and support fast feedback loops. Other prioritization models exist, and many Agile and iterative methodologies can be implemented for the planning loop. As long as the planning loop employs a system that is able to iteratively plan at a pace that matches the speed of delivery and feedback, the value stream has all of the components in place needed to establish the feedback portion of the Outcome Loop. In the following chapter, we will dive into connecting the planning loop to the delivery loop.

From Frenzy to Flow at TUI Group

Pieter Jordaan is the group chief information officer at TUI Group and has been spearheading the transformation of the world's largest travel organization into an AI-native organization. I first met Pieter in 2020, when he asked me to present the concepts of *Project to Product* to TUI's CEO and board. Pieter's approach to TUI's very rapid cloud transformation immediately made an impression on me. While it was clear to me that he was a hands-on and deep technologist, his approach to the transformation was different from what I had seen from his peers.[11]

What stood out first was Pieter's focus on business outcomes. Rather than the multiyear cloud plans that I was used to seeing, Pieter had managed to move TUI's e-commerce, which supported 50% of its revenue, to a brand-new cloud native platform within six months. This started him on a journey to accelerate toward dedicated product teams.

During the COVID-19 pandemic, while many travel businesses shut down, Pieter moved TUI from disparate business units supporting legacy databases and systems onto a consolidated cloud platform with teams leveraging the Product Operating Model. He also established a new leadership structure aligned to product value streams and instrumented all the value streams with flow metrics.

Turning TUI into a technology innovator was only possible thanks to their move from functional silos to value flow, which enabled rapid delivery, continual feedback, and ongoing experimentation loops. This approach not only contributed to their rapid recovery after the COVID-19 pandemic but also set them up for their AI transformation.

Over the following four-year period, the average flow time for TUI's value streams accelerated from two hundred days to just fifteen days in key products.

This foundation could not have been timelier. Pieter and his team were some of the fastest to lean into transforming both their distribution model and their software delivery the moment the 2022 ChatGPT demo made it clear how disruptive AI would be to their business and operations.

To underscore the point, during one of his executive briefing sessions to his board, Pieter pointed Claude Code to their website and turned it agentic e-commerce ready for answer engine optimization and agents, demonstrating the power and speed of agentic workflows and outcome-driven AI agents. This gave his board a visceral understanding of the scope of the shifts coming in the Age of AI.

As part of his initial cloud transformation and Product Operating Model implementation, Pieter had already put in place a single-threaded structure with dual-leadership for product and engineering. This meant the leadership structure was properly aligned to company outcomes as well as product and platform value streams through two-in-the-box product and engineering leaders for each. With that in place, the next step was shifting to AI-native engineering in the organization at the same pace as the original cloud transformation. To accelerate this process, Pieter created a four-level AI literacy framework to steer internal discussions about upskilling and development.

The first level is Explorer, basic chat skills; the second level is Practitioner, advanced prompting and steering skills; the third is Builder, multi-agents with humans in the loop; and the fourth level is Strategist/Innovator, with outcome-based agentic workflow design skills. Pieter believed the biggest obstacle for scaling AI will be humans' ability to learn and adapt.

To assist with the journey, Pieter personally coded an internal AI mentor that coached employees through these levels and uses interactive training to learn and evaluate skills. He set an aggressive goal for his whole organization to reach the Builder level, ensuring all employees have the AI literacy to transform the organization's processes and value streams. Furthermore, Pieter put AI in the hands of all employees across all business units through an internally developed AI assistant builder, which has been used to create over three thousand agents that are being leveraged by TUI's staff.

While the single-threaded leadership structure was in place, along with OKRs and the Outcome Tree, Pieter realized how profound the AI shift would be for TUIs leaders. In large organizations, senior managers are accustomed to owning large sets of teams and supporting those teams. A shift was needed from "owning people" to "owning outcomes."

At the individual contributor level, another shift was happening. Many of the typical skills workers focused on were becoming less relevant. However, their domain expertise, combined with AI and agents, would become increasingly relevant in an outcome-based agentic value flow. To help with this, Pieter and I met with the TUI board again to outline a plan for the Seven Shifts from output to outcome. It is this kind of end-to-end organizational awareness and buy-in from senior executives, combined with transformation leadership, that is going to be the hallmark of organizations that thrive in the Age of AI.

Conclusion

Organizational structures shape the dynamics that drive business outcomes. Functional structures were effective for managing work that was easy to decompose into specializations of labor. AI has upended all of that and requires a shift from functions to flow-, customer-, and outcome-oriented organizational design. The new top-level structure is a value-stream oriented organizational design, which is decomposable into the value stream units that underpin the Outcome Tree. To ensure this structure is effective and durable, the leadership structure of the organization must be aligned to the Outcome Tree via the Dedicated Leadership Model. This scalable and explicitly partitioned leadership structure establishes the value streams that we can then accelerate with agents. However, before we put that acceleration in place, we need to establish the additional telemetry and mechanisms for measuring and managing value streams to enable the second shift, from Slop to Substance.

In Summary

- Functional silos create costly handoffs between the various specializations or roles, fragmenting delivery and introducing wait states that impede flow.

- In Outcome Management, value streams are the new organizational units that deliver end-to-end outcomes, with functions treated as secondary structures.
- Dedicated leadership is essential to ensure alignment and accountability for outcomes and to drive empowerment for teams.
- Dedicated leadership can be supported by a single-, dual-, or multi-leader structures as long as they adhere to the principle that the value stream's leader or leaders have a singular commitment to their value stream.
- Value Stream Management operationalizes flow optimization by ensuring capacity-based funding and outcome-based planning for value streams.

Key Takeaways

- Shift from functions to flow by replacing siloed organizational structures with an Outcome Tree.
- Dedicate leadership to each value stream whether via single or multiple leaders, each of who is aligned directly to a single value stream in the Outcome Tree.
- Manage flow, not functions, by making value streams transparent, measurable, and connected to strategy and outcomes.

Prompt

Objective: Help humans shift from functional silos to value streams and dedicated leadership aligned to the Outcome Tree.

Operating protocol (assist, don't act unilaterally):

- Map today's structure: List core functions (e.g., product, engineering, design, ops) and identify key value streams (products, platforms, services) that actually deliver outcomes.
- Propose designs for a value-stream–oriented org: Each value stream as a node in the Outcome Tree with its own Outcome Loop, objectives, and budget.
- Design dedicated leadership for each value stream: Default to a single leader; suggest dual/triple-leader only where domain + tech + AI expertise clearly require it. Make ownership of outcomes explicit.
- Check MECE: Ensure every person and team belongs to exactly one value stream; surface overlaps, gaps, and matrix tangles.
- Define flow visibility: Recommend basic flow metrics and how to connect them to strategy and objectives for each stream.

Guardrails: Do not "re-org" autonomously. Always present options, trade-offs, and risks, and flag when functional reporting lines diverge from the Outcome Tree and threaten flow.

Chapter 5

Second Shift: Slop to Substance

With AI flooding organizations with cheap and scalable artifacts, output-centric metrics are becoming meaningless and misleading. An AI-centric operating model must instead focus on the end-to-end measurement of outcomes. Many organizations and teams are challenged on this front, as they have only invested in metrics that are easy to measure and those that focus on their limited functional area. Outputs tend to be the easiest to measure and myopic enough that they make it easy for leaders to show progress even if that progress is delivering AI slop and disconnected from outcomes. Until instrumentation is implemented end-to-end and connected to outcomes, metrics cannot effectively guide decision-making and delivery in the Age of AI. Organizations must invest in outcome-oriented metrics, instrumentation, and telemetry supporting every value stream in Outcome Tree.

In this chapter, we explore making all work visible and measurable through mechanisms, including Plan Distribution, Flow Distribution and the *Flow Metrics Model*. The chapter concludes with a practical approach to operationalizing data-driven continuous improvement via improvement objectives that accelerate flow and amplify future outcomes.

Measuring outputs is easy. However, if we cannot connect those outputs to outcomes, output metrics are meaningless. For example, a value stream could be producing the most amazing conversational user experience, but that user experience has no value unless it is being adopted and delighting its customers. When organizations manage by measuring what is easy, they fall into the trap of vanity metrics.[1] Output vanity metrics can include the number of features delivered by a development team, the number of deployments completed by an operations team, or the lines of code or pull requests contributed by agents. None of these output metrics are inherently bad, and each should be measured at some level in the organization. However, they are meaningless unless connected directly to an outcome.

Dysfunction: Vanity Metrics: Metrics that make a value stream appear effective but fail to provide insights into business or customer outcomes.

So, why do so many organizations track vanity metrics instead of the outcome metrics that represent business and customer value? The reason goes back to what organizational structures make easy to measure. If the dominant organizational structure is functional, it makes it easy to measure the performance of the various organizational functions. For example, a functional structure makes it easy to measure how many designs the user experience teams produced, how many features the development teams implemented, how much code agents generated, and how many deployments the agents and operations team performed. Each of these throughput metrics represents output that may or may not correspond to a customer outcome.

For example, if customer sentiment has shifted away from using a traditional mobile interface to using an AI-native conversational interface, each of these throughput metrics could be irrelevant until the team shifts its roadmap. Overly narrow time metrics have a similar pitfall. For example, measuring the cycle time from code commit to code deploy provides visibility into a single stage of development. But this metric tells us nothing about whether the right code and artifacts were delivered to meet the customer's needs.

Shift: Slop to Substance: Measuring outputs is easy and, in the Age of AI, increasingly meaningless. Functional silos default to silo metrics, products degrade with vanity metrics, and leadership falls prey to lagging indicators. To ensure you are delivering substance not slop, measure outcomes.

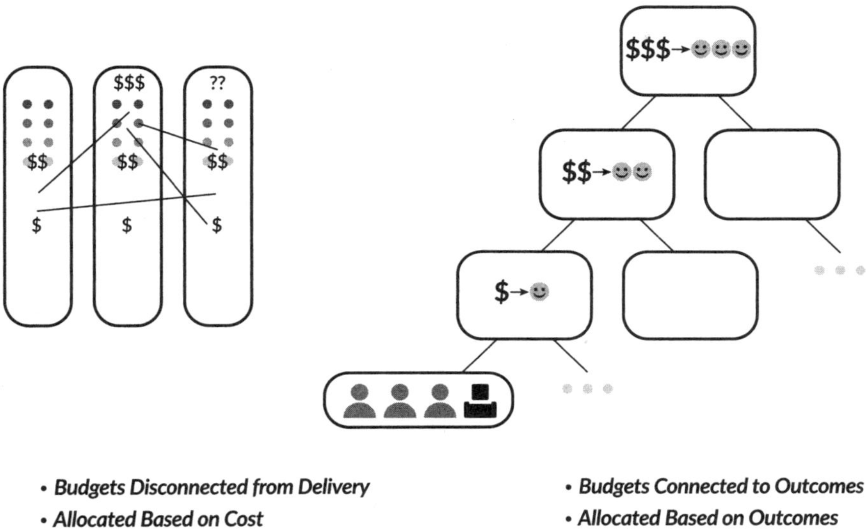

FIGURE 5.1: Moving from Slop to Substance

Flow Metrics Model

Output metrics are a necessary part of Outcome Loop instrumentation. In this chapter, we will dive deeper into the output metrics that are the most meaningful to track as part of the Outcome Loop. However, if they are disconnected from outcome metrics, all output metrics become vanity metrics. If we optimize for output metrics, we are optimizing for producing more of something without assurance whether that thing has any value. In the simpler complexity domains, this can work, as delivering value may be as obvious as building the next physical widget. However, in the complex domain, with changing markets and customer sentiment, value is often not obvious and requires feedback. Thus, we need to connect output metrics to outcome metrics, then connect the outcomes back to the planning process via the feedback loop. When connected to outcome metrics, output metrics become a leading indicator. To drive outcomes, we need to ensure that we optimize our organization not around outputs, but around the end-to-end flow through the Outcome Loop.

Flow Metrics Model: A framework for assessing the flow of work through a value stream using flow-based metrics, including Flow Time, Flow Velocity, Flow Efficiency and Flow Load. Used to track the delivery portion of a value-stream's Outcome Loop and provides Flow Metrics that connect delivery to outcomes.

The Age of AI is amplifying outputs in ways that were previously incomprehensible. In some problem domains, humans working with agents are already able to produce a hundred times the code that a human could alone. Agents are also able to perform a growing number of tasks working autonomously. And this is just the beginning. Whereas a user experience designer might take two weeks to produce a compelling user interface design output, we can easily envision dozens of agents creating dozens of designs in the span of minutes. In other words, in creating our management systems we should assume it will be easy to create ten or one hundred times the outputs with the same budget. This renders output metrics even more meaningless unless they are connected to outcomes.

Dysfunction: Local Optimization of Value Streams: When value streams optimize around output metrics, they maximize activities not outcomes.

The Outcome Loop Model is made for measuring and optimizing outcomes. It shifts away from function- and output-oriented management to Outcome Management. As such, measuring and optimizing the flow of value through the Outcome Loop provides us with a mechanism for maximizing outcomes.

Avoiding Local Optimization

With Outcome Management, our goal is to continually optimize the flow of value through the Outcome Loop. Given that the Product Operating Model is designed for the complex domain, we need a data-driven approach to optimization. Complex systems exhibit emergent phenomena where a small change to an input can have a dramatic change to an output.[2] For example, a budget reduction that might have minimal impact on the overall organization can mean a critical member of the staff is no longer part of the company, and if that person were producing a key output that many other value streams depended on, the impact on outcomes can be outsized. To gain visibility into these dynamics, we need instrumentation for measuring every Outcome Loop in the organization as well as the flow of value across the entire Outcome Tree. In the following sections, we will examine the instrumentation and measurement mechanisms for each part of the Outcome Loop.

Guidance: Invest in Outcome Loop Telemetry: Measuring flow and feedback across the Outcome Loop requires a unified, end-to-end infrastructure. Continue to empower specific roles with function-specific tools, but ensure a unifying layer connects all of the artifacts and workflows across the entire Outcome Tree in a way that is curated for both humans and agents to act on.

Connecting Inputs to Outputs

The strategy and budget inputs needed for the Outcome Loop tend to be well defined and managed in most organizations and well documented through best practices, such as strategic budgeting or the balanced scorecard.[3] Connecting those inputs to outputs and outcomes is critical for Outcome Management.

Budget inputs are specified by the organization's budgeting process that typically produces some version of a profit and loss statement. Strategic planning can take many forms, but the process usually results in a vision and strategic initiatives that the organization will focus on. These processes typically run on annual and quarterly cycles. We will take a close look at how to connect annual and quarterly planning cadences to the Outcome Loop in the next chapter (Chaos to Cadence). For now, we can assume that the planning process produced a first draft of a budget and a strategy that will provide inputs to the top-level Outcome Loop of the organization.

The Outcome Loop must connect inputs to outputs and outcomes. A common dysfunction is for inputs to be disconnected from outputs, which makes it unclear which activities performed by teams are connected to strategic initiatives within budget. This connectivity may seem straightforward, but the data from the *Project to Product State of the Industry Report* makes it clear that it is far from the norm.[4]

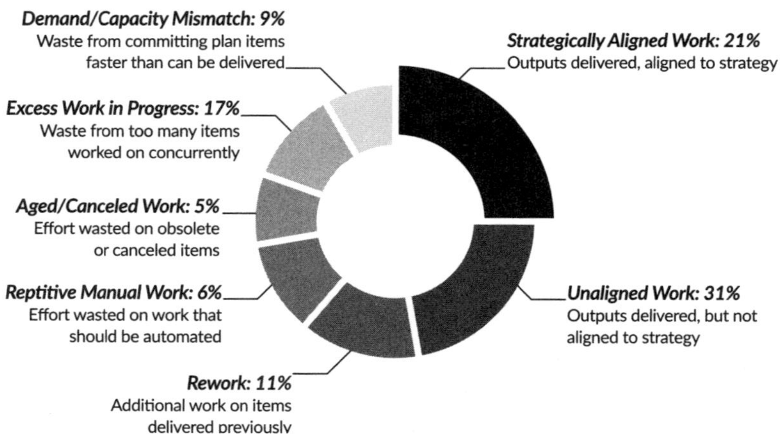

FIGURE 5.2: Sources of Waste and Misalignment

$150M illustrative budget. Source: Planview. The *2024 Project to Product State of the Industry Report*, Planview. 2024.

This data, summarized in Figure 5.2 on the previous page, indicates that only 25% of work done by the value streams observed in the study was aligned to the busines's strategic priorities. This means 75% of the productive capacity delivered work that was outside of what was planned.

In other words, the majority of the work was disconnected from inputs. We will dig into the sources of misalignment and waste are visible in Figure 5.3 later in this chapter.

Dysfunction: Disconnected Outcome Loop Inputs: When strategy and budget inputs are not connected to outputs and outcomes, team capacity is spent on unaligned work.

This lack of connectivity stems from strategic planning processes that are disconnected from delivery. The disconnects range from tooling to reporting and planning cycles. The strategy and budget input disconnect must be bridged to implement Outcome Management. The initiative is similar to the shift from value stream mapping to Value Stream Management that was discussed above. Value stream mapping is static, which means the maps and flows become stale as soon as the mapping is completed.

In contrast, Value Stream Management relies on live telemetry and flow data. Similarly, strategic planning must shift into the live and data-driven activity of Strategic Portfolio Management.[5] Both Strategic Portfolio Management and Value Stream Management provide methodologies supporting Outcome Management in the Outcome Loop.

Definition: Strategic Portfolio Management: The discipline of aligning investments and initiatives with the overall business strategy to maximize the delivery of value and outcomes by connecting strategy to delivery.

To support Outcome Management, strategic planning must evolve from a static process that produces a set of inputs to a practice of continual operation across the Outcome Tree. Strategic Portfolio Management is already a well-established practice at many leading organizations and works effectively when providing continual process and connectivity to the delivery loop. While Strategic Portfolio Management provides us with the planning mechanics, the challenge many organizations struggle with is in implementing mechanisms for connecting the strategic plan to the increasingly rapid pace of delivery.

In Part I, we reviewed the budget portion of the Outcome Loop. Budgets cascade down the Outcome Tree, with actuals that represent what was spent cascading back up. What we will review now is how to connect the strategy to outputs and outcomes, as well as the metrics that we will use for tracking that part of the Outcome Loop.

Guidance: Connect Strategy to Delivery: Ensure that the Strategic Portfolio Management layer is directly connected to the planning loop and delivery loop so every activity links back to funded strategic initiatives.

Connecting Strategy to Delivery

The outputs produced by a focused team of humans can be tremendous. In a matter of weeks, a single team could deliver the code for an entire mobile application by hand. However, working with AI and agents, a single person can produce more output than a typical team. As the outputs of entire teams and value streams are amplified by increasingly capable AI, the rate of activity and artifact production is going to continue to grow at what may be an exponential rate. What we saw in the study data discussed above is that three-quarters of outputs were already misaligned with strategy prior to the productivity gains achievable with AI. Without a new mechanism between strategic planning and delivery, this misalignment will grow the amount of unaligned slop produced to unmanageable levels. Organizations need to shift from the impedence mismatch between the activities and artifacts produced by value streams with what is typically a much higher-level strategic plan. In Outcome Management, we employ two mechanisms to bridge this gap.

Dysfunction: Strategy Drift: The gradual misalignment of an organization's strategy and what is being delivered by the teams executing on that strategy.

The Outcome Loop uses objectives and feedback for continuous alignment. Each strategic input must be connected to an objective and its key results. Objectives define the outcomes that will determine if and to what degree the value stream has delivered on the strategy, given the budget provided. While key results define and quantify the strategic outcome we are after, each roadmap item supports a specific objective. This is the basis of the Outcome Roadmap, which defines all of the work that is connected to outcomes (for more, see Chapter 2).

The connectivity can be transitive. For example, a team could decide it needs to explore a new AI model's capabilities. This work may occur several layers down the Outcome Tree. When that work supports the corresponding roadmap item and objective, all of its activities and artifacts are linked to that roadmap item and thereby aligned to the strategy. Another way to visualize this is that the roadmap items have child items for work done at each level below that node of the Outcome Tree. The activities and artifacts produced by the teams are the work that delivers on the roadmap item.

The *Project to Product State of the Industry Report* data indicates there are four distinct ways that work flows from what is planned to the outputs that are created. First, we have *planned work*, as discussed above. In the Product Operating Model, all of this work is connected via a roadmap item to a strategic plan item and objective. In our Teen-Wellness example, all of the work under the "passwordless signup" item is explicitly connected to a key result and to the strategic plan item "becoming the #1 daily wellness app for teens." This work results in features being delivered from the corresponding backlog. Across the value streams studied, planned work aligned to the strategy added up to 25% of the work.[6]

The second plan category is *unplanned work*, which represents another 25% of the work in our data-driven study[7] and substantially more in other reports, such as 81% in a survey-based study done by PagerDuty.[8] Unplanned work is work that was determined by teams to be necessary without being directly connected to a plan. For example, when implementing "passwordless signup," the team may have realized their Mobile Apps architecture does not support providing two different signup mechanisms. New work was then added to the backlog for updating the architecture to support this and removing the technical debt that impeded it. This work supports the objective and key result but was not originally planned. Defects and urgent customer requests are other common sources of unplanned work.

The third plan category is *canceled work*. This is work that was planned but has either been removed from the plan explicitly or has aged beyond the relevance of the plan. This category makes up a very significant 7% of the work analyzed.[9] There are many scenarios that result in work being canceled. One of the most common explanations is that something changed materially since the planning process, and the work is no longer as high a priority as other items on the backlog. This could happen because of rapidly shifting customer needs, overly slow delivery times, or gaps in the planning process. As we will see later in this chapter, accelerating the delivery loop reduces the amount of canceled work due to faster delivery and planning feedback cycles.

The fourth plan category is *aged work*. Aged work is work that the team has not started and is unlikely to start in the near term, but that was previously planned. The most common scenario is that a new plan has been created, and the work is no longer relevant but has not officially been taken off the roadmap or the value stream's backlog. For example, the value stream may have had some work on the backlog from the last planning cycle related to implementing a second authentication technology. The "passwordless signup" plan item could have rendered that irrelevant. But if there was a gap in visibility, that work may not have been removed from the backlog. This work will then age, and the team will revisit it periodically. Our study data shows that revisiting aged work of this sort takes up a meaningful portion of a value stream's delivery capacity. Another way to think of aged work is items that have not been explicitly removed from the roadmap but should have been.

Plan Distribution: The proportion of work items categorized by their relation to the plan, including planned work, unplanned work, aged work, and canceled work.

As we will see throughout this chapter, our first goal needs to be to make the work flowing through the Outcome Loop visible and measurable. The aggregate percentages of planned, unplanned, canceled, and aged work that we found in the study are much less important than measuring and analyzing the actual numbers for your organization. Making all work visible means knowing the proportion of the four *Plan Distribution* categories for every value stream in the organization. A value stream that is riddled with tech debt might be very slow at implementing roadmap items, resulting in a high proportion of canceled work. A value stream building your latest AI product may result in a very high proportion of unplanned work if its planning cycles are long, such as quarters or months, while the learning cycles are short, as is typical in a rapidly changing technology landscape. In Chapter 9 (Divisions to Domains), we will cover the tailoring of Plan Distribution to different product life cycle contexts. What is key for implementing Outcome Management is ensuring that the Plan Distribution is visible and actively managed as part of the planning process.

Once the Plan Distribution is visible for each value stream's Outcome Loop, our goal is to optimize the proportion of planned work by reducing the portions of unplanned, canceled, and aged work accordingly. This does not imply reducing those latter two categories to zero. For example, reducing all canceled work to zero would imply a planning process that perfectly predicted the roadmap. Given that we are in the complex domain, fast feedback and responsiveness to change are typically better goals than perfect predictability. As such, we want to be deliberate about monitoring the portion of canceled work to ensure it does not exceed a level that creates excess waste in the system and excess toil for the teams. Goodhart's Law states, "When a measure becomes a target, it ceases to be a good measure."[10] This is particularly relevant to every Outcome Loop metric, as our goal is to maximize outcomes, not to overly fixate on an ideal Plan Distribution.

A similar pattern holds true for planned versus unplanned work. While we generally want to maximize planned work, this also depends on context. For example, in research-heavy and exploratory work, or when rapidly scaling, it can be appropriate to set unplanned work to be as high as half of the capacity of the value stream. In this scenario, the overhead of planning in high-uncertainty scenarios may not be worth the overhead. Part of this context can come from the life cycle stage of the product, as we will cover in detail in Chapter 9 (Divisions to Domains). It can also come from market or macro conditions. For example, at the start of the COVID-19 pandemic, I deliberately removed any constraints on unplanned work for all the value streams at Tasktop so we could focus on quick response to rapidly changing conditions. In general, the more we move from the complex domain to the chaotic domain, the higher the portion of unplanned work is appropriate. Conversely, if we are delivering a new product to a well-known market, the vast majority of the work should fall into the planned work category.

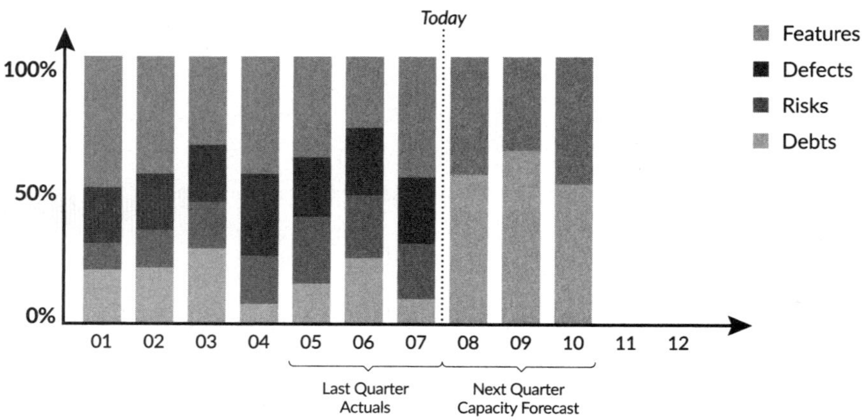

FIGURE 5.3: Plan Distribution Example

Guidance: Maximize Planned Work, Manage Unplanned Work, and Minimize Waste: Ensure that the majority of capacity goes to planned work, and tailor the amount of unplanned work to the business context. Keep canceled and aged work to a minimum.

Connecting Outputs to Outcomes

The vast majority of organizations I have worked with have mature processes for measuring and managing outputs. Agile literature provides the guidance that many organizations follow for creating and tracking the scale of outputs that humans can generate. We have now entered the Age of AI with dramatically augmented capacity for output generation. For example, we are already seeing evidence of developers being able to produce an order of magnitude more artifacts per unit time, as summarized in Gene Kim and Steve Yegge's book *Vibe Coding: Building Production-Grade Software with GenAI, Chat, Agents, and Beyond*, and that is just the beginning.

For the purpose of Outcome Management mechanisms, the rate of output generation can be unlimited. Outputs are being created through activities, whether those activities are being done by humans, humans working with agents, or agents working autonomously. These activities produce the flow of value to the customer. For example, features added to a product provide the customer with new capabilities, while defect fixes provide the customer with a better experience. In software, the delivery artifacts can include lines of code, containers, documents, and AI models.

To connect these outputs to outcomes, we use the concept of flow. In *Project to Product*, I introduced the Flow Framework® 1.0, which defined an end-to-end approach for measuring the flow of value through a product value stream.[11] Outcome Management builds on the Flow Framework and introduces the simplified Flow Framework 1.1. The 1.1 version is backward compatible with the 1.0 version, with the only changes being the hiding of the detailed "Activity Model" layer, removal of the index labels, and the renaming of "Business Results" to "Business Outcomes."

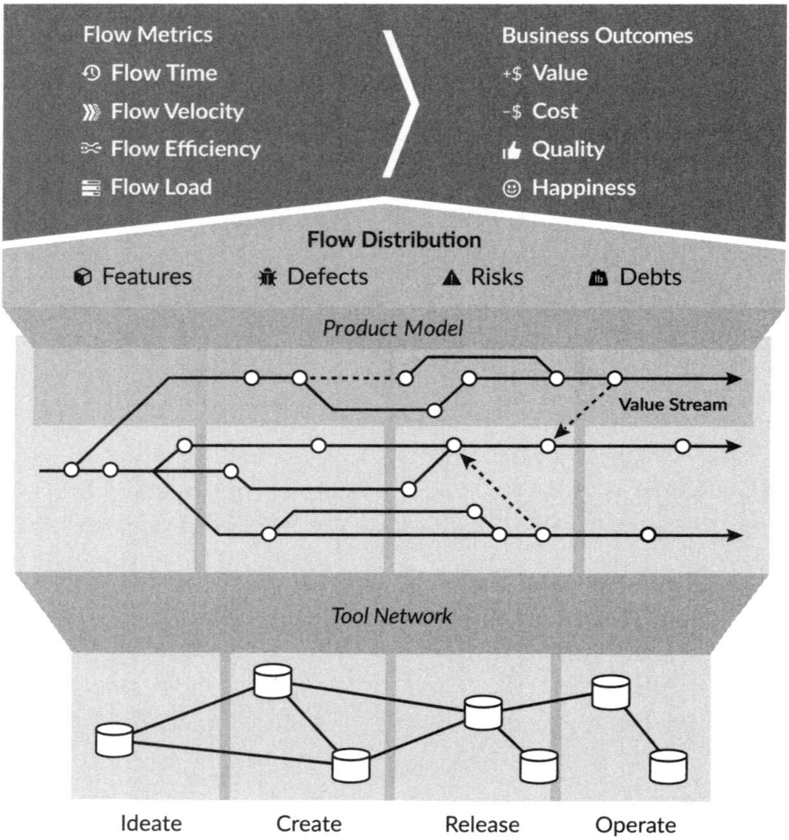

FIGURE 5.4: Flow Framework 1.1

The Flow Framework® was created by Mik Kersten and originally developed at Tasktop/Planview. Diagram adapted for *Output to Outcome*.

One of the key contributions of the Age of Oil & Mass Production to how we think about digital delivery is operational excellence for manufacturing that came from the rise of Lean Manufacturing and the Toyota Production System.[12] Lean Manufacturing is all about minimizing waste and maximizing flow through a production process. The Flow Framework leverages and expands on these concepts to apply the same concepts of flow to delivering digital artifacts. At the core of the Flow Framework are the *Flow Items*, which define the units of value that flow through a value stream. These are analogous to the flow of widgets, such as cars, through a manufacturing line.

Flow Item: A unit of work that flows through a value stream and is expected to contribute to a customer or business outcome, including features, defects, risks, and debts.

Flow-based systems, such as Lean Manufacturing and the Flow Framework, rely on the concept of pull. Pull is based on customer demand. The goal of the four Flow Items is to provide a high-level categorization of all the value that is pulled through a value stream in order to drive a business or customer outcome. As such, these Flow Items must comprehensively categorize all the work that flows through a value stream. In this respect, they must be mutually exclusive and collectively exhaustive to ensure we cover all work and are able to distinguish between the types of output without double counting. The four Flow Item types are features, defects, risks, and debts.

Features represent new business value that is delivered. They are pulled by customers and include work items, such as epics, user stories, and requirements. *Defects* are also pulled by customers and represent quality improvements. These include bug fixes and incident resolutions. *Risk* items are pulled by the business. These include work to address security vulnerabilities, privacy, compliance, and governance issues. Finally, *technical debt*, or *debt items*, are also pulled by the business. Technical debt arises when technologists or agents take shortcuts in order to deliver work, and these shortcuts impede the flow of future work through the value stream. Debt items include improvements in the software and operational architecture, such as API additions, refactorings, and automations. For example, ensuring that agents can work effectively on a production portion of the codebase can require refactoring and specification work. Collectively, these Flow Items represent all of the flow of outputs that will drive outcomes.

TABLE 5.1: The Four Flow Items

Flow Item	Delivers	Pulled By	Description	Examples
Features	New business value	Customers	New value added to drive a business outcome, visible to customer	Epic, user story, requirement
Defects	Quality improvements	Customers	Fixes for quality problems that affect the customer experience	Bugs, problem, incident, change
Risks	Security, governance, compliance	Security and risk officers	Work to address security, privacy, and compliance issues	Vulnerability, regulatory requirement
Debts	Remove of impediments to future delivery	Engineers and architects	Improvements of the software and operational architecture	API addition, refactoring, infrastructure, automation

The work activities that deliver Flow Items to the customer and business can produce many artifacts connected to numerous work items. For example, delivering the "passwordless signup" feature can mean the team and agents resolve a dozen different user stories, fix many defects along the way, create numerous unit tests, and build and deploy tens of thousands of lines of code. The purpose of Flow Items is to encapsulate all of those activities and artifacts so that we can track them at a higher level and connect them to our objectives and outcomes.

Flow Items provide us the units that flow through the value stream's Outcome Loop. In order to understand what is being delivered, we need to measure the *Flow Distribution* of the Flow Items. For example, it is feasible that a product's roadmap only includes feature work. However, given the complexity of software, it is very unlikely that the team will not need to allocate capacity to the other Flow Items. If capacity is not allocated to defect fixes and security improvements, as well as the management of tech debt, then it is unlikely that the planned outcomes will be delivered. For example, a team may have delivered the "passwordless signup" feature in a way that is full of bugs and inadvertently exposes customers' private information. Stakeholders involved in planning may be surprised when this happens, but this is a common dysfunction that results from the planning loop ignoring Flow Distribution and over-allocating capacity to features.

Flow Distribution: A measure of the proportion of the four Flow Items delivered by a value stream over a specific time period.

Dysfunction: Feature Factories: When roadmaps focus only on features and ignore defects, risks, and debts, the result is fragile systems, security issues, and a failure to deliver longer-term outcomes.

The solution is to ensure that all roadmaps are categorized by Flow Item. As with the Plan Distribution types, our goal here is first to make the outputs being worked on visible, to set them explicitly for the business context, and to avoid one-size-fits all approaches. For example, the guideline of dedicating 20% of a value stream's capacity has been suggested by many as a best practice.[13] However, the amount of technical debt can vary greatly, with greenfield products having very little debt and legacy software having very high levels of debt. Instead of targeting a fixed percentage, the goal should be to deliberately set a value stream's capacity for each of the Flow Items to maximize the outcomes for the value stream.

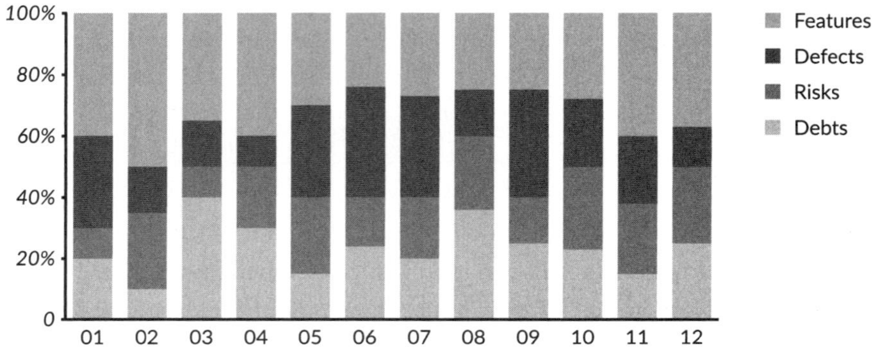

FIGURE 5.5: Flow Distribution

Dysfunction: Fixed Tech Debt Allocation: Rigidly dedicating a percentage of capacity to tech debt may appear disciplined but ignores the context of each value stream and what allocation will drive the desired outcomes.

Flow Distribution is present in two parts of the Outcome Loop. In the delivery loop, output capacity for each value stream is a zero-sum game of Flow Distribution. If we ask a team to dedicate twice the capacity to feature work, their capacity for defects, risks, and debts will be reduced proportionally. For example, a common failure mode is not accounting for the portion of defect work that a value stream needs to work on and ignoring tech debt. This can cause a value stream to enter into the "tech debt death spiral" described in *Project to Product*, where the more feature work is planned, the less capacity the team has for future feature work.[14] My team and I once showed a Flow Distribution chart to the CIO of a global bank, with feature work shaded green and defect work shaded red. He was shocked and stated, "I thought I was paying for green, why is most of our funding going to red?" This realization gave the bank's teams the air cover they needed to focus on tech debt reduction and accelerate feature delivery dramatically only weeks later. In my recent experience modernizing a legacy solution, having agents focus on tech debt reduction while developers focus on architectural improvements and features can be a great way to both avoid the tech debt death spiral and improve developer happiness.

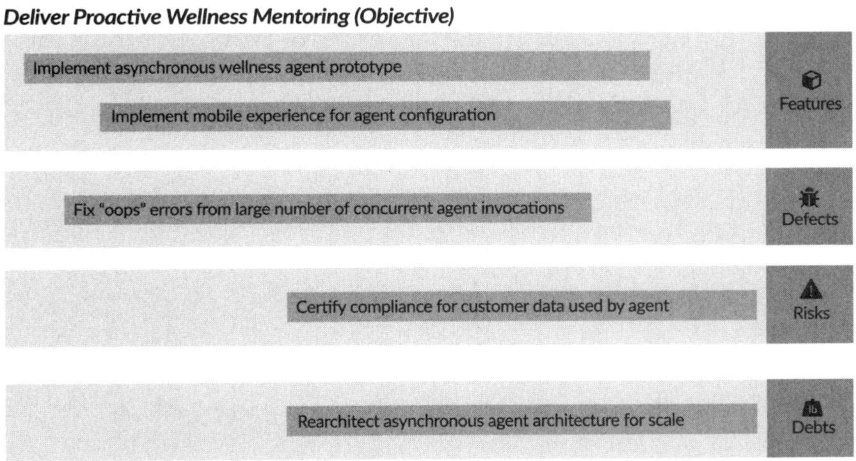

FIGURE 5.6: Outcome Roadmap Categorized by Flow Item Type

Given that Flow Distribution is a key measure of the delivery loop, we must also account for it in the planning loop. Deliberately allocating a percentage of the value stream's capacity to features, defects, risks, and debts ensures that the planning we do accounts for all of the work done by the team. To accomplish this, we can categorize the Outcome Roadmap by Flow Distribution. This allows us to see the proportion of the roadmap that is committed to delivering net new customer value via features, as well as how much capacity will go to reducing risks and technical debt. The categorization ensures that the trade-off decisions in planning are deliberate. For example, if the plan included two consecutive quarters with a Flow Distribution weighted toward debt reduction, we should expect the resulting tech debt payoffs to enable significant capacity increases for feature delivery. If they don't, this could be indicative that the tech debt work that was done was not aligned to the desired outcomes. This is exactly the kind of feedback we want between our planning and delivery loops.

With Flow Distribution as part of both the planning and delivery loops, we are able to compare what was planned versus what was delivered, in other words, the plan versus the actuals. We can do this both at the planning level, tracking roadmap attainment for a particular planning cycle, and at the Flow Distribution attainment level. For example, take the scenario where agents produced a large number of features, but architectural limitations meant the additional work needed to assure the quality and stability of those features was not factored into the planning cycle. In this scenario, we would see overachievement on features delivered on the roadmap, followed by unplanned work on defects. These issues become straightforward to diagnose using Flow Distribution and Plan Distribution.

Measuring Time and Velocity

The final things we need to measure in the Outcome Loop are how quickly value is flowing through the system and how much value is flowing through the system. To do this, we leverage flow metrics.

There have been countless approaches to measuring developer productivity, team productivity, and the flow of value. There has also been a significant amount of inconsistency in the terminology used for developer productivity. For example, lead time is often used in a way that is inconsistent with the definition of this term in its use in Lean Manufacturing.[15] The flow metrics definitions match those of Lean Manufacturing and reflect those detailed in *Project to Product* and summarized here. The goal is to be precise and specific about the span of work we are measuring and to ensure we are measuring from the perspective of business and customer outcomes. With output metrics becoming increasingly meaningless as agents scale outputs, it is critical to have precise definitions and accurate telemetry for measuring flow to quantify the benefits of AI.

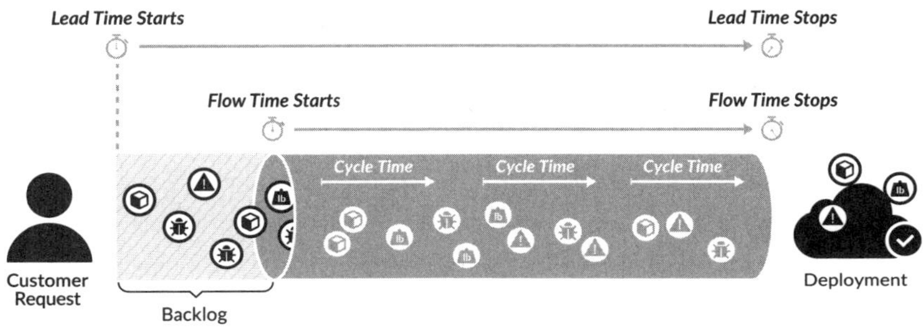

FIGURE 5.7: Measuring Flow of Time
This figure was created by Mik Kersten and originally published in *Project to Product*. Diagram adapted for *Output to Outcome*.

To consistently measure flow, we need to determine when we start and stop the measurement clock that turns Flow Items into the business and customer value that drives outcomes. To do this, we employ three different time metrics corresponding to different segments of the Outcome Loop.

The broadest metric is *lead time*. This is analogous to measuring how long it takes from when a customer orders a car to when the customer receives the car. The lead time clock starts when a request from a customer, or a representative of a customer or business value, is added to the backlog. This backlog request is then included in the planning loop as a candidate for the roadmap for that cycle. If the request is included in the roadmap, it is expected to be delivered in that planning cycle. If it is not, it will remain on the backlog for that value stream.

With software and other digital assets, lead time exhibits some additional dynamics beyond those of manufacturing. A car maker is expected to deliver every car that is ordered. However, in any given planning cycle, digital product delivery tends to deliver only a fraction of the requests that have been made. It is not uncommon for popular products or open-source solutions to fix only a fraction of open feature and defect requests simply due to the breadth and popularity of the projects. For example, as of 2025, some of the most popular open-source projects, such as Linux, Kubernetes, and VS Code, had thousands of open requests visible in their issue trackers.

We want to make sure we track lead time, but for digital solutions this is not the metric we want to optimize. Instead, we want to optimize *flow time*. Car manufacturers also focus on the flow time metric when they want to scale production of a new car model. For a car manufacturer, the flow time clock begins when construction on a new car starts in a plant and ends when the car leaves the assembly line. For technology, the flow time clock starts when we start work on the item and stops when that item is deployed to the customer. The starting point is comprehensive of any kind of work beginning, including analysis, discovery, or design. In the delivery loop, this is precisely the time we want to optimize, as it represents how quickly we can deliver the outputs that drive outcomes.

Within flow time, there are multiple *cycle times*. In manufacturing, these are the different workstations, such as the paint shop, the wire harness install, and so on. For technology, these are the various phases involved in delivery, such as design, coding, adding tests, scaling operations, implementing security and compliance controls, and performance tuning. In elite organizations, these activities have become highly iterative. For example, a "you build it you run it"[16] team is responsible for each of those aspects of delivery. Cycle time is a more relevant metric when there are handoffs between specialized functions but a less relevant metric in highly iterative product delivery. As such, the main metric we employ for measuring time to value in the Outcome Loop is flow time.

Flow velocity measures the throughput of the value stream. For a car manufacturer, this is the number of cars built in the plant over a span of time, such as a day or a quarter. For digital value streams, it's the number of Flow Items delivered over a span of time. Flow velocity is the measure of productivity in the delivery loop.

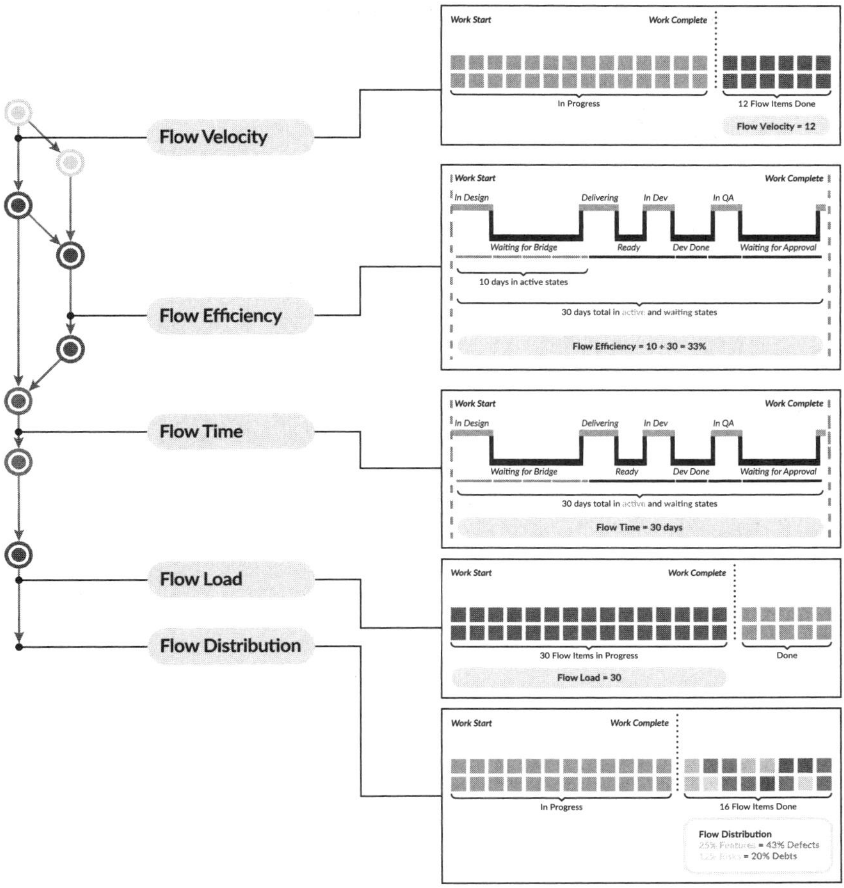

FIGURE 5.8: Flow Metrics and Flow Distribution Illustrated

In my work with with large organizations, I have repeatedly been asked about leveraging flow metrics to measure an individual's productivity. For example, leaders have wanted to know if flow metrics can help them understand if one individual is more productive than their colleague. Flow metrics are not intended for this, by design. In all of my experience with productivity metrics, metrics that focus on the individual, not the team and value stream, are error prone, misleading, and ineffective to optimize around. Individuals in a team are constantly helping each other and reviewing each other's work, meaning the portion of work spent on individual Flow Items cannot be easily attributed. In addition, agents are amplifying both individuals' and team members' work, further blurring the attribution. Flow metrics work precisely at the value stream level that they were designed for. Instead of measuring an individual's productivity, we should focus on measuring the flow velocity of the value stream in aggregate. As value streams cascade in the Outcome Tree, we can measure every level right up to the entire tree.

If metrics finer grained than a value stream are needed, those are available through artifact metrics. For example, we can measure the number of lines of code delivered by an agent or the number of defects fixed by a developer. However, in Outcome Management we focus on the metrics that drive the Outcome Loop. Artifact metrics are not meaningful unless they are connected to an outcome, and it is at the value stream level that we can connect outputs to outcomes. As such, there is no fixed flow velocity number that represents an ideal target. What we want to see is a correlation between flow velocity and an outcome metric. For example, we want to see that the more features work or prototyping that we deliver for our chat application, the more adoption and customer satisfaction we see due to the quality of the user experience improving.

Managing Unlimited Capacity

Consider a scenario in which we can accelerate our roadmap a hundredfold by employing a large fleet of agents to dramatically increase our flow velocity. This could come at a very high cost due to the inference costs of running the agents. The question is, how should a value stream leader determine whether and how much to invest in accelerating flow velocity, especially in scenarios where AI makes velocity this elastic? This is where we need to query the connectivity from flow back to the Outcome Loop inputs. It only makes economic sense to accelerate flow velocity if we are driving the specified outcome within the parameters of the budget input.

For many value streams, flow velocity and flow time will identify the key constraint of the Outcome Loop. For example, for my teams at Tasktop and Planview, I ensured that flow time was always under two weeks, which matched the length of our sprint cycle and feedback loop. Yet in the study data, we saw an average of 120 days.[17] In a fast-moving market, the speed of decision-making is far too slow if it takes a quarter or more to get new functionality deployed. Once flow time is no longer the constraint on the feedback speed of the Outcome Loop, the metric to focus on is the end-to-end throughput, as measured by flow velocity.

Measuring Load and Efficiency

The remaining flow metrics for helping you manage value streams are *flow efficiency* and *flow load*. Flow efficiency is the ratio of active work to wait states. Wait states are one of the main sources of waste in a production process.[18] For any value stream, the main source of wait states indicates the bottleneck of the value stream. For example, if agents are producing a lot of new code overnight, but that code has to be reviewed and integrated by the most senior developer, the time waiting on the review from that developer will be the main contributor to reduced flow efficiency and represent the bottleneck. If the value stream has a dependency on another platform or API that is delayed in providing it with the functionality it needs, that might be the main source of wait states. Flow efficiency allows us to identify the bottleneck for any value stream. We can then feed that information back into the planning loop to ensure we invest capacity in resolving the bottleneck. For example, we might do that by allocating more capacity to the development of that API or by increasing the number of senior developers dedicating time to reviews.

Flow load is a measure of work in progress. It tells us how many Flow Items are currently active in the value stream. In the *Project to Product State of the Industry Report*, the most common source of reduced flow velocity was overly high flow load.[19] This often happens when teams take on more work than they have capacity to do and is exacerbated when all of the work that has been put on teams is not visible in planning, such as when the risk and debt work the teams are doing is ignored and the roadmap only tracks feature work.

Based on its human and agentic capacity, at any point in time each value stream has an ideal flow load. If that is exceeded, flow time will increase and flow velocity will decrease due to the overload and thrashing that results. This is true for manufacturing lines as well, which is why car plants are not run to 100% capacity. Continually monitoring and adjusting flow load ensures teams have a sustainable workload and that capacity is allocated to removing toil from the system, as we will review in the following sections.

TABLE 5.2: The Four Flow Metrics

Flow Metric	Measurement	Example
Flow Velocity	Number of Flow Items completed in a given period of time.	Debts resolved: Number of total Flow Items completed.
Flow Time	Time elapsed from when a Flow Item enters the value stream to when it is released to the customer.	Average time for Flow Items to move through a value stream.
Flow Load	Number of Flow Items with a flow state of active or waiting.	Too many features being worked on concurrently impacts velocity.
Flow Efficiency	The proportion of Flow Items that are actively worked on to the total time elapsed.	Flow efficiency decreases when dependencies increase.

Flow Capacity Planning

In project work, capacity planning is done by allocating resources to tasks based on skills and availability.[20] This does not work for Outcome Management, which is built around creating persistent capacity for value streams rather than reallocating people to projects or allocating a single person or team to multiple projects. However, when turning strategy into plans, understanding what capacity is available is just as critical for product plans as it is for project plans. The intersection of planned work and flow velocity provides the solution.

The historical capacity of a value stream to deliver on future roadmap items for a particular planning cycle is defined by its historical flow velocity of planned work for that same interval. Using this measure provides us with an accurate history of how much planned work was delivered. It also provides us with the foundation for capacity planning. A value stream's future capacity will be its past capacity multiplied by a productivity increase or decrease.

The simplest, and in my experience most effective, approach to capacity planning in the Product Operating Model is to use the flow velocity of planned work from the last period. In other words, not to bake in a productivity increase. The length of the historical period being used should be at least as long as the period being planned. For example, a team can use last week's flow velocity to predict next week's capacity, but for planning a quarter ahead, we may want to use the past three quarters to avoid skews from seasonal effects such as holidays.

In the next section, we will review strategies for improving flow velocity. However, assuming sufficiently short planning intervals, any increase in productivity, or an improvement in the proportion of planned work, should be reflected in actuals in the following iteration. This approach avoids the pitfall of overly optimistic forward-looking assumptions about productivity increases. There are exceptions, such as if a new team will be added to a value stream or a new set of agents leveraged to increase capacity. In this case, it is feasible to extrapolate a percentage increase in capacity based on the expected productivity gains. However, end-to-end flow velocity can take time to ramp up due to other constraints in the Outcome Loop, so this approach should be used judiciously.

Using one-to-one mapping of historicals to futures tends to be more effective as it avoids over-allocating the team. Over-allocation can quickly increase flow load to the point where the actual flow velocity for the iteration turns out to be lower than planned. This counterproductive overplanning is what we saw so much of in the study data. Although AI and agents can dramatically increase capacity, teams often need time to resolve other constraints, such as ensuring there is sufficient time allocated to reviewing all the additional output produced by the agents.

Guidance: Plan Only Around Historical Flow Velocity: Base capacity planning on historical actuals of the flow velocity of planned work for each value stream. Avoid factoring in productivity gains unless supported by structural changes, such as adding already ramped up teams or AI agents.

Flow velocity–based capacity planning allows us to close the loop all the way back to inputs. It enables us to determine how we convert budgets into outputs. The final part of the loop that we need to measure is outcomes.

Outcome Metrics

The last set of top-level Outcome Loop metrics we need to define are the outcome metrics that determine whether we have delivered on our strategy. Outcome metrics tend to be well understood and established in organizations, with best practices managed by Finance and Operations teams. Outcome Management relies on these outcome metrics and stipulates that every value stream must have outcome metrics specified as part of its Outcome Loop, that the objectives must include outcome metrics as their key results, and that each of the key results must be quantifiable.

Quantifying the key results follows the best practice discussed in Chapter 2. For example, a poorly defined key result would state that "more users are using our app," whereas a well-defined key result would state that we "increased monthly active users from 10K to 20K" if usage is the strategic outcome. Revenue growth or profit per user may provide an even better outcome metric.

EMPLOYEE OUTCOMES	+	CUSTOMER OUTCOMES	=	BUSINESS OUTCOMES
Eg. Employer Net Promoter Score		Eg. Customer Net Promoter Score		Eg. Revenue Growth

FIGURE 5.9: Employee Outcomes + Customer Outcomes = Business Outcomes

In general, outcome metrics should include financial metrics, such as revenue, retention, and profit. They can also include product adoption and engagement metrics, such as signups, daily usage, stickiness, growth, and feature adoption. They can also include sentiment metrics, such as Net Promoter Score and customer satisfaction metrics. Some forward-looking companies also include sustainability metrics, such as power consumption or carbon footprint. As we will see in Chapter 9 (Divisions to Domains), these metrics should be tailored to the product segment and life cycle stage.

Outcome metrics fall into the employee or the customer outcomes buckets. For example, for organizations that value company culture, employee Net Promoter Score is an effective employee outcome metric, while customer Net Promoter Score is a valuable customer outcome metric. Note that for value streams delivering products to internal customers, we still maintain the distinction between the outcomes of the employees working on the value stream and those of the employees who are the consumers of that work.

In addition to ensuring that the outcome metrics are quantified and cascade down the Outcome Tree, we must also ensure they drive the feedback mechanism of the Outcome Loop. A common failure mode is that outcome metrics do not support sufficient granularity to provide value streams lower in the Outcome Tree with actionable input. For example, if there are three mobile application value streams, it is critical that adoption is tracked separately for each. If they are only tracked in aggregate, the three value streams will not know if it is their efforts or the efforts of others that are driving the metric up. If these value streams are monetized with customers, either via sales or indirectly via advertising, it is critical that the revenue for each value stream is collected and reported to that value stream separately. If the products are bundled into a single offering, the attribution of each value stream's contribution to that offering must be established. Without clear attribution, the outcome feedback mechanism for the value stream is broken, breaking the Outcome Loop. A common dysfunction occurs when the attribution is only clear at higher levels of the Outcome Tree, yet we know that the majority of the work happens at the lower levels. If this is the case, the Outcome Tree cascade is broken, and establishing that connectivity and attribution becomes the key priority.

> ⓧ **Dysfunction: Disconnected Outcome Loops:** When outcome metrics lack granularity, value streams cannot attribute their outputs to outcomes. This breaks the feedback mechanism of the Outcome Loop.

Data-Driven Improvement

With the Outcome Loop established, connected, and measured, we have all of the telemetry we need to apply the Theory of Constraints to value streams. The goal of doing so is to identify the bottlenecks for a value stream and then implement mechanisms to systematically resolve those bottlenecks. As we are optimizing flow through a dynamic system, resolving one constraint has the tendency to introduce another.

This is why we need to make improving flow a top-level component of the Outcome Loop itself.

The mantra I find most powerful here was stated by Gene Kim and coauthors in *The Phoenix Project: A Novel About IT, DevOps, and Helping Your Business Win*: "The improvement of daily work is as important as daily work itself."[21] Since we are dealing with a dynamic system that varies from organization to organization, there is no linear roadmap that indicates which constraint to focus on first and which to focus on next. Instead, we need the Outcome Loop telemetry to see the constraint at each point in time.

The metrics summarized in this chapter give us all the data needed for continuous improvement of the Outcome Loop. So far, we have defined the plan item types of planned, unplanned, aged, and canceled. We also have the Flow Item types of features, defects, risks, and debts. Together, these express all of the planning and delivery involved in the Outcome Loop. The final thing we need to define is a mechanism for tracking improvements to the Outcome Loop based on the flow and feedback through the loop. To capture that, we add the *improvement mechanism* (or *improvement work type*) to the Outcome Loop.

Outcome Loop Improvement Mechanism: A special kind of work type that does not directly deliver business outcomes but instead accelerates the flow of value through the Outcome Loop by removing constraints to delivering future outcomes.

Outcome Loop improvements are a special type of work that accelerate the delivery of outcomes. We can think of them as a meta type of work item, as they do not directly contribute to a customer outcome. However, they accelerate the flow of value through the loop, thereby enabling a faster pace for delivering future outcomes. For example, if we are not getting the expected yield from agents working on a production system, we can schedule improvement work to enhance the system's modularity and specifications accordingly. If employees are struggling with adopting agents, accelerating outcomes may require additional capacity to be allocated to AI coaching and training.

For any Outcome Loop that is not already optimized, each planning cycle should allocate capacity to improvements. For example, if the flow diagnostics are telling us there is too much flow load on a value stream, simply reducing the load on the team can have an immediate and dramatic effect on the outcomes within the same cycle. If there is a hypothesis that a new kind of agent can remove the manual toil of dealing with old tech debt issues by modernizing a tech stack, allocating roadmap capacity to that improvement work can have an outsized impact on accelerating flow for the next cycle. What is critical is that we take the same data-driven and quantitative approach to tracking improvements as we do to planning and tracking other kinds of work.

Outcome Loop Improvement Objectives: Objectives and Key Results focused on accelerating the flow of value by removing constraints and investing in people, processes, and agents that accelerate flow.

To do this, we simply employ the same objective tracking mechanism for improvements as we do for other outcomes. However, the difference with Outcome Loop improvement objectives, or improvement objectives for short, is that the key result is not a business or customer outcome, but a quantifiable improvement in the planning loop, delivery loop, or feedback loop.

Each of the Outcome Loop metrics is a candidate target for improvement key results. For example, we might want to increase the proportion of planned work from 30% to 60% of a value stream, so we express that as a key result and then plan the corresponding improvement work on the roadmap, such as refining the planning process. We may want to increase the flow velocity of a value stream by 10% each quarter, which means the roadmap must contain debt work in the form of improvement automation and agent integration as well as subsequent training for engineers. In each case, the improvement is defined as an objective, with roadmap work allocated to generating the outputs and process changes that realize it. At the end of the next cycle, we can then measure the impact of those improvements on business outcomes.

As we are dealing with a dynamic system, we must explicitly balance internally facing improvement work with the work that delivers customer outcomes. A team that has been struggling for years with an inefficient Outcome Loop may make a valid case that improvement objectives need to be prioritized over everything else. However, if those improvement objectives take the majority of the value stream's capacity for multiple quarters, at the end of that journey the value stream may not have any customers left. This zero-sum balancing becomes a core part of the planning process by making improvements a first-class entity and ensuring that these trade-offs are explicit.

Improvement objectives are a great opportunity to elevate the working conditions of the value stream. This is because the lowest hanging fruit for accelerating flow is often removing waste and toil from the system. For example, if cognitive load is raised too high for a team by adding too many autonomous agents, a counterbalance is needed.

In our measurements of outcomes at Tasktop, we almost always saw a strong correlation between the improvement in flow velocity and employee happiness, as measured by the employee Net Promoter Score. The easier we made it for teams to build value and deliver outcomes, the happier those teams were. Once the major toil was removed, we continued to have an annual aggregate flow velocity per person improvement target of at least 10%. We needed a counter-balancing mechanism to ensure we were not increasing velocity by overworking engineers and burning them out. So, we always paired the flow velocity improvement with an employee happiness improvement. We did not want to see the former improve at the cost of the latter. This is another example of the pairing of an improvement objective to an outcome objective, as improving employee happiness was always one of our top-level goals.

While CTO at Planview, I worked with our teams to build AI agents that would actively review the integrity of each product value stream's Outcome Loop. These agents actively monitored for problems and suggested improvements to product managers. For example, if a value stream was consistently overloaded, an agent would suggest specific roadmap items to remove and propose dependencies to resolve to accelerate flow. The key learning from this was the power of agents to not only accelerate outputs but also accelerate the Outcome Loop as a whole. Agents can similarly be deployed to continually inspect and improve the integrity of the entire Outcome Tree.

Scaling the Ideation Cliff at Vanguard

Technology is central to Vanguard's mission to uncover, create, and deliver new ways to drive positive outcomes for more than 50 million clients. With such a large client base, delivering a seamless digital experience across mobile and web platforms is critical. I had the opportunity to collaborate with Mike Carr, Vanguard's chief technology officer, and see Vanguard's methodical and data-driven approach to modernization as an effective model for others to emulate.

Vanguard has advanced through key phases of modernization. It started by adopting modern cloud technologies followed by implementing a microservice architecture, deploying end-to-end Agile practices, and then transitioning to the Product Operating Model. Their efforts have driven significant improvements in the space of technical change paired with a reduction in the frequency of major incidents. But even more important, Vanguard's data- and metrics-driven approach throughout this journey has resulted in four foundational layers from which they are now deploying their AI transformation.

While deploying the Product Operating Model, the team rallied around the principle: "You can't improve what you don't measure, and you can't measure what you can't see." Outcome metrics were clear and well-specified from the start of the journey. With their focus on developer productivity, Vanguard had a mature delivery pipeline as well as release and Agile team metrics in place. However, the team realized the need for visibility into the entire end-to-end Outcome Loop. They then introduced new instrumentation that adopted measuring the flow metrics. What was once only suspected became clear when the data arrived. The "create" phase of Vanguard's value streams, during which teams wrote and shipped the software, took twenty days on average. Development was already best in class. The release phases, which included testing and validation, took fifty days, meaning there was some room for prioritizing improvement work on that front. What was surprising is that the ideating phase, predevelopment, took 120 days.

The team identified the main constraint across Vanguard's value streams and called this effect the "Ideation Cliff." They measured very high work in progress and flow load, with an average of over fifty major features and initiatives in progress concurrently for each team. The bandwidth taken by all that work in progress was a major impediment to delivery bandwidth. After ensuring each value stream and team was clearly mapped, the team set a goal of improving flow by 15% within a year. Ten months into the initiative, thanks to this data-driven approach to measuring and prioritizing improvement, that objective was far exceeded with flow improving over 35%, resulting in much higher throughput from ideation to development. By implementing clearly defined product value streams, Outcome Loops, and telemetry, the teams laid the critical foundation needed to further scale and measure productivity improvements with the adoption of AI-native engineering practices.

Conclusion

The Age of AI brings with it an abundance of outputs. AI-native organizations that have been born leveraging amplified outputs have managerial systems in place that ensure these outputs drive strategic outcomes. However, established organizations have managerial systems that are focused on tracking vanity metrics focused on maximizing production. With constraints on outputs removed, this results in overproduction of AI slop rather than delivery of outputs that drive outcomes with substance.

Value streams are a feedback loop. Without outcome-oriented telemetry and metrics, value streams often devolve into tracking output metrics, which results in local optimization. In other words, outputs are maximized without connectivity to outcomes, resulting in further slop and waste. Whereas agents should be increasing productivity substantially, without the investment in tracking flow and outcomes, agents amplify the problem rather than the solution. Implementing flow and outcome-oriented telemetry is critical for establishing a feedback loop that ensures all agentic amplification of outcomes delivers on the strategy. Once this closed Outcome Loop is implemented, data-driven continuous improvement of value streams has been established.

With that in place, we will next review the planning, meeting, and reporting cadence needed to optimize the value flowing through the Outcome Tree.

In Summary

- Tracking outputs disconnected from outcomes is meaningless and degrades technical metrics, such as pull requests and features delivered, to vanity metrics.
- Local optimization creates organizational waste, as it encourages optimizing for output instead of outcome.
- AI agents amplify the problem by multiplying output capacity, rendering output metrics even more misleading when disconnected from customer and business outcomes.
- Outcome Loop telemetry is the essential data needed to optimize flow, detect bottlenecks, and connect delivery to outcomes.
- Improvement objectives balance near-term outputs with enabling future outputs by reducing toil, removing constraints, and accelerating flow to drive both employee satisfaction and customer outcomes.

Key Takeaways

- Measure and optimize outcomes, not vanity metrics.
- Make all work visible and measurable via Plan Distribution, Flow Distribution, and flow metrics.
- Invest in continuous improvement by creating capacity for improvement objectives to remove constraints and accelerate flow.

Prompt

Objective: Help humans replace vanity output metrics with outcome- and flow-based measurement across their value streams.

Operating protocol (assist, don't act unilaterally):

- Identify current "vanity metrics" (deploys, story points, LOC, tickets closed), and show how they are disconnected from customer, employee, and business outcomes.
- Discover Plan Distribution for each value stream (planned, unplanned, canceled, aged work), and make it visible; highlight waste, strategy drift, and overplanning.
- Classify work into the four Flow Items (features, defects, risks, debts) and calculate Flow Distribution; look for flow dysfunctions and constraints.
- Help introduce the Flow Metrics Model (flow velocity, flow time, flow load, flow efficiency), and link trends to concrete outcome metrics (e.g., revenue, retention, NPS, employee NPS).
- Propose improvement objectives that target specific telemetry changes (e.g., reduce flow time, lower flow load, increase percent planned work) while guarding against burnout.

Guardrails: Do not optimize for output volume alone; always reconnect metrics to outcomes and to a closed Outcome Loop.

Chapter 6

Third Shift: Chaos to Cadence

Accelerating the delivery of outcomes with AI requires precise organizational alignment and rapid decision-making. Disparate meeting, reporting, and planning cadences undermine both speed and coherence. A unified cadence is needed to support the decision-making speed needed to leverage the output amplification of AI.

In this chapter, we will review the *Unified Cadence Model*, which synchronizes the entire organization to shared annual, quarterly, monthly, and weekly cycles designed around fast feedback. The chapter concludes with a summary of how a unified cadence empowers value streams to pivot quickly and transparently while staying connected to organizational strategy and outcomes.

I have witnessed many large organizations invest billions in Agile transformations only to question whether delivery had become more difficult at the end of that journey. How is it possible that such massive investments, made with all of the right intentions, could possibly bring an organization backward in terms of performance? It is hard to envision a car manufacturer retooling a plant only to be surprised that fewer cars were being delivered after the fact. Yet we are now seeing the same questions being asked about large-scale AI transformations.

The first challenge is that most organizations do not have adequate measurements of productivity in place prior, during, or after the transformation. Without accurate measurement, it is impossible to objectively determine whether things are going faster or slower. Due to the high stakes of these transformations, I have repeatedly witnessed leaders avoid putting in place outcome measurement, opting for basic output measurement to hide behind due to a fear of failure at organizations that lacked sufficient psychological safety or learning orientation. The lack of a data-driven approach to improvement, coupled with the complexity of today's organizations and technology stacks, means it is easy for transformations to go astray. Given that, it is unsurprising that so many people in post-transformation surveys report that things seem to be going slower than before.[1]

Consider the change that a car manufacturer makes when retooling a plant to increase robotic automation. Nothing has changed in that organization's operating model. All that has happened is the delivery loop has accelerated, which means other parts of the business, such as the shipping of finished cars, may need to adapt to the increased pace.

In contrast, with an Agile transformation there is a fundamental change in ways of working for teams. New processes are created, such as sprint planning and program increment planning.[2] New ways of tracking, such as backlogs and Agile boards, change how work is managed. If the operating model of the business does not change to match, the resulting layering of disparate management systems can wreak havoc on organizational processes and communication.

Going back to the metaphor of trees in nature, it is as if we found a way to engineer leaves that could grow and photosynthesize at twice the rate but did nothing to change the roots, trunk, and branches supporting those leaves. In this scenario, the tree could not consume all the energy the leaves produced, nor could it support the nutrients needed by those leaves. Similarly, I have observed organizations that have an effective Outcome Tree are able to productively consume much higher rates of tokens per team than those operating with legacy models.

Guidance: Unify the Entire Organization's Management Cadence: Establish a single management review and meeting cadence across the organization and all value streams.

The typical rollout of a large Agile working model overlays it on top of existing planning systems. That means that an Agile meeting cadence is deployed on top of the established business planning cadence. Business planning cadences tend to be well established and integrated with core functions, such as Finance and Human Resources. If the Agile ceremonies are orthogonal to the monthly, quarterly, and annual reporting and planning of the business, chaos can easily ensue.

This chaos can wreak havoc with decision-making, communication, and the effectiveness of business and technology feedback loops. When this happens, even if delivery is moving faster, to key stakeholders it can easily feel like it is moving slower. This is the challenge with overlaying Agile as a "second operating system" for the organization. The complexity of managing and synchronizing two operating systems introduces coordination costs that can exceed the productivity gains provided by the transformation.

Dysfunction: Separate Planning Cadences: When product and business cadences run separately, the result is misaligned priorities and rising coordination costs from constant attempts at realignment.

This explains the very stark difference between the way AI and digital native organizations plan and the way incumbent organizations plan. Digital natives tend to have their plan/build/run loop established as a core part of their top-level business operations. In this way, their operations are similar to those of a car manufacturer. There is no separate set of Agile ceremonies; there is just planning. The corresponding plan/build/run loop is a core part of the operating cadence of the business.

We can also contrast this with how other parts of the business function. Consider a large sales organization that underwent a transformation to adopt a new sales methodology. Now imagine that all of the sales teams, often made up of five to ten salespeople each, adopt a new and more agile forecast management model and meeting cadence. However, Sales leadership continues to operate on the old model and cadence.

In this scenario, the sheer number of meetings and translations between the two systems would inundate both the team leaders and the executives and get in the way of effective execution. Even more problematically, delays and any inaccuracies in the data would easily lead decision-making astray. Every time a forecast was released, people would be questioning which methodology produced the numbers. Instead of making decisions during a meeting, they would be doing mental mapping between the methodologies and questioning numbers. This would make for a very ineffective and uncompetitive sales organization. Yet this is exactly what so many business and technology organizations accept when they create a messy matrix of meetings, reports, and ownership structures.

In this chapter, we will unwind the chaotic matrix of meeting cadences. In the chapters following, we will tackle the unwinding of matrix reporting lines and tangled ownership structures.

Shift: Chaos to Cadence: Replace the confusion of parallel meeting structures and mismatched reporting cycles with a single, unified operating cadence that supports planning, delivery, and feedback across the entire organization.

Unified Cadence Model

The solution to the mess of overlapping and interdependent meetings is simplification. The organization needs a unified meeting and reporting cadence. This may seem obvious, and most organizational functions tend to follow a single cadence. However, many large-scale digital and Agile transformations have created a separate planning loop from the one used by the rest of the organization. There are many names for these processes, such as annual strategic planning and quarterly business reviews. They tend to be well-honed processes that run a cascade of annual, quarterly, monthly, and weekly meeting cadence and supporting reports.

Why have so many technology organizations layered in a whole new cadence rather than connecting to the well-honed one that the rest of the organization runs on? In my experience, the main reason for this is that when Agile ways of working were deployed, there was not an appetite to alter the business planning cadence in a way that would support the more rapid and flexible Agile planning cadence. As a result, the secondary cadence was established, and the problem surfaced. In other words, this dysfunction arises from a resistance to changing the primary planning cadence.

The core issue stems from the fact that the business planning cadence of an established organization is not designed to handle the fast feedback and iterations that come from more Agile and Lean ways of working. For example, if a quarterly business review is focused on status reporting and does not have embedded mechanisms for making business-level prioritization decisions, it is not the right cadence vehicle for supporting the input that value streams need from leadership. It is this mismatch that creates the duplicated meeting structures and all of the inefficiencies that follow.

Unified Cadence Model: An organizational planning mechanism that adopts a single unified meeting and reporting cadence whose goal is supporting feedback and prioritization across the entire Outcome Tree.

The Unified Cadence Model provides the planning cycle mechanisms for Outcome Management. For organizations that have separate business and technology planning cadences, this approach requires changes to both. The changes should result in an overall simplification of the meeting cadence and a reduction of meetings. For organizations that already have a single meeting cadence, the Unified Cadence Model offers some potential refinements for connecting the Outcome Loop and value streams to top-level planning processes.

Some Agile practitioners suggest that annual and quarterly planning processes are not suitable for Agile ways of working.[3] The Unified Cadence Model takes the opposite approach and states that we have to make the team- and value stream–level planning function run on the same annual, quarterly, monthly, and weekly basis, and make each of these lean and iterative. It also asserts that we need to change the structure of the entire cadence to support the Outcome Loop while supporting highly agile and just-in-time planning at the team level.

Aligning the Planning Cascade

An organization's vision and strategy often span multiple years. For some organizations, such as those creating products that involve long regulatory processes, the strategic and scenario planning may stretch into decades. This process can create very high-level objectives or use other approaches to strategic and scenario planning. The first point at which we want to unify cadence is when connecting that strategy to an Outcome Loop that will deliver on that strategy. As such, the connection between the top-level organizational strategy and the Outcome Loop can support a multiyear window of time. For the sake of simplicity, we will use the illustrative example of a one-year window in the discussion below. Shorter time scales for top-level planning are feasible as well. For example, very small or nimble organizations may do the equivalent of the annual planning described below on quarterly or monthly cycles.

We start by ensuring that the top-level planning process, which typically rolls up to the CEO or similar director for the organization, is connected to the top-level Outcome Loop. This top-level Outcome Loop represents the value stream that contains all of the other top-level value streams. The strategy is then translated directly into the objectives for the top-level value stream's Outcome Loop. The capacity to deliver on the strategy, with the budget provided, must be based on the historical output capacity of the top-level value stream as reviewed in Chapter 5 (Slop to Substance). If the historical capacity is insufficient to deliver on the strategy, then the strategy must be revisited as it is not grounded in historical performance. This is the top level of feedback needed for the strategic planning process.

Strategy and Outcome Planning

For organizations that have been doing project-based planning, this is a very significant change. In that mode, the strategy is defined and, if the budget allows it, resources are added to the projects that will deliver on that strategy. With Outcome Management, we assume a fixed capacity for each value stream when planning, and we separately plan investment to increase capacity. This is not dissimilar to how a car manufacturer needs to plan. It can take two to four years to build a new car plant. As such, when doing annual strategic planning for how to win market share, the car company needs to determine how to leverage its existing plant capacity to drive the most impactful outcomes. It is possible to make significant strategic pivots with fixed capacity. For example, a plant that can produce electric, hybrid, and gas-powered vehicles might shift more production to electric if market or supply chain conditions allow it. Those plans and pivots are still based on fixed plant production capacity.

With software, we do not need to wait years to spin up new teams and agents, and thereby more capacity. However, the teams are only part of the story, and the value stream structure supporting the teams must evolve as well. As discussed in Chapter 5 (Slop to Substance), until we have evidence of new capacity being online, we should plan based on historical capacity, and we should track plans to grow capacity via improvement objectives.

The top-level value stream's Outcome Loop gives us everything we need for turning the strategic plan into an annual roadmap and objectives that match the annual strategy and budget. The plan that results provides the objectives that define the outcomes and an Outcome Roadmap that defines the Plan Distribution and Flow Distribution. In another major departure from project planning, the outputs do not need to be specified as part of the plan. Value streams should have autonomy on how they will deliver the outputs that drive the outcomes.

The Outcome Roadmap can provide high-level guidance on what outputs are considered most likely to drive the planned outcomes. In our TeenWellness app example, the furthest-out item on the roadmap is "add sleep tracking feature." However, if the previous item, "add caffeine tracking feature," proves more popular, the value stream should have the autonomy to reallocate priorities to whatever will maximize the outcome, even if that means postponing the sleep tracking feature.

Dependencies exist between value streams as well as between value streams and the rest of the organization. For example, the marketing team may have started prework for a campaign on sleep tracking. The Outcome Roadmap is the vehicle for connecting these kinds of dependencies. With Outcome Management, if changing a roadmap item helps deliver on that outcome, the value stream needs to have the autonomy to do so. But given the issue of dependencies, any changes to the plan must be visible and cascaded. This is exactly where the Unified Cadence Model comes in. The mechanism of connected Outcome Roadmaps ensures that other teams, such as marketing, are made immediately aware of changes to outputs.

Guidance: Manage Dependencies with Outcome Roadmaps: All value stream dependencies should be captured and coordinated at the Outcome Roadmap level when planning.

With the strategy, budget, objectives, and Outcome Roadmap defined, we are ready for the delivery portion of the loop to begin iterating. The delivery loop does not stop during planning, as the teams will continue delivering on the previous iteration's priorities. The new plan is simply a new prioritization and set of objectives that alter what is being delivered. For the annual planning cycle, the objectives should be specified ahead of the start of that cycle. For example, an organization with a January 1st fiscal year start should have their objectives defined, finalized, and communicated well ahead of January 1st and to provide enough time for the full cascade of value streams to create their Outcome Roadmaps.

How far ahead the plan needs to be communicated varies between organizations. The key constraint here is that this plan must cascade all the way down the Outcome Tree so every value stream can repeat the process above. For example, a child value stream may determine that "passwordless signup" depends on both provisioning a new authentication provider and rearchitecting the internal authentication platform. This requires the corresponding value stream to do the same roadmapping and capacity planning and then feed that back into the parent value stream. In this way, the planning process is recursive. In other words, the parent value stream cascades its inputs, objectives, and Outcome Roadmap down to the child value stream. Then, each of the child value streams cascades those down to their children.

The Outcome Tree is an exponential structure, which means the planning cascade can efficiently reach many team levels without excessive coordination. For simplicity, consider an Outcome Tree with a branching factor of ten (i.e., where each team has on average ten people at each level of the tree). In this scenario, an Outcome Tree that is four value stream levels deep can support up to 1,111 teams. With five levels, it can support up to 11,111 teams, or 111,110 employees, and each of those teams can be amplified by a large number of agents. As long as there is a clear cascade and planning cadence established for the cascade, even the largest organizations can get through this planning process in a matter of days or weeks.

Guidance: Provide Enough Time to Cascade Planning: Communicate the top-level plan early enough to allow every level of the Outcome Tree time to process the inputs and create the roadmaps and objectives that feed back up to the top loop before planning is finalized.

Once the initial strategic planning is completed, the delivery loop for each value stream can kick off. This is where it is critical that we have established our Unified Cadence Model in order to ensure that feedback from both the delivery process and the outcomes delivered is feeding back into the planning loop.

When doing a business review, whether weekly, monthly, or quarterly, we want to ensure visibility into each value stream's input, output, and outcome metrics. Table 6.1 outlines a simple visualization, generalized from the approach I created across the value streams I have managed over my career.

The table represents all of the value streams for one node of the Outcome Tree. For Product A, we see the input cost in terms of number of staff, cloud hosting spend, and AI token spend. We then see the outputs in terms of the number of Flow Items delivered in the iteration, as well as the Flow Distribution (i.e., percentage of features, defects, risks, and debts delivered). The flow time metric is excluded from my top-level reports as the value streams I managed had sufficiently fast flow time, though all flow metrics were available by drilling into the report. We then see the state of outcome metrics, including recurring revenue, as well as customer and employee Net Promoter Scores. The same metrics are used for a platform value stream, though the platform has no direct revenue.

If Product A were composed of multiple value streams, the metrics of those child value streams would be presented in the same way and roll up to the parent. For each metric, we always included a visible delta, such as the increase in token spend since the last iteration. This approach makes it easy to track changes in inputs, outputs, and outcomes for each value stream as part of the review cadence.

TABLE 6.1: Example Value Stream Report

Value Stream	Inputs			Outputs		Outcomes		
	Staff	Cloud	Tokens	Flow Velocity	Flow Distribution	Recurring Revenue	Customer NPS	Employee NPS
Product A	#	$	$	#	[%, %, %, %]	$	#	#
Platform B	#	$	$	#	[%, %, %, %]	-	#	#

Quarterly Planning

The core of the Outcome Loop planning cadence is the planning cycle or iteration. We need to ensure that this approach to planning is not a separate process from business and operations planning but merged into a single process. Agile frameworks often recommend planning windows of eight to twelve weeks. But our goal is to align both the process and the cadence. This implies that we have the following durations to choose from: annual, quarterly, monthly, and weekly. While an organization can follow all of the methodology specified by planning frameworks, or create its own methodology, the invariant characteristic of Outcome Management is that the planning cadence lines up with the calendar windows of years, quarters, months, and weeks. This supports getting the entire organization on one cadence

I have observed organizations devise many reasons for staggered planning cadences. A common one is that one function's planning needs to be completed before the planning for the technology organization can begin. For example, Sales and Marketing need to complete their quarterly business reviews, which can take two or three weeks at the start of the new quarter, after which the results of those reviews can provide input into the tech teams' planning.

Guidance: Align the Planning Cadence with the Calendar: The planning cycles must line up with business and calendar boundaries–annual, quarterly, monthly, and weekly–so the Outcome Loops and organization operate on a single cadence.

This results in multiple overlapping time boxes and incurs significant coordination cost between them. It also means that, in this example, Sales and Marketing are disconnected from the technology planning process. For example, if it takes one week to do the full quarter plan for the product organization, it is at week four of the quarter that we might learn about the fact that the sleep tracking feature in our example is not being implemented until the following quarter. If Sales and Marketing started their work assuming that this feature would be available, they now have to abandon those efforts, resulting in substantial waste. And in the process of abandoning that work, multiple meetings, each with a coordination cost, will typically be held to look at various ways of salvaging the original plan.

The Unified Cadence Model means the quarterly business cadence and the technology planning cadence are one process. How you implement this in your organization depends on how you approach business planning, but this does mean that including the review of at least the top-level value streams in your quarterly business reviews and plan definition is critical. For example, if your organization's goal is to have that done by the third week of the quarter, the entire planning loop cascade and Outcome Roadmap creation must be completed by that third week. The resulting unification dramatically reduces coordination costs, is much more responsive to feedback, and enables the speed of decision-making that is key to effectively leveraging the output amplification of AI.

Unifying the Meeting Cadence at Planview

When Planview acquired Tasktop, the planning cadences of the two companies had to be integrated. Razat Gaurav, then CEO of Planview, and I sat down and expected a fair amount of work for our teams in terms of merging all of the related meetings, reports, and processes. To our surprise, this turned out to be very easy. Early in his career, Razat had been a product manager at i2 Technologies, a leader in supply chain planning and optimization. He had leveraged a Product Operating Model and quarterly product reviews at each of his companies since. I had thought I would need to push to elevate product value stream reviews, but all of this was in place, and the entire executive leadership team was attending those quarterly meetings. We simply had to take the objective, flow, and outcome structure from Tasktop's process and embed it into the existing processes. Notably, Razat had all Planview functions running on a quarterly planning cadence, including Finance and HR. Planview was using a subset of the SAFe® framework for cross-company planning, which made it easy to integrate Tasktop's Outcome Tree cascade.

However, there was one significant difference. The quarterly product review cadence was offset by multiple weeks from the quarterly business reviews. This was foreign to me, as I was accustomed to a single company cadence. The reasoning was logical. The Product teams wanted input from the Sales and Marketing teams' planning activities before they completed their planning.

During the seventeen years I spent running Tasktop, I had experimented with dozens of planning cadence schedules. In the end, what worked best was taking the last two weeks of the quarter to come up with the draft objectives and roadmaps, first for the whole company in the second to last week, then for the cascade of value streams in the last week. We would then have all of our financial numbers completed in the first week of the new quarter, run quarterly business reviews and planning for those first two weeks, and have the objectives, roadmaps, and all other plans updated by the end of the second week. It took a decade of experimentation, fine tuning, and creating processes that made it easier for dealing with end-of-quarter sales crunches as well as other hard deadlines. But once in place, this process proved highly effective for years and kept the company aligned and executing through across both stable and turbulent periods.

After a year of attempting the staggered cadence at Planview, I reached out to Dean Leffingwell, pioneer of Agile at scale and creator SAFe® and defined its planning interval (PI) process, asking him if he knew of these staggered PI cadences working for his or other organizations. Dean stated that having a single time box across the company lowered overhead in every instance he had encountered. Dean had himself tried the multiple cadences but ultimately returned to using a single cadence. This is precisely what we ended up doing at Planview. Whatever your process, these experiences highlight the need to run it on a unified cadence. After unifying the planning cadence, we were able to substantially reduce the number of meetings and cut the overhead of meeting preparation and reporting by half.

Conclusion

Change initiatives, transformations, and AI deployments have wreaked havoc on the meeting, reporting, and planning processes of organizations. At the core of this is a tendency to layer on additional processes and ceremonies instead of replacing entrenched ones. The result is a planning process that is overly convoluted. The Unified Cadence Model solves this by reanchoring the entire planning cycle in a nested set of cadences that span the entire organization and can process, react to, and learn at the speed of outputs delivered by agents. Leveraging the Unified Cadence Model as the heartbeat of the organization, we will next explore the containment and coupling structures between value streams in the Outcome Tree.

In Summary

- Agile transformations often increase complexity and chaos by laying on top of existing organizational structures and planning cadences.
- Parallel cadences create dysfunctions by creating misaligned priorities. This, in turn, results in waste as departments attempt to reconcile and realign mismatched priorities and time horizons.
- The Unified Cadence Model provides the solution by aligning annual, quarterly, monthly, and weekly planning cycles across business and technology.
- A unified cadence enables autonomy and adaptability, as value streams can independently reprioritize based on outcomes.

- The cascade of planning down the Outcome Tree enables the scaling of a unified meeting and planning cadence across very large organizations.

Key Takeaways

- Adopt the Unified Cadence Model across the entire organization aligned to shared annual, quarterly, monthly, and weekly cycles.
- A unified cadence empowers value streams to pivot quickly and transparently while staying connected to organizational strategy and outcomes.

Prompt

Objective: Help humans replace fragmented planning rhythms with a single, unified cadence that drives faster, outcome-oriented decisions.

Operating protocol (assist, don't act unilaterally):

- Map today's cadences: List all major annual, quarterly, monthly, and weekly meetings for business, product, and technology; highlight overlaps, gaps, and conflicting cycles (e.g., quarterly business review vs. iteration planning).
- Propose a unified single cadence: One shared annual strategy cycle, one quarterly planning/review cycle, plus simple monthly and weekly check-ins tied directly to Outcome Loops and value streams.
- Merge, don't stack: Recommend where Agile ceremonies should be merged into existing business reviews instead of added as a "second operating system."
- Tie each cadence to decisions: For every recurring meeting, clarify which outcome metrics, flow metrics, and roadmap changes it should review and what decisions it must enable.
- Design the cascade: Show how top-level objectives and Outcome Roadmaps must be ready in time for child value streams to do their own planning and feed back up.

Guardrails: Do not introduce new parallel cadences; always push toward fewer, shared cycles, and flag any process that forces teams to reconcile two different time boxes.

Chapter 7

Fourth Shift: Matrix to Modularity

AI and agentic solutions can create tremendous output, especially when working within modular structures. The challenge for most incumbents is that their organizational, product, and technical structures are far from being modular and instead form a messy matrix of dependencies, communication paths, and reporting lines. In this chapter, we will review an approach to rewiring your organization into modular structures within the Outcome Tree. We will then examine how to provide each value stream with autonomy and empowerment by leveraging the Independent Action Model. The chapter concludes with practical approaches for operationalizing modularity to reduce coordination costs and accelerate flow.

Reorganization efforts start with the best of intentions. A typical catalyst is a missed business outcome that triggers a performance review. Consultants may then be brought in to comb through the organizational structure. The current structure is blamed, a new organizational structure is proposed as the target model, and the better part of the following year is spent implementing the new structure. The primary hierarchy changes from business unit–based to functional, or vice versa. This creates gaps between leaders and teams who should be collaborating, at which point the gaps that are created are turned into matrix or "dotted" reporting lines. The dependencies that span the new hierarchy get encoded in these matrix lines.

For example, a director level engineering manager may report to a vice president in their region. But they could be matrixed to their functional vice president at the company headquarters in another country and then matrixed again to a chief technology officer with whom they work closely. All of this makes logical sense, as these three roles are intertwined. However, for that manager to make a decision, they now need to involve up to three different managers. And this is just the start of the matrix lines, as managers up and down the hierarchy will be similarly matrixed to each other. The matrix lines that span an entire organization can quickly get so complex that not a single consequential decision can be made without multiple meetings.

In the previous chapter (Chaos to Cadence), we reviewed the way Agile rollouts and digital transformations have produced new meeting cadences that are layered over existing ones. A similar thing happens when a transformation or reorganization results in an Agile matrix line being layered over existing organizational charts. I have worked closely with several companies that have tens of thousands of team members and organization charts that are incapable of indicating who is working on what. In most cases, those companies have deployed an Agile, Scrum, or Spotify Model[1] structure without significantly altering the organizational chart. This creates a dysfunction that parallels the meeting cadence issue. The resulting increase in coordination costs and lack of clarity wreak havoc on decision-making, planning, and communication. The next step is usually to create a parallel organizational chart system that needs to be referenced to understand who is on which team and to ensure that both are kept up to date.

ⓧ **Dysfunction: The Messy Matrix:** Reorganizations and Agile transformations that add matrix reporting lines create overlapping hierarchies, diffuse ownership, and incur high coordination costs. Decision-making slows to a crawl as new meeting and reporting cadences form around matrix lines and must be coordinated across them.

Consider the example cascade we discussed in the previous chapter. In the four-value stream deep tree that has 1,111 nodes (i.e., teams), there are over 1.2 million ways of connecting just the managers in the matrix. This excludes the ability to matrix team members, which would bring us to over 123 million potential matrix lines. While it is very unlikely that anywhere near this many matrix lines would be put in place, the potential for additional complexity when connecting just a fraction of the organization this way is massive. This is why these overlay structures so quickly create "the messy matrix."

Shift: Matrix to Modularity: Replace the complexity and coordination cost of matrixed organizational structures with modular value streams that have clear ownership, boundaries, and the autonomy to deliver outputs in support of organizational outcomes.

Independent Action Model

Our goal with Outcome Management is to make the Outcome Tree a core part of the primary operating model, not a secondary overlay structure. In other words, to make the second operating system become the first. This means we need a model for structuring the organization that minimizes the matrix structure. As we will discuss in this chapter, this organizational streamlining around the Outcome Tree has the effect of minimizing coordination cost. The question is, what do we want to maximize? The answer proposed in this chapter is that we want to maximize the independence of action via value stream modularity.

The power of good modularity ensures that modules can evolve independently. In the Product Operating Model, the modules are value streams. As such, our goal is ensuring that value streams can act independently by taking end-to-end ownership of turning their inputs into outcomes. Enabling the Independent Action Model is the goal of value stream modularity.

Independent Action Model: Ensures that leaders and teams can act autonomously to deliver outcomes within their value streams without excessive cross-team coordination or process overhead.

Value Stream Modularity

Modularity is a property that allows us to organize a system into clear and self-contained components, which can be connected, composed, and interchanged. Modularity enables the separation of concerns, allowing complex systems to be decomposed into components that can be built and evolved independently. For many of us, our first tangible experience with modularity was playing with LEGO® or other interchangeable bricks. That experience proved fun and popular enough that LEGO has become the number one toy company globally. The power of modularity is fascinating to many and, when employed effectively, allows humans to create, assemble, and reassemble both physical and knowledge artifacts of tremendous complexity. These range from particle accelerators to AI models.

Two of the key principles of modularity are cohesion and coupling. Good modularity means each module has *high cohesion*, meaning it encapsulates common functionality. In our TeenWellness example, the password system for our mobile applications relies on some kind of identity management system that provides information on users. If we have high cohesion of that identity management service, it will enable us to plug in a third-party identity management service that also encapsulates that same functionality.

High Cohesion: A module encapsulates a closely related set of functionality that it can deliver independently, making it easy to swap out or replace. For a value stream, high cohesion includes aligned functionality, expertise, and ownership.

High cohesion alone is not enough to make this easy, as we also need to worry about coupling. For example, if our mobile application contains many rules about how to deal with groups of users, it is likely that when a new group is being created it will rely on numerous connections to the identity management service. This is called high coupling, and it occurs when many connections between modules are needed for normal operation. As research shows, systems with good modularity have low coupling.[2] *Low coupling* relies on high cohesion, such as when a single module contains everything related to user management, like handling groups of users and access control. Employing the principle of low coupling ensure that our mobile application is loosely coupled to the identity management service. In other words, it has zero or few dependencies on the details of how that service implements its various user management capabilities.

This combination of high cohesion and loose coupling is the kind of good modularity that will make it easy for us to plug in various identity management services, such as the passwordless service in our example. Good modularity of this sort is what has made the world's most successful software systems evolve gracefully even as their usage and functionality skyrockets. As examples of the power of good modularity, consider the success of the Linux, iOS, and Android ecosystems.

Low Coupling: Modules interact through well-defined and minimal interfaces so that they can be changed independently without materially affecting the functionality and outputs of the overall system.

TABLE 7.1: Good vs. Bad Modularity

	Software	Organization
High Cohesion	Encapsulate common functionality	Encapsulate expertise and ownership
Low Coupling	Decrease dependencies between modules	Decrease dependencies between value streams

Sociotechnical Congruence

Those who have been directly involved with larger technology projects will be familiar with the way that good modularity makes systems easier to maintain and scale. On the flip side, those who have had the displeasure of dealing with large monolithic systems will know how difficult it is to make changes to those systems, both for people and for agents. Bad modularity impedes the flow of value, making the delivery loop highly inefficient. This happens when not enough capacity is allocated to improvement work, as discussed in Chapter 5 (Slop to Substance), causing technical debt to increase to the point of hindering flow. It can also result from problematic design decisions or technological dead ends, such as tools and frameworks that do not scale to the needs of the organization.

Modularity is not a function of technology layers alone. Since the earliest days of the Age of Software & Digital in the 1970s, the effects of Conway's Law have been well documented. Conway's Law states that organizations tend to produce the architecture that mirrors the organization's internal communication patterns.[3] This implies that if an organization's communication is a messy matrix, a tangled architecture with poor modularity is the likely outcome. It is common for organizations to blame technology teams for making poor architectural decisions. However, even with the best architectural intentions, a tangled organizational structure will create a tangled technical architecture.

Sociotechnical Congruence: The alignment between organizational structures, such as teams, ownership, and communication patterns, and technical structures, such as software and agentic architectures.

The solution to this problem goes by the mouthful *sociotechnical congruence*.[4] This concept means that we need alignment between the organization's social structures, such as the organizational hierarchy and team communication patterns, and the organization's technical structures, such as the software architecture, agentic framework, and service design. Several studies indicate that sociotechnical congruence is not automatic and that organizational complexities and flawed talent sourcing strategies can move organizations in the wrong direction.[5]

The question becomes one of how we achieve sociotechnical congruence. How can we create good modularity that will make it easy for teams to deliver value and ensure alignment between the technical architecture and the organizational structure? The answer lies in applying the same modularity principles that we apply to software to the design of our organizations. In other words, we need to implement effective people, technology, and agent-centric modularity in the Outcome Tree.

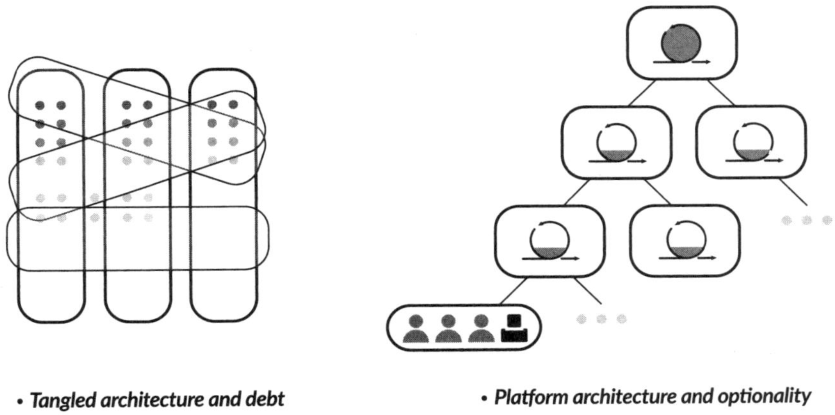

FIGURE 7.1: Matrix to Modularity

Maximizing Value Stream Cohesion

The goal of each value stream in the Outcome Tree is to provide end-to-end value delivery to the customer. In order to ensure that we create a highly modular Outcome Tree, we need to follow the two key principles of good modularity.

To start, we need to ensure high cohesion for each value stream. This means the value stream encapsulates everything it needs in order to deliver value to a customer. *Value stream cohesion* comes from allocating domain ownership in a way that optimizes each value stream for a common and coherent set of functions specific to a customer or customer segment. For example, if an organization had two highly overlapping products but built them as part of two different value streams, it would have low value stream cohesion.

As an example, consider Google's multiple online meeting solutions, which at one point included Hangouts, Chat, Meet, Duo, and Allo. The availability of so many overlapping solutions created confusion both internally and for their customers and ultimately led the company to begin steadily combining the product value streams. Value stream cohesion is just as important for platform products. If we had two different parts of the organization offering an identity management service to our application, and a third-party service as well, we would be in a state of low cohesion for these value streams in the Outcome Tree.

Value Stream Cohesion: The degree to which a value stream encapsulates the capabilities, expertise, and ownership required to deliver its intended outcomes.

The goal of high value stream cohesion is for each value stream to move as fast and as independently as feasible while delivering outcomes, which means removing as many of the wait states from process and technology dependencies as possible. What we want for each value stream is independent action. This concept was introduced in Gene Kim and Steven Spear's *Wiring the Winning Organization*[6] and is key to enabling each part of the organization to move at its optimal speed for delivering outcomes. For example, if implementing a change to how we access customer data in a mobile app requires going to two internal and one external team to validate that nothing will get broken, flow velocity is likely to grind to a halt.

To ensure the highest levels of cohesion, each value stream would need to have complete autonomy and ownership of its entire technology stack. This goal is aspirational, as it is very unlikely that every value stream will create its own data storage technologies or AI models. As such, while we want to maximize cohesion, in any complex Outcome Tree we will end up with some dependencies on other value streams and will need mechanisms for managing and minimizing those dependencies.

If the dependencies are on child value streams, the process is relatively easy, as we manage the dependencies through the Outcome Roadmap, as we described in Chapter 2 (The Outcome Loop). However, it is possible that two different value streams want to depend on an internal, or an external, service. For example, in addition to the TeenWellness app's value stream, a reporting value stream may want access to customer data that comes from an identity service. In this scenario, we have three choices. We can either recreate another identity service in our part of the Outcome Tree or create a dependency to another part of the Outcome Tree or to third party service.

In my experience, defining mechanisms for managing such dependencies over time is one of the most important aspects of building complex systems. So much so that I created a quarterly process of analyzing dependencies to ensure that my teams were optimizing this trade-off between embedding, at the cost of duplication, and creating dependencies, at the cost of increasing coupling. My peers at other organizations have experienced similar challenges in structuring their technology organizations and have implemented similar mechanisms to ensure that these dependencies are visible and actively managed.

After realizing that there is no ideal answer, just a trade-off to optimize over time, dependency management became a part of our planning process at Tasktop and then Planview and a key driver of improvement objectives. Ensuring sociotechnical congruence then meant that organizational changes could be made every quarter, and most quarters involved at least incremental dependency-related changes of some kind. The majority of changes were not made to the teams, or leaves in the Outcome Tree, but to the branches. Changing the composition of teams is expensive, as teams can take many quarters to ramp up. However, changing the structure of the tree carries much less overhead as it does not directly impact the productivity of teams. Each of these changes helped pave the path to achieving sociotechnical congruence.

Maximizing cohesion and managing dependencies is a question of optimization, and one that is inherent to managing complex modular systems. For example, we have witnessed this trade-off play out in the verticalization or supply chain breadth of car manufacturers. At times of high innovation, the verticalization and lack of supply chain dependencies between hardware and software have made car companies successful, as witnessed by the architectural approach of the crop of modern electric vehicle makers. At times of slower innovation, the cost efficiencies of broad supply chains and de-verticalization can provide a competitive advantage.[7]

Guidance: Optimize Cohesion and Coupling for Flow: Regularly review the encapsulation of each value stream and cross-value stream coupling to maximize flow. Embed these reviews into the regular planning cadence and leverage improvement objectives for making structural changes to the Outcome Tree.

What mechanisms can we employ to balance this trade-off of coupling and cohesion? Given that this is an optimization problem, we need to determine what we are optimizing for. This is precisely where the Outcome Loop comes into play. We want our modularity strategy to optimize for the flow of outputs that drive the planned outcomes over a specific time period.

Consider the simple example of our "passwordless signup" roadmap item. Completion of this item depends on an identity service. In support of value stream cohesion, we determine that the identity service is sufficiently standalone as to warrant its own value stream. This is because it can be used independently of the mobile application by other applications in our product portfolio. We now have two choices. We either have a child value stream implement the identity service, or we create a dependency on a value stream elsewhere in the organization.

The principle of value stream cohesion cascades down the Outcome Tree. If the parent value stream is Mobile Apps, we want the child value streams to be closely related to Mobile Apps as well. Identity services are more broadly applicable, so we know that, from a value stream cohesion point of view, the identity service does not belong within this part of the Outcome Tree. As such, the first step in planning should be creating a dependency on the platform value stream that provides these services. If the platform value stream can commit to this on their roadmap for this quarter, we can proceed. If they cannot, we have another choice to make. We can either implement the identity service within the Mobile Apps value stream, or we can push out this roadmap item to the following quarter.

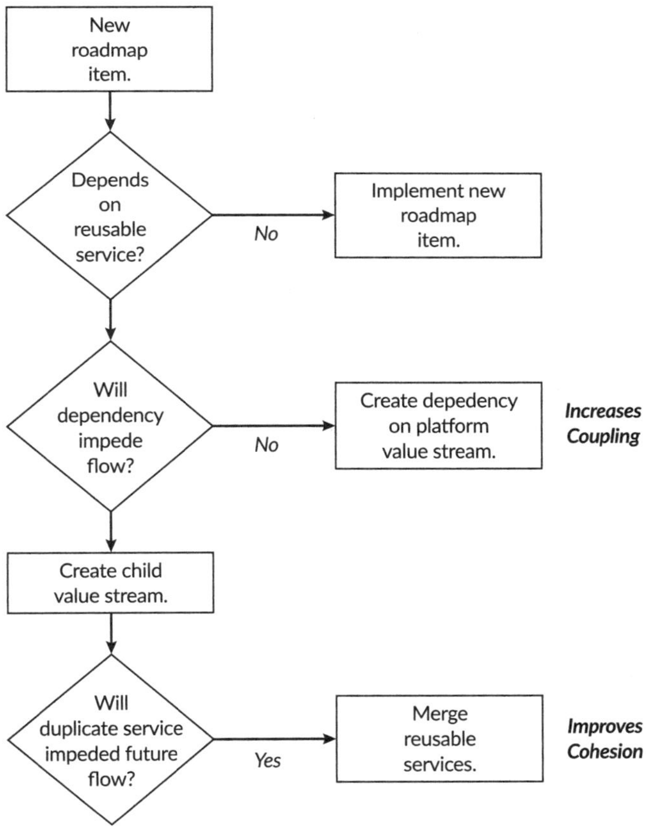

FIGURE 7.2: Example Flow Chart for Managing Coupling and Cohesion

If we implement the identity service in the Mobile Apps value stream, we are reducing *value stream coupling*. This puts the implementation in the control of the Mobile Apps value stream, removing the dependency and risk associated with the implementation being out of the span of control of Mobile Apps, and reduces wait states. This inlining of dependencies has the effect of accelerating flow. However, it also has the effect of reducing global cohesion. In other words, it is a near-term optimization of the Outcome Loop, as it accelerates flow in the near term but will impede flow in the long term.

If we consider what happens a few quarters out, we are likely to have two different parts of the organization implementing an identity service and will now need to coordinate between those two implementations to ensure that they remain consistent and compatible. We just introduced a form of technical debt, increased coordination cost, and created new coupling and matrix communication lines across the Outcome Tree.

These near-term optimizations can be the right decision in terms of maximizing velocity as long as we have a mechanism for avoiding their long-term implications and as long as we avoid the "one-way doors"[8] that create long-term lock-in. As we discussed in Chapter 5 (Slop to Substance), improvement objectives are the mechanism for improving future flow. As such, in this scenario we add an improvement objective and roadmap item to extract a common identity service platform service in a future planning cycle and put the various tech debt work items under that roadmap item so we have a sense of the scope of this future work.

We then need to determine where in the Outcome Tree this new improvement roadmap item should reside. If we put it on the Mobile Apps value stream, it may get pushed out multiple quarters as, having implemented its own identity service, Mobile Apps will be incentivized to move onto the next set of roadmap items that will drive previously defined outcomes rather than invest in reworking something that they begrudgingly took on because the platform value stream did not have enough capacity. If we put it on the platform value stream, we could end up with the same problem of this work being too far down their queue to get prioritized in a meaningful timeframe, as we know from planning that they did not have enough capacity in the first place. It is this adversarial dynamic that so often results in improvement work not getting sufficient priority, causing tech debt to increase, modularity to decrease, and overall organizational capacity to decline over time. The solution to this is to put the improvement roadmap item on the common parent value stream of Mobile Apps and Platforms and to ensure that it is connected to a sufficiently elevated improvement objective.

Guidance: Elevate Improvement Work: Improvement roadmap items must reside on the parent value stream's roadmap in the Outcome Tree and be tied to an improvement objective. This ensures that they are prioritized at the appropriate level and not deprioritized by competing near-term.

In our simple example Outcome Tree, the common parent of Mobile Apps and Platforms is the top level of the product organization. We will dive deeper into the ownership implications of this in the next chapter (Objectives to Ownership). This implies that the dedicated leader for the entire product development organization, such as the chief product and technology officer, must now determine which objective this work is related to and where this roadmap item fits in terms of priority. In our example, the objective would likely be the top-level one of "become the #1 daily wellness app for teens." The leader of the top value stream may determine that affecting capacity in this way will make this annual objective too hard to hit and schedule this roadmap item for later in the year. Or when confronted with this escalation, they may decide to bite the bullet now and reprioritize the work of the platform team. In either scenario, there is a clear set of mechanisms for managing near-term or long-term optimization in a way that maximizes flow and outcomes within the window specified by the strategy and objectives.

Minimizing Value Stream Coupling

We have established how to manage the balance of coupling and cohesion between value streams. With clear mechanisms for when to maximize cohesion in place, we need strategies for minimizing coupling between value streams. The goal of the loose coupling modularity principle is to make it easy to configure and reconfigure value streams to maximize value delivery as the strategy evolves. In our LEGO example, the way components are loosely coupled is with standardized brick interfaces. For value streams, loose coupling similarly comes from standardized interfaces, such as Application Programming Interfaces, or APIs, provided by each value stream. Whichever convention or protocol is used, what matters is that the interfaces make value streams pluggable. In other words, we can reconfigure our Outcome Tree by moving value streams to best match the outcomes we are optimizing for. For example, we may determine there is a suitable third-party identity service that we can employ. Loose coupling enables the Mobile Apps value stream to easily shift from the internal service to the external one. It also allows us to repurpose the capacity from the internal Mobile Apps value stream to other work. In other words, the loose coupling has to function at the technology level as well as at the team level. This enables sociotechnical congruence.

Value Stream Coupling: The degree of interdependence between value streams, as defined by their reliance on shared capabilities, interfaces, and delivery processes.

Loose coupling of technology modules and layers is a well understood domain with clear best practices.[9] The challenge that many organizations face is the effects of the messy matrix creating coupling at the team level, making it difficult to easily reallocate or reprioritize value stream roadmaps and work. Part of the challenge with technology work is just how deep teams' expertise needs to grow for them to be effective in their complexity domain.

Consider the Identity Service value stream. Let's assume the team has been working on this service for the year. They have become experts in the various complexities related to the identity management domain, such as user management and access control. They have created numerous agents specific to this domain of work. If we now switch to an external identity service provider, we cannot expect this team to quickly switch to building mobile user interfaces. This limits our ability to plug this team and its value stream into another part of the Outcome Tree.

Dysfunction: Cognitive Overload of Value Streams: When a team is spread across multiple complexity domains, it can experience cognitive overload. Even with the assistance of agents, team boundaries that cut across with complexity domains lead to overly complex roadmaps and thrashing.

Referring back to our LEGO example, not all LEGO pieces can be connected in a productive way to all other LEGO pieces. The same goes for our organizations. People, teams, and the agents they employ specialize in particular complexity domains. This both supports our goal of high cohesion and enables loose coupling. As such, we need to understand what those complexity domains are and use that information to determine what can be plugged in and reconfigured with ease and what requires the more expensive process of team reskilling or reconfiguration.

Returning to our example, the team working on identity management may have exactly the right skill set to take on another platform service that we need to build and be productive out of the gate in tackling those new roadmap items. But it could take them months to ramp up on mobile application development, and those team members may be inherently motivated by platform service work and not front-end work. In Chapter 9 (Divisions to Domains), we will further explore aligning types of individual and team expertise to various delivery and Outcome Tree segments.

Guidance: One Complexity Domain Per Team: Each leaf value stream's team must focus on a single complexity domain to ensure cohesion and avoid the costs of cognitive overload.

Loose coupling cannot be implemented at the team level alone. This is where value streams come in, as they allow us to encapsulate the expertise of both a single team and teams of teams. At the leaf levels of the organization, we need to ensure that each value stream and its leaf team only work on a single domain to avoid cognitive overload, as described in *Team Topologies*.[10] As strategy and priorities evolve, this allows us to easily determine which new roadmap work should go to which team. If priority changes are substantial, it may mean we need to invest in upskilling a team. For example, we may know that our Identity Service team has expertise in graph databases, as the service they created leveraged a graph database. If the new roadmap priority is creating a new platform service for generic graph data storage to support a new set of AI agents, we can provide this team with a bootcamp to learn the latest graph technologies and then have them take on the corresponding roadmap work.

Guidance: Roadmaps Must Be Easy to Change: If it is difficult to reassign roadmap items as priorities shift, it is time to fix the coupling and cohesion of the corresponding value streams.

With the expertise of the leaves established, we employ the cascading aspects of the Outcome Tree. For example, a well-partitioned Outcome Tree will ensure that all platform services teams will combine into a single Platform Services value stream at a higher level in the Outcome Tree. This will ensure that the leadership of that Platform Services value stream can best partition the work to the various value streams below it while managing both the talent and the technology architecture to ensure loose coupling and high cohesion between the various Platform Services value streams and their consumers elsewhere in the organization. This is an ongoing journey with improvement objectives that need to be planned to ensure investment in both the people and the technology aspects of value stream modularity.

Once we have mechanisms in place to ensure we are continually working on maximizing value stream cohesion and minimizing value stream coupling, we have created a modular Outcome Tree. A modular Outcome Tree is critical in maximizing flow. Perhaps even more importantly, it is the key component of creating option value in our organization.

Outcomes from Option Value

The power of modularity for creating company and market value has been studied in detail by Carliss Baldwin and her team at Harvard.[11] In short, modularity creates option value for organizations. This means that the organization has the option to double down on investments when market conditions support expansion. It also provides organizations with the ability to defer or adapt investments when market conditions require pivots or retreat. The result is material economic benefits, as it allows organizations to minimize risk and maximize returns by deciding which options to invoke in their strategy given changing market conditions. In summary, it enables flexibility with the same resources. Dr. Baldwin's work provides empirical evidence that a company with better modularity will deliver better innovation and economic value.[12] Another way to frame this is that modularity enables more efficient Outcome Trees by enabling the same inputs to drive better economic outcomes.

A key goal of Outcome Management is to enable the option value that results from creating a modular organization. This is key to achieving the productivity gains provided by constantly changing technology and markets in the Age of AI. In addition to supporting software modularity, value streams and the Outcome Tree create modular organizational structures. The combination of the technical and the organizational structures into a single modular architecture provides option value when adapting to a rapidly evolving technological landscape. Furthermore, it directly enables organizations to harness the productivity of AI in accelerating the Outcome Loop.

Encapsulating for Agents

The modularity and encapsulation of value streams play a critical role in structuring the organization to leverage agents. While it will be suitable for some value streams to focus on amplifying the work of human teams with agents, for others the most productive answer may be to have agents own the entire delivery loop of the value stream and, in some cases, to own the entire Outcome Loop.

Consider a value stream that is maintaining a legacy batch reporting infrastructure. This reporting could be critical to the Finance organization and involve integrations with many different systems. The roadmap for the value stream involves updates to the reporting data sets and defects that need to be fixed. In my experience, this is the last thing that developers enjoy working on. However, such value streams may still produce critical data sets that other value streams depend on. Ensuring clear encapsulation makes it possible to provide the agents with the autonomy and independent action needed to successfully own the end-to-end delivery of those value streams.

By encapsulating the expertise and conceptual domains of value streams, we enable such value streams to be entirely delivered by AI. For organizations that adopt this, a portion of the leaves of the Outcome Tree will be composed entirely of agents delivering on the corresponding value streams' roadmaps. The structure of the Outcome Tree above that layer will ensure that the delivery meets the inputs defined at the higher levels of the organization. By establishing loose coupling between the work done by agentic value streams, human value streams, and human and agent hybrid value streams, we can optimize the allocation of people and agents to the outcomes we seek for the organization. We will explore the mechanics of such autonomous value streams in detail in Chapter 10 (Managers to Makers).

The reduction in coupling is so key to leveraging agents that organizations who fail to undertake this are likely to have difficulties unlocking the value of AI for their domain. For example, Justin Watts was charged with deploying agents to streamline food and goods deliveries at John Lewis Partnership, a large UK-based, employee-owned retail group.[13] The initial attempts at deploying agents yielded only incremental gains without significant cost savings or customer experience improvements. Justin is a Lean expert, and when he analyzed how the agents were deployed, he noticed a high number of handoffs in the current delivery process. The handoffs spanned national regions and various communication channels. He realized that in this envionment, even a tripling of the AI investment would not yield a meaningful outcome. Instead, he redesigned the entire delivery process to increase cohesion and reduce coupling, allowing agents to work effectively within far fewer value streams. The result was an impressive time reduction in food and goods delivery from 10 days to 1.3 and the ability to further scale with additional AI capabilities.

Parallelizing the Delivery Loop

The flexibility offered by modularity extends beyond the delivery of roadmap items. Recall that everything we deliver is a hypothesis in the Outcome Loop. In other words, we expect that delivering a new feature will drive the business and customer outcome we expect. Given that this is a hypothesis, we will only be correct a portion of the time. With the flexibility of modularity combined with AI, we can use *parallelized hypothesis testing*. In other words, rather than treating the hypothesis testing as serial, where a team implements a feature and we get feedback, we can leverage AI to test multiple hypotheses in parallel. This means we can run many more experiments at the same time, further leveraging the option value provided by modularity.

For example, consider the "caffeine intake" tracking feature on our roadmap. There are many ways this can be designed, ranging from leveraging the augmented reality capabilities of a mobile device to manual entry by the user. We could spin up ten sets of agents in parallel to create and then deliver these ten designs while the standard feedback portion of this parallelized delivery loop lets us know which had the best customer outcomes. Value stream modularity allows scale not only in terms of organizational capacity but also in terms of time via parallelization.

Parallelized Hypothesis Testing: The practice of leveraging AI agents to test multiple solution hypotheses for the same desired outcome in parallel rather than validating sequentially.

Optimizing Outcome Tree Modularity at Priceline

Leading a fast and effective deployment of the Product Operating Model and Outcome Management at a single organization is an impressive feat. I first started collaborating with Sejal Amin in 2018, when she was the chief technology officer, tax and accounting at Thomson Reuters. She then implemented several more of these transformations at Shutterstock and, most recently, at Priceline, the pioneer of the online travel category and a world leader in travel deals.

When Sejal took on the chief technology officer role at Priceline, she immediately saw an opportunity. Fifty projects were in motion, and many had multiple dependencies to realize their full potential. After reviewing the landscape, she recognized that only a handful of those initiatives could be delivered within the current planning cycle—not because of a lack of vision or talent, but because the existing operating model was not yet optimized to unleash the full capacity of Priceline's teams. She noticed symptoms familiar to many scaling organizations: individuals stretched across multiple teams, functional silos creating unnecessary handoffs, and a structure that had grown far more complex than the work required.

The foundation was present for positive change. Sejal quickly understood that the talent, the teams, and the product structure already existed to achieve far more—and that with the right model, Priceline could accelerate its ability to innovate. After aligning the executive team on the Product Operating Model and Outcome Management methodology, she partnered closely across Product, Technology, and Commercial to define a clear, cohesive product hierarchy, value stream structures, and an integrated Outcome Tree. For example, the Flights Product value stream evolved into a unified Product Portfolio value stream supported by Native App, Front-End, FinTech, Data, and Customer Care capabilities, enabling teams to collaborate with greater focus and purpose. Sejal's goal was straightforward: maximize cohesion and minimize unnecessary coupling so teams could deliver outcomes with dramatically fewer handoffs and far more speed.

To shortcut this process, she took a new approach that I had not previously witnessed. She introduced an innovative "Operating Model testing" initiative. Instead of waiting for dependencies to resolve organically, she and the leadership team proactively simulated the delivery of the most complex flows, such as launching a new product across the Outcome Tree. These simulations allowed teams to redesign boundaries, optimize platform services, and reduce friction with each iteration. In effect, Sejal created a dynamic, learning-oriented environment to continuously strengthen modularity and reduce delivery wait states. Supported by new flow and outcome telemetry, the organization gained ongoing visibility into how to refine and improve. The results were profound: Complex flows that once required fifteen handoffs now required only five, unlocking value, speed, and clarity for Priceline.

With a highly modular Outcome Tree in place, Sejal established a strong foundation for her next set of initiatives. This included championing "extreme ownership," ensuring that leaders fully owned the end-to-end outcomes of their value streams, and amplifying the impact of each value stream through agents. Because of the early investment in rewiring Priceline's Product Portfolio, these initiatives gained immediate traction, ultimately accelerating the customer outcomes that are core to Priceline.

Conclusion

Modularity is a mechanism that has made it possible for us to build increasingly complex systems by decomposing them into independently functioning parts that make up a cohesive whole. An effective Outcome Tree needs to apply the principles of good modularity to ensure the independence of action for each value stream while enabling the aggregation of multiple value streams to produce outcomes greater than the sum of the parts without incurring overly high coordination costs. The principles of coupling and cohesion enable us to define and redefine the boundaries of value streams and the scope of supported agents as organizations evolve. With these mechanisms that support the clarity of value stream scope in place, in the next chapter we will proceed to further define the scope of ownership and leadership.

In Summary

- Matrix structures create dysfunctions by adding reporting lines that diffuse ownership, multiply coordination costs, and slow decision-making.
- Replace the messy matrix, Agile overlays, and second operating system constructs with the Outcome Tree as the primary model.
- Leverage value stream modularity to ensure clear ownership, boundaries, and autonomy while minimizing dependencies and maximizing flow.
- Value stream modularity requires high cohesion and loose coupling to ensure each value stream can minimize dependencies and maximize autonomy while remaining connected to company outcomes.

Key Takeaways

- Replace the messy matrix with modular value streams organized into an Outcome Tree.

- Optimize for flow with modularity by continually improving value stream cohesion and minimizing value stream coupling.

Prompt

Objective: Help humans replace messy matrix structures with modular value streams that enable independent action and faster flow.

Operating protocol (assist, don't act unilaterally):

- Help them map the current "messy matrix": Functional org chart, dotted lines, squad/tribe overlays, and key cross-team dependencies. Highlight where ownership is unclear and decisions require multiple managers.
- Propose a modular Outcome Tree view: Define value streams as modules with clear outcomes, leaders, and teams; suggest where matrix lines can be removed or replaced by value stream boundaries.
- Analyze cohesion and coupling: For each value stream, identify whether it encapsulates the capabilities needed to deliver outcomes (high cohesion) and where it is over dependent on other streams (high coupling).
- Recommend structural options: Embed capabilities to reduce fragile dependencies or create shared platform value streams with clear interfaces and SLAs.
- Tie changes to metrics and improvement objectives: Show how modularity changes should improve flow time, flow efficiency, and coordination cost.

Guardrails: Do not automatically "reorg" anything; always present modular options, trade-offs, and risks so human leaders decide how to unwind the matrix.

Chapter 8

Fifth Shift: Objectives to Ownership

AI agents amplify the outputs that a single team can deliver. For a growing number of domains, they will also enable fully autonomous value streams. Both require clear ownership structures to channel the expanded output of hybrid human-agent teams and to enable autonomy for fully agentic value streams. Ownership must be aligned with leadership structures, yet in many organizations accountability is diffused by ambiguous or shared accountability. In this chapter, we will review replacing this ambiguity by aligning every leader and team to objectives that cascade through the Outcome Tree. The chapter will conclude with a summary of how to align incentives by directly matching compensation, promotion, and recognition to outcomes.

In the preceding chapters, we defined the structure of the Outcome Tree as well as the dynamics of Outcome Loops. We reviewed how objectives connect inputs to outputs and outcomes. But who in the organization is responsible for each of these mechanisms? What is the ideal ownership structure for Outcome Management?

Ownership structures are as varied as organizational designs. Functional ownership is common and optimizes for specialization and expertise, with leaders responsible for areas such as engineering, marketing, and finance. However, functional ownership is a structure that is detached from customer outcomes, as it is internally facing. Matrix ownership is often introduced to ensure that specialization is paired with "horizontal" structures that are aligned to business or customer outcomes. However, as we saw in the last chapter (Matrix to Modularity), those matrix lines result in ambiguous ownership and excessive coordination costs. Shared or collective ownership is often deployed as a part of Agile transformations in order to foster broader collaboration around outcomes in a way that spans the organizational chart. However, the lack of clarity on responsibilities can grind the speed of decision-making to a halt. This goes against our goal of deploying a management system that accelerates Outcome Loop decision-making.

In Chapter 4 (Functions to Flow), we reviewed the Dedicated Leadership Model for value streams. In this chapter, we will define how to map that leadership and management structure onto the Outcome Tree via the *Outcome Ownership Model*.

> **Shift: Objectives to Ownership:** Replace ambiguous and siloed ownership with dedicated accountability for outcomes, ensuring that every value stream, leader, and team has clear authority and capacity to deliver the outputs that drive those outcomes.

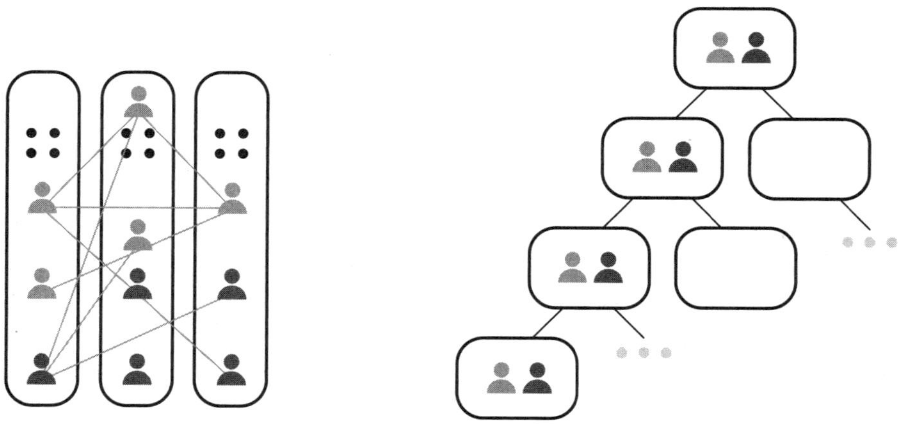

- ***Complex decision making***
- ***Independence of action***

FIGURE 8.1: Moving from Objectives to Ownership

Outcome Ownership Model

Most executive leaders I have worked with are wired to drive business and customer outcomes. They seek speed of decision-making and success for themselves and their organization. However, no matter how effectively Outcome Management is implemented, if the ownership and incentive structures are not aligned to the Outcome Tree, the incentives of the broader population of managers will get in the way of delivering those outcomes.

Consider the vice president responsible for one of the TeenWellness app's value streams and a scenario where their incentive structure is entirely based on delivering sales targets for the next two quarters. A rational interpretation of that incentive structure could be securing as many large deals as possible. This could result in all of the value stream's capacity going to features that help showcase the solution to partner organizations, which help land large deals. However, this approach may be misaligned with the company strategy.

A balanced set of objectives for that value stream should include tracking active usage to ensure the app is engaging and useful, as well as managing quality, performance, and tech debt. In this case, we have created a system where the objectives for a value stream are misaligned with the incentives of the leader for that value stream. Even with the best of intentions, this will create a constant tension that impedes outcomes.

Another way to look at this is that the performance loop for the individual, which is the basis for compensation and promotion, is misaligned with the Outcome Loop for the value stream. At best, this will create conflicting priorities. However, it is more likely that it will create an environment where the team on the value stream realizes that outcomes are not rewarded, but outputs, such as the features that are constantly being requested, are. This creates a highly dysfunctional value stream that will exhibit all of the issues of Output Management.

> **Outcome Ownership Model:** Aligns leadership accountability and incentive structures directly with value stream outcomes rather than outputs.

Dysfunction: Incentives Misaligned with Outcomes: When leadership incentives are tied to outputs or only near-term outcomes, accountability drifts away from strategy, creating tension between leaders and fostering a culture in which teams are disconnected from outcomes.

Incentivizing Outcomes

The solution to misaligned incentives is to make the value stream leader's incentives be a one-to-one mapping to the objectives of the value stream. Given that we are using the Dedicated Leadership Model, this means the leader has the exact same incentive structure as we created for the value stream. If there is a dual-leader structure, it is critical that both leaders are incentivized with the exact same objectives to avoid the same misalignment between the leader and the value stream. For example, an engineering leader may determine that an objective concerning training technical staff on the latest AI capabilities is key for long-term success. The dual leader from Product Management will be responsible for the exact same objective, otherwise they would be incentivized to reallocate the training capacity to another objective, such as more feature delivery capacity. The resulting discussions and negotiations are what helps create a balanced set of objectives for the value stream. This simple focus on incentivizing for outcomes can become the basis for helping leaders explicitly allocate capacity to developing people, such as by establishing mentoring and coaching initiatives to help individuals and teams grow in support of longer-term organizational outcomes.

Guidance: Align Leadership Incentives to Outcomes: Leadership incentives, compensation, and promotion criteria must match the objectives that cascade through the Outcome Tree so that accountability is directly connected to outcomes.

Incentives to Impact

Many organizations want to create a mentality of "one company, one team" in order to help unify company culture.[1] However, to foster an outcome-oriented culture, each individual and each leader need to know how their work contributes to the organization's success. For example, revenue and profitability are common metrics for company performance. But it can often be difficult or impossible for a manager of a team, or an individual contributor, to map between the outputs they are producing and how those affect a metric like profitability, especially when working for a large organization.

To address this, the Outcome Tree provides a very direct and clear map of how the work of every individual and team rolls up to the company strategy and outcomes. This enables each individual to understand how the impact of their efforts contributes to the success of the organization. Too often the "one team" mentality easily translates to the top-most ranks of the organization, where the mapping to business outcomes is obvious, but it becomes more disconnected the deeper in the organization you go.

In some cases, it may be desirable to allocate additional weight to objectives that are particularly important at a point in time. For example, in a market downturn, a company may be churning many customers and want to overweight the top-level objectives to support retention.

Rather than creating a separate incentive structure for managers to double down on retention, this overweighting to retention should be reflected in updated objectives, ensuring that the retention key result for the whole company cascades down to each value stream. This can incentivize one product helping drive retention for another product by prioritizing roadmap work to make the two function better together and become even more useful to customers. This can also be additive to retention goals specific to a value stream. The key is to ensure that this objective cascades down the Outcome Tree just as any other does.

Dysfunction: Conflicting Priorities: When objectives overlap and roadmaps are not aligned to key results, teams face competing demands.

Objectives and Key Results tracking best practices often specify a priority ordering of the objectives, but not a weighting.[2] In contrast, incentive structures, especially ones that are connected to compensation, often specify a weighting. For example, if there is both a revenue and a retention objective, we need to understand what percentage each contributes to the variable pay of a manager. In this case, for every value stream, we need a weighting for how much each objective will contribute to the incentive structure of the leadership of that value stream. This weighting should be derived from the priority order of the key results.

In our TeenWellness example, the "increase monthly active users" key result is ranked higher than the "app store star rating" key result. The percentage weightings should be allocated accordingly. If they are not, for example, if "adoption" is made to be 99% of the incentive structure and "star rating" 1%, we will again have leadership incentives that are misaligned to value stream incentives. This weighting can be useful as objective wording and ordering may be hard to specify to sufficiently distinguish the relative priorities of various key results in a way that is robust enough for compensation structures. However, if the weighting diverged significantly, it should be made explicit in the objectives themselves, such as by surfacing that retention is 70% of the company priority and new bookings are 30%.

With Outcome Management, our goal is to ensure that we are incentivizing the organization for outcomes. The incentive mechanism itself is up to the organization. Common monetary incentive structures, such as variable pay and equity grants, are one mechanism. But the same approach works for incentivizing career progression. For example, a leader should be more likely to be promoted up the Outcome Tree if they have helped their value stream achieve its objectives.

Some organizations may use nonmonetary approaches to drive intrinsic motivation in employees. For example, they might follow Dan

Pink's autonomy, mastery, and purpose approach from his book *Drive: The Surprising Truth About What Motivates Us*[3] or Matt Beane's approach from *The Skill Code: How to Save Human Ability in an Age of Intelligent Machines*, which proposes creating an environment of healthy challenge, complexity, and connection to help employees thrive in the Age of AI.[4] The Outcome Tree is aligned to these dimensions by design, and the individuals who drive the most outcomes should see the most intrinsic motivation through a direct mapping to the business outcomes they have impacted. And the reward system for achieving objectives can be as simple as recognition by peers across the organization.

Oversharing Objectives

In the same way that we untangled the matrix structure in Chapter 7 (Matrix to Modularity), we will now untangle the leadership structure needed to support optimizing for outcomes. In the Outcome Tree, each value stream is responsible for delivering on its set of objectives and managing the productivity of its Outcome Loop. Outcome Management ensures a clear and complete alignment between the leadership structure and the Outcome Tree. What follows is that each objective has a singular leadership, following the Dedicated Leadership Model, responsible for the attainment of that objective.

> **Guidance: Each Objective Must Have Dedicated Ownership:** Every objective in the Outcome Tree should follow the Dedicated Ownership Model, with a single- or dual-leadership structure, to avoid diffused accountability and unclear ownership.

This may seem like an obvious rule. However, in the hundreds of objective tracking deployments I have seen, it is the exception, not the norm. Best practices on this topic abound. Google, one of the earliest adopters of OKRs, ensures that each objective has a named owner, usually the team leader.[4] Apple takes a similar approach to task and objective tracking by ensuring that each objective has a "directly responsible individual."[5] Given that these principles of singular ownership have scaled so well for these tech giants, why is it that organizations so readily fall into the trap of oversharing objectives?

Many organizations want to create a spirit of collaboration. Having multiple individuals responsible for a particular objective might seem like a good way to formalize that collaboration and ensure that people feel they are "in the same boat." However, the moment that multiple people own an objective, we have introduced ambiguity of ownership. This leads to an increased coordination cost because two or more people must be consulted in order to effect change on the objective, impeding independent action.

If the objectives that sit above and below in the Outcome Tree also have multiple owners, the costs are multiplicative. When this happens, organizations need to pull large numbers of people into multiple meetings in order to affect what should have been a localized change. This is wasteful purely from a meeting time perspective, but even worse, it slows decision-making and can disempower leaders from owning the outcomes that should fall within their value stream. In the more severe scenarios, decisions that should be made by a leaf value stream in the Outcome Tree involve multiple executives or the CEO.

> **Dysfunction: Ambiguity of Ownership:** When multiple people own an objective, accountability becomes unclear, slowing decisions and undermining independent action by escalating localized issues to executives.

To avoid these dysfunctions, Outcome Management does not support shared objectives. However, we can still formalize lines of collaboration. The primary mechanism for this is aligning the objectives in the Outcome Tree. We covered this in Chapter 3 (The Outcome Tree), and with this we can make sure that the cascade rolls up to a common set of objectives and that teams collaborate as part of that rollup. For example, if one of the TeenWellness value streams creates a useful augmented reality widget that is driving more engagement with the app, other mobile apps may want to set up a meeting to learn more and suggest a roadmap item that will enable reuse of this widget. The second and more expensive mechanism we have is to introduce a dependency to ensure the collaboration. For example, if we need new capabilities from one of the Platform Services value streams to create a new set of agents to be used in our mobile app, we create a dependency that makes it clear that design discussions will be needed to determine how these agents will be produced by Platform Services and consumed by the apps.

The one exception when it is appropriate to have individuals share an objective is when we are applying the dual-leader or multi-leader model to the value stream. This still follows the Dedicated Leadership Model, and the singular ownership of the objectives is supported by a partnership of the multiple people in the leadership box of the value stream. In this scenario, it is key that the incentive structure of the multiple leaders match so that we preserve the alignment of ownership. This clarity and precision create a culture of ownership and accountability.

Guidance: Align Multi-Leader Incentive Structure: Value streams with dual- or multi-leader structures must ensure that all leaders share the same incentive and compensation structure matching the objectives of the value stream.

Leadership Leveling

The alignment of various organizational roles and titles to the Outcome Tree should be a direct mapping as both structures represent an ownership hierarchy. The simplest way of implementing this is to ensure there is a title level that corresponds to each level of the Outcome Tree. For example, if the top technology title for the product development organization is chief product and technology officer, then this person is responsible for the top level of the Outcome Tree. Their staff could be at the senior vice president or vice president level, each owning the next layer of value streams. Different organizations will use different titles for these levels, such as directors and managers. What is key is that there is a leadership level that corresponds to each level in the Outcome Tree. Some organizations may have exceptions to this.

For example, if a vice president reports to another vice president, then one vice president will have more scope in the Outcome Tree than the other. While this tends to be an anti-pattern from a Human Resources best practices point of view,[6] the Outcome Tree can make the ownership scope of each role clear. In addition, the Outcome Tree structure always has humans reporting to humans, meaning that autonomous value streams can only appear as leaves of the tree and must be connected to a human leader's scope of ownership.

In the Dedicated Leadership Model, the mapping of leadership level to the Outcome Tree is a direct one-to-one mapping. Each level in the tree corresponds to a level in the organizational hierarchy. However, as we reviewed in Chapter 4 (Functions to Flow), many organizations will have separate functional hierarchies that map onto the Outcome Tree.

For example, there may be one hierarchy of engineering leaders and another of product leaders if the organization is using a dual-leader model. In this case, the key principle to apply is to ensure that the functional organizational chart hierarchies are aligned, ideally at the same title levels. This means that a vice president of product responsible for a mobile app should be a dual leader with a vice president of engineering for that mobile app. This ensures that the seniority and scope in the org chart are aligned to the Outcome Tree. In such a structure, there is still a single-threaded owner at the top of the organization, such as the CEO.

Guidance: Align Titles to the Outcome Tree: Organizational hierarchies must map cleanly onto the Outcome Tree. If multiple functions provide leadership, their title levels should be aligned, for example, vice president to vice president if using a dual-leader model.

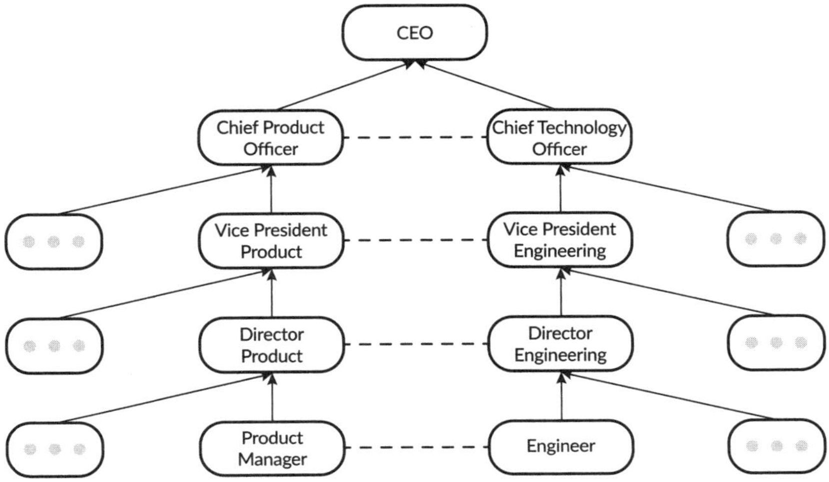

FIGURE 8.2: Aligning Title Levels to the Outcome Tree

Many organizations stray from this alignment of titles to the Outcome Tree. A common pattern of legacy organizations is that the closer the leader is to business functions, the more senior the title. For example, a product leader may have a vice president title while their dual-leader engineering partner has a lower director title. The effect that this has organizationally is to communicate that the product leader is more senior and therefore has more ownership of that particular value stream.

This breaks the dual-leader model, where ownership is an equal partnership. It can also cause severe dysfunctions in the Outcome Loop, such as work specific to one function being overly prioritized. For example, the vice president of product should be prioritizing feature work over technical debt work and training of engineers on key new skills such as agentic coding. If there isn't a partnership with a vice president of engineering, the healthy tension is often replaced by the senior person's functional priorities dominating. This creates the dysfunction and short-term optimizations in the corresponding value stream.

Dysfunction: Title Imbalance in the Outcome Tree: When dual-leader value streams assign mismatched titles, such as vice president and director, the more senior titleholder's functional priorities will tend to dominate. This skews toward functional goals and undermines the dual-leadership balance of the Outcome Loop.

Directly aligning the title hierarchy to the Outcome Tree results in a clean partitioning of the ownership structure. This makes ownership and accountability clear. There is never any ambiguity on who to go to in order to get clarification or an escalation on any particular roadmap item. Budget, capacity, and outcome ownership are simple, particularly if we avoid matrix lines per Chapter 7 (Matrix to Modularity).

Crosscutting Concerns

We will always need to manage dependencies between value streams. These can get particularly tricky with complex technology stacks and platform and service dependencies. Who should be responsible for managing those dependencies? Given how critical it is to manage dependencies in a way that maximizes flow, Outcome Management relies on dedicated roles for this: the *technical program managers*. Technical product managers tend to focus on the intersection of product strategy with deep technical involvement on delivery, and technical program managers focus more closely on the technical delivery of platform products and other services. In the Outcome Tree, these tend to apply to external products and internal platforms respectively, but many organizations use the acronym TPM for both roles.

Technical Program Manager: A dedicated role leveraged by Outcome Management that is responsible for coordinating value stream dependencies to accelerate flow.

Consider the scenario where we want to replatform our TeenWellness mobile suite to use an entirely new data storage technology that will provide twice the performance to AI agents at half the cost. The business outcomes of implementing this are clear. However, during the planning process, the engineering team notices there is a high degree of coupling between each of the mobile apps and the storage technology. Rather than having a platform service that abstracts away the data storage, the mobile apps use the storage layer directly. This means that switching the data storage technology will affect each Mobile Apps value stream, and it could do so in complex ways. For example, if changing data storage architectures involves a shift from relational to graph storage, there may need to be significant changes in each of the mobile apps.

The role of the technical program manager is designed precisely for managing these kinds of dependencies that can span the value streams, leaders, and roadmaps in the Outcome Tree. The role includes cross-team and cross–value stream coordination, as well as all of the technical program and risk management needed to deliver complex initiatives that span multiple value streams and roadmaps. Technical program managers help streamline and de-risk the planning process, ensuring that the appropriate technical deliverables, such as architecture and tech debt work, are on the roadmap to ensure the crosscutting initiatives are delivered. During delivery, they help manage and de-risk dependencies by regularly inspecting the delivery loop for dependencies that may be falling behind and blocking progress and flow. They will typically report to a leader high up enough in the Outcome Tree to have purview over the multiple value streams being coordinated. Minimizing dependencies also implies minimizing the number of technical program managers that should be needed.

As technology stacks continue to increase in complexity and the scope of agentic contributions grows, so does the complexity of the technical program manager role. Consider a scenario in which a single team's capacity is affected, say, due to an unforeseen staffing challenge. If the work this team is doing is deep within a dependency chain, this single delay can cause a cascade of delays that will force each dependent value stream to replan their work. The replanning is likely to bring in another set of complex dependencies and capacity questions.

Gathering all the relevant data and running the scenario analysis can be extremely complex. As long as the Outcome Tree data is properly structured and curated, AI agents can provide significant benefit of value to value stream leaders in curating and running scenarios for roadmap planning and Outcome Loop optimization. For large and complex organizations, Outcome Tree optimization and dependency management requires AI due to their combinatorial complexity. Additionally, AI amplification for the technical program manager role allows a single individual to manage across many more value streams.

Constraining the Cascade

In this chapter, we have covered the incentive and leadership aspects of outcome ownership. Strategy cascades from the top down the Outcome Tree, with clear ownership objective setting cascading up the tree. The remaining consideration is how we avoid overloading the Outcome Tree with too many outcomes.

This challenge parallels the one we saw with roadmaps in Chapter 2 (The Outcome Loop). If everything is a roadmap priority, then nothing is a roadmap priority. Similarly, if a leader has two dozen objectives to achieve in a quarter, the resulting cascade could quickly become intractable. Even when prioritized, the product and technical diligence needed to determine how to deliver on those objectives can easily overwhelm the capacity of value streams to execute that many priorities.

With Outcome Roadmaps, we use flow velocity–based capacity to ensure that we do not overload a value stream. In addition, we leverage the relationship between flow load and flow velocity to indicate when we have overloaded the capacity of a value stream. Unlike roadmap items, objectives do not directly consume team capacity. As such, as long as value stream capacity is managed, it should not matter whether the team is delivering roadmap items in support of one or one hundred objectives.

However, each objective brings with it communication and coordination overhead. Each objective must be communicated to stakeholders up and down the Outcome Tree and tracked as part of the planning cadence. In addition, each item on the Outcome Roadmap must be connected to an objective. This means that if the number of objectives significantly exceeds the number of roadmap items being worked on, multiple objectives will be mapped onto a single roadmap item, which brings into question whether the objectives were broken down too finely. In summary, there is a coordination cost to each objective that we add to the Outcome Tree.

Given that each objective incurs a coordination cost, we need to constrain the number of objectives cascading through the Outcome Tree. This means implementing a mechanism that limits both the number of objectives and the number of key results per objective. There is a broad range of best practice guidance on these limits, ranging from keeping the number as small as two to three key results per objective[7] to allowing a team to set any appropriate number.[8] I have tried countless variations on limiting the number of objectives and always came back to the simple rule of a maximum of five objectives per value stream and a maximum of five key results for every objective.[9] This is exactly the guidance provided by Andy Grove, who pioneered the OKR framework, as well as John Doerr, who popularized it in *Measure What Matters*.

Guidance: Limit Objectives and Key Results to Five: Each Outcome Loop should have no more than five objectives, and each objective should have no more than five key results. This balances ambition with coordination cost and prevents overly complex cascades of objectives across the Outcome Tree.

In addition, in the Outcome Roadmap, we have the constraint of ensuring that each roadmap item supports a specific objective. This means that in aggregate, for each value stream, the number of objectives should not exceed the number of roadmap items the team has capacity to deliver in the current iteration. If the number of objectives is larger, it is an indication that some should be pushed to a future plan.

Guidance: Match Objective and Key Results to Roadmap Capacity: The number of objectives should not exceed the number of roadmap items that the team has the capacity to deliver in the planning iteration.

Stretching the Truth

The final principle of adopting objectives for Outcome Management relates to the fact that we need to support work in the complex domain and, at times, in the chaotic domain. The complex domain has an inherent uncertainty in both the planning and delivery portions of the Outcome Loop. For many objectives, we cannot definitively know ahead of time if the outputs we deliver will drive the desired outcomes, as the process is one of hypothesis testing. If we were planning in the clear domain, the process of connecting a roadmap item to an outcome would be an easy one.

For example, if we were building a new bridge to offload traffic from an overloaded bridge, we could easily derive the key result for the new bridge traffic from the existing traffic pattern and then ensure the outcome matched. In the complex domain, where customer, market, and competitor behavior can be difficult to predict, there is a higher degree of uncertainty in the correlation of outputs to outcomes.

The ability of AI to forecast in the complex domain is also limited due to emergent phenomena creating chaotic dynamics that put fundamental limitations on predictability.[10] This can cause leaders and teams to set overly conservative key results as they do not have the up-front information on what will drive outcomes during planning. This is similar to the practice of "sandbagging"[11] in forecasting sales targets during times of uncertainty, when giving a low-ball forecast seems like the sounder approach. However, this over-conservativism can result in misallocation of resources when a higher target is attainable.

There is a common objective setting best practice, originating with Andy Grove at Intel, of setting "stretch key results."[12] This means that objective attainment is achieved at a value lower than 100% of the key result. For example, for my teams I always set stretch objectives that would be achieved at 70% of the key result specified, as popularized by Google.[13] In our TeenWellness example, we have the key result of "increase monthly active users from 10K to 20K." If this were marked as a stretch objective, full attainment of it would be hitting 17K users. Hitting 20K would be further cause for celebration. Setting stretch objectives helps leaders and teams strive to hit their key results when working with uncertainty without overly penalizing a miss if some of the assumptions in the outcome hypothesis were incorrect.

Guidance: Use Stretch Objectives: Set some objectives to have full achievement reached below the 100% value of the key results, such as 70%, to encourage ambition without penalizing teams working in domains with inherent uncertainty.

Refactoring the AI Teams at Planview

I was the chief technology officer at Planview when the breakthrough ChatGPT demo launched in November 2022. I already had a sizable data science team working on our machine learning capabilities, but it was clear that generative AI would change everything. We quickly went to the board to secure an out-of-cycle budget for additional AI hiring and immediately reallocated internal teams to the effort. With so many other tech companies scrambling to find AI talent, I thought that hiring would be our main constraint, but it turned out to be the easy part. A couple of months into the journey, it became clear that organizing the teams for outcomes was the bottleneck.

Prior to our adoption of AI models and agents, we had a well-established cohesion within the AI and Data Science value stream and clearly defined coupling between it and the various product value streams. The AI team produced research and prototypes that provided features such as strategic scenario planning for Planview. The engineering teams would then incorporate these features, at first by using a service provided by the AI team while in a "labs" type preview mode, then by taking over development and operations of those features if they had been validated by initial customer adoption.

Large language models disrupted all of that as we quickly validated how much better they worked than the models we had been training in-house. The AI team pivoted to focusing more time on creating an agentic framework for frontier models than on training our own models. That was straightforward, as our agentic framework was self-contained. But every product was affected by the capabilities introduced, with major changes to the user experience, new chat-based support, and agentic interaction. All of this meant that any kind of handoff process between the AI team and product teams was too slow to be feasible. In addition, the data foundations of the products had to be transformed to populate a knowledge graph and new semantic layer, which was critical to reasoning models and agents effectively working with our product data.

To support all of this change to the product and technology landscape, we needed a new organizational design and a refactoring of our Outcome Tree and ownership structure to match. We also needed that design to align to a new set of architectural and scaling constraints. For example, the teams were accustomed to architecting both our software and organization around cloud hosting costs, but we saw quickly that the agentic architecture had an even more outside impact on the interaction between architecture and cost structure.

While I remained impressed with the velocity of what the teams were delivering, I heard growing concerns from the engineering teams that what we were creating would become increasingly difficult to support at scale. The AI engineers and data scientists were working with the Python programming language, while the data and product engineers preferred our more complex systems to be written in the Java programming language. The Python codebase was growing at a very fast pace, and there was enough concern that I decided to personally review the entire codebase. It was clear to me that we were back in a world of throwing work over the fence between the AI and engineering teams. We were falling on the wrong side of Conway's Law, meaning our organizational structure would soon become a blocker to our progress. We were running into the usual pitfalls of misaligned incentives, with the AI team wanting to move as quickly as possible on enabling new capabilities, the product team pushing for the greatest amount of minimum viable features while trading off the data foundation investments we needed, and the engineering team pushing for the data investments that would enable future capabilities and scalability and slowing the AI team in the process.

These misaligned objectives and incentives made the next step on organizational change clear. I had not created a triple-leader structure to date, but it was time. Our chief data scientist, vice president of product, and vice president of engineering formed a new value stream and became its "three-in-the-box" leaders. The four of us created a single set of objectives, which then underpinned their and their teams' objectives and incentive structure. This structure provided the value stream cohesion that we needed and enabled autonomy for the team solving its own problems in support of achieving their objectives.

For example, the AI engineers and the product engineers created a single codebase for the multi-agent architecture and then a decentralized model, allowing their various teams to build and operate their own agents. This effort paved the path for other teams in the company to create and operate their own agents as well, dramatically accelerating how quickly new agents were delivered. Six months later, we launched Planview Copilot (now Planview Anvi). This ownership structure was critical for sustaining the pace of innovation that we needed to get to a production-grade offering while learning and adapting to an entirely new technology.

The benefit of the consolidated structure was very high cohesion of this new AI value stream. However, Planview's many other product teams became overly dependent on the AI value stream providing all of their core AI capabilities. This was a problem as the domain expertise for offerings, such as investment and capacity planning, lay within those product teams. In addition, nearly every aspect of the product footprint was being transformed by AI. In other words, while the AI team had great cohesion, the other product value streams had become overly coupled to it.

I reached out to Scott Densmore, who at that time had built and was leading the GitHub Copilot team. Scott's teams had followed a similar path, but as GitHub Copilot grew to be an increasingly foundational component that others integrated with and built on, he decentralized his AI engineers and data scientists to be embedded across numerous GitHub product value streams. This had the effect of increasing the cohesion of those product value streams and removing a bottleneck on a single team. It was clear that the teams at Planview needed to take a similar step to further optimize ownership and flow.[14]

The journey of Outcome Tree design never ends, and using the concepts of value stream cohesion and coupling has provided me and my teams with an invaluable guide. However, that design is only as effective as the ownership and incentive structures that support it.

Conclusion

Every management system needs control mechanisms and feedback signals. In the Outcome Tree, the primary control mechanism is ownership. Objectives without clear ownership result in the diffusion of responsibility and impeded decision-making. The Outcome Tree can only function effectively if every node has clear and dedicated ownership. This ownership structure must be a foundational element of the organizational design and the structure along which feedback flows.

In support of that, the incentive structures of the leaders in the Outcome Tree must match the cascade of objectives that defines the desired outcomes. If these structures are misaligned, the pitfalls of matrixed organizations, dependencies, and excessive coordination costs take over. In contrast, clear ownership enables the independent action and the autonomy needed at scale to harness the amplification provided by AI.

This shift, together with the previous ones, defines how to optimize the flow of value through the organization. In the next chapter, we will examine how to structure the organization itself in order to support different kinds of outcomes.

In Summary

- Functional, matrix, and shared ownership structures fail to optimize for outcomes by diffusing accountability.
- The Outcome Ownership Model provides clarity by ensuring every value stream leader is comprehensively accountable for outcomes.
- Aligning incentives directly to value stream objectives is critical to avoid output orientation or short-term incentive optimization.
- Ownership of objectives must be single-threaded to the leadership structure of the Outcome Tree for both single and multi-leader value stream structures.

Key Takeaways

- Replace ambiguity with ownership by aligning every leader, team, and objective to the Outcome Tree.
- Align incentives to outcomes by matching compensation, promotion, and recognition to objectives.

Prompt

Objective: Help humans align ownership, incentives, and objectives to the Outcome Tree so accountability tracks outcomes, not outputs.

Operating protocol (assist, don't act unilaterally):

- Map current ownership: For each value stream, list leaders, their objectives, and what actually drives their bonus/promotion. Highlight where incentives track outputs instead of outcomes.
- Propose an outcome ownership view: Ensure every value stream has a single owner (or dual/triple leaders) whose incentives mirror that stream's Objectives and Key Results.
- Enforce single-threaded objectives: For each objective, identify one directly responsible leader; flag ambiguous/shared ownership as a risk to decision speed.
- Check hierarchy alignment: Compare HR titles and reporting lines to the Outcome Tree; surface title mismatches that skew ownership.
- Right-size the cascade: Recommend 3–5 objectives per value stream and 3–5 key results per objective, and ensure KR count does not exceed roadmap capacity. Suggest where "stretch" objectives (e.g., 70% = success) are appropriate.

Guardrails: Do not alter pay, titles, or reporting lines yourself; always surface options, trade-offs, and risks for human leaders to decide.

Chapter 9

Sixth Shift: Divisions to Domains

During the Installation Period of the Age of AI, winning with AI requires mastering disruptive innovation. But disruptive initiatives cannot be managed with the same sets of input, output, and outcome metrics as existing initiatives and sustaining innovations. In this chapter, we will review the concept of outcome domains, which tailor different parts of the Outcome Tree to specific business goals, such as incubating AI initiatives and then transforming the business with the most promising incubations. We will review how to set Plan Distribution and Flow Distribution according to both market contexts and product life cycle stages. The chapter concludes with guidance on aligning leaders to *outcome domains* based on their unique mindsets and risk appetites.

The goal of Outcome Management is to create a structure that supports the dynamics of rapid iteration for delivering business and customer outcomes. In earlier chapters, we defined the Outcome Tree and the Outcome Loop as the key models supporting the target dynamics of fast flow, innovation, and rapid hypothesis testing and iteration. So far, we have treated the Outcome Tree as a uniform hierarchy of value streams, each with their own specific inputs, outputs, and outcomes. We noted that these may vary depending on the type of outcome we are after. For example, a customer-facing product may focus on a revenue outcome, whereas a platform product may focus on a scalability and performance outcome.

Consider a large organization's Outcome Tree. Would we see commonalities in the various Outcome Loops? There are likely to be a number of platform value streams, and we should expect their outcome metrics to exhibit similarities. The organization may also have both early-stage and mature products. In terms of outcomes, we should expect the early-stage products to be less profitable than the mature products. But an early-stage product could be critical to an organization's survival. If we consider Outcome Trees across various organizations, we will see similar patterns of outcomes converging, say, between those supporting early-stage startups and scaleups focused on growth and those for public companies focused on profitability.

In this chapter, we will explore how each Outcome Tree should be partitioned into various segments, how these segments apply to various company stages, and how each segment defines the nature of inputs, outputs, and outcomes for its various value streams. This segmentation will also provide us with guidelines for the kinds of AI amplification that can be applied to the different domains. For example, whereas vibe coding and rapid prototyping can accelerate iterating on incubation stage initiatives, fully autonomous value streams may be easier to deploy to support more mature and constrained product offerings.

> **Shift: Divisions to Domains:** Replace uniform, siloed managerial structures with segmented value streams grouped according to the types of customer and organizational outcomes they drive. This includes customer-facing, platform, early-stage, and mature products, each with input, output, and outcome metrics tailored to its context.

Outcome Domain Model

One of the most common struggles I have witnessed in larger organizations is an under-investment in platforms. Whereas I'm accustomed to tech companies investing around half of their technology budget into platform services and components, I commonly hear that enterprises tend to invest only in the 10% to 20% range. Another struggle for many large organizations is the inability to get innovative new offerings out of an incubation state and into a position where they are gaining market share. Elite technology companies are great at this, but most others struggle and cite *The Innovator's Dilemma*–style[1] challenges and frustration with the technology part of the organization being too slow to deliver. This is all in spite of CEOs and other leaders continually saying that more platform investment is needed and that innovation is key to survival. What took me much longer to realize is that these problems stem from the same flaw in these organizations' operating model: the lack of a mechanism for effectively segmenting value streams.

How much of the Flow Distribution of a product should be dedicated to new feature delivery? How profitable should a value stream be? What percentage of the overall budget should be dedicated to platform products? What portion of the platform budget should be dedicated to developer and agent productivity tooling? How much should be invested in new versus sustaining innovations? The answers to each of these questions depend on the segmentation of the various domains in the Outcome Tree.

Ⓧ **Dysfunction: Fragmented Outcome Metrics:** When value streams define outcome metrics independently, the cascade drifts out of alignment with the higher-level strategic context of each outcome domain.

Organizations tend to see segmentation of their value streams emerge organically over time. For example, earlier-stage initiatives tend to be grouped under one leader and managed to a slightly different set of metrics than the core products supporting the majority of the company's top line. The challenge is that this segmentation is often ad hoc. In addition, the measurement of outcomes for platforms is all too often mixed up with core products, and outcomes for existing products are often tangled up in outcomes with new and transformative initiatives. Instead of having each value stream define their own outcomes from the ground up, we can segment the Outcome Tree into domains. Each outcome domain defines the kind of contribution that the value stream makes to the Outcome Tree and helps parametrize the Outcome Loop metrics accordingly. This segmentation disambiguates and simplifies the types of outcomes that each value stream contributes.

Outcome Domain Model: A partitioning of the Outcome Tree into domains specific to various product life cycle stages and market segments. It categorizes value streams and outcomes into distinct zones (core, platform, incubation, and transformation) based on business goals and product life cycle stages so that each is managed with appropriate objectives and metrics.

From Horizons to Domains

There are numerous options for dividing up high-level areas in an organization. A common one is establishing divisions, each of which may contain multiple functions. For example, a car manufacturer may have divisions that include mass market vehicles, trucks, and rental fleets. Each division may have its own sales, marketing, and technology functions.

In addition to creating logical divisions according to customer and market segments, we can partition an organization according to innovation, life cycle, and technology diffusion phases. The Three Horizons Framework can be used to segment product investment, where Horizon 1 is core business, Horizon 2 supports emerging growth, and Horizon 3 enables future options.[2] For example, a company's existing mobile apps can be considered a Horizon 1 investment as they monetize in the near term. In contrast, research efforts around new AI-based interfaces might take more time to monetize and, as a result, fall into the longer-term Horizon 3. A key benefit of this appraoch is that it helps a company apply performance and profit metrics specific to each horizon.

For the first few years of running Tasktop, I leveraged the Three Horizons Framework in this way. However, the model was insufficient when it came to handling life cycle issues, such as the end of life of products. Furthermore, it was of limited use in helping us take a more structured approach to managing early-stage and disruptive innovations.

When Geoffrey Moore created the Zone Management model in his book *Zone to Win: Organizing to Compete in an Age of Disruption*,[3] I adopted it instantly, documented how to apply it to product portfolios in *Project to Product*, and continued to leverage it successfully over many iterations of bringing product innovation to market. Zone Management builds on and extends the idea of the Three Horizons Framework.

As summarized in *Zone to Win*, Zone Management has been applied at leading tech companies including Microsoft, Cisco, and Adobe. It creates a split between initiatives that consume investment and those that deliver material revenue to the organization. In addition, it creates a clear distinction between disruptive innovations and sustaining innovations. Sustaining innovations include all of the productivity tooling of an organization in the *productivity zone*, as well as all of the products that deliver revenue and evolve via incremental evolution in the *performance zone*. In contrast, disruptive innovations include the new incubation initiatives that prepare companies for the next disruptive wave (the *incubation zone*) as well as those that can help the company transform to catch the next technology wave (the *transformation zone*).

While Zone Management is one of several segmentation models, the concepts of the four zones map well to how an Outcome Tree should be segmented into domains. For Outcome Management, we need to ensure that the input and outcome metrics we set for each value stream match its life cycle stage. For example, incubation products can benefit from smaller budgets revisited regularly. The outputs and delivery loop must also support the life cycle stage. For incubation value streams, the feedback cycle should be measured in days and not weeks, requiring a fast delivery loop. The same is less likely to be true for a product that is far along its life cycle stage and being considered for end of life.

Over the years, I evolved what started as Zone Management into the Outcome Domain Model described here. The Outcome Domain

Model builds on the concepts of both Zone Management and the Three Horizons Framework and expands on them to support value streams, the Outcome Tree, and AI agents.

> **Guidance: Segment the Outcome Tree by Life Cycle Stage:** The Outcome Tree should support domains that reflect the life cycle and market stages of products and value streams. Input, output, and outcome metrics should be tailored to each domain, ranging from incubation to maturity.

Product to Profit

In his seminal book, *Product Development Flow,* Donald Reinertsen makes the case that economic outcomes across the full product life cycle should be the guiding metric for product development.[4] When we take the long view of the product life cycle, this principle holds. For commercial endeavors, we should only be investing in products that contribute to making an organization profitable, by some metric of value, in the long run. For established companies, that metric will simply be financial profit. For startups, profitability may not be attained until a much later stage, such as a public listing or acquisition event, but the goal remains. For government institutions that create products to deliver citizen services rather than revenue, a nonmonetary outcome metric, such as health span improvements, must justify the lifetime investment in the product. For the sake of simplicity, we will refer to both as "life cycle profitability," whether the "profit" outcome is measured using a monetary or nonmonetary outcome metric.

Early-stage products, for example, those still in a stage of validating product-market fit,[5] are likely to consume much more investment than is offset by the revenue they produce. Products at scale-ups, companies pursuing high growth and market dominance, may consume very significant amounts of investment for many years before producing a profit. However, at some point in its life cycle, a product needs to produce a return on that investment. Segmenting products into outcome domains that correspond to their life cycle stages and business contribution makes that differentiation explicit, and it also creates a mechanism in the Outcome Tree for moving products from one life cycle stage to the next.

We leverage a similar segmentation for the Outcome Domain Model. Instead of managing a set of company divisions, we leverage a model that places each value stream in one of four domains based on the value stream's contribution to the business and where it sits in the innovation life cycle. This is not to say that value streams in the core or platform domains do not innovate as much as those in the transformation or incubation domains, but we must measure and manage those innovations according to the outcome needs of the domain. We can make all of this explicit by applying the Outcome Domain Model to the Outcome Tree.

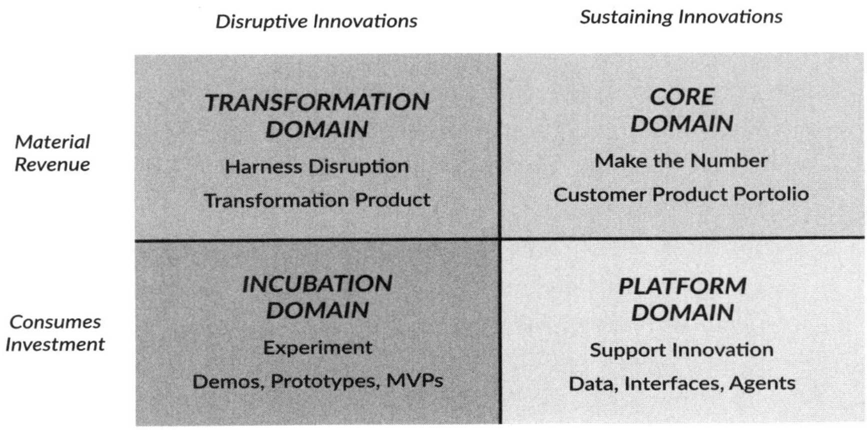

FIGURE 9.1: The Outcome Domain Model

The Outcome Domain Model categorizes all value streams into those that are disruptive or sustaining on the horizontal axis and those that either produce material revenue or consume investment on the vertical axis. The *platform domain* contains the value streams that support all of the other value streams with common services, shared data repositories, and agentic frameworks. The platform domain's value streams do not produce revenue or profit directly but support other value streams and enable both sustaining and disruptive innovations to be built on top of common platform components.

Next, we have the *core domain*. This is where the customer-facing portfolio of product value streams resides, where the vast majority of the revenue or other value metric is produced, and where the outputs are all about delivering sustaining innovations for growth in the core customer base and target market.

During times of rapid change, such as the Installation Period of the Age of AI, many companies need to invest in disruptive innovation. There are many approaches to managing disruptive innovation, such as those outlined in *The Innovator's Solution*.[6] Regardless of approach, from the point of view of the Outcome Tree, what we need is a portion of the value streams to be dedicated to incubating new ideas and innovations. This is the *incubation domain* and includes demos, prototypes, and minimum viable products.

When one of these new offerings shows promise in the market, it can be moved into the *transformation domain*. This domain is for a newly incubated product that has shown enough promise to become a material part of a company's revenues in the future and is ready to start scaling up, but is not yet at the maturity level of the core domain.

To define the four domains and the mission and focus for each, we need clear criteria for how an organization's products can move through the domains. As an example, consider an organization that needs to address AI as a disruptive wave in its market. In our TeenWellness example, this organization makes its top line revenue from subscriptions to the mobile applications that populate the core domain. It can then incubate multiple AI solutions, such as voice and augmented interfaces, in the incubation domain. When one of these has the potential to become 10% of the company's revenue, per Moore's specific guideline, it is moved into the transformation domain. It is managed separately there, under dedicated leadership supported by the CEO. For most organizations, there should only be one product in the transformation domain at a time due to the focus it requires from senior leadership. Once it has been validated by delivering 10% of the revenue, it is moved into the core domain and becomes a part of the core product portfolio.

Product innovation can either take a sustaining or a disruptive trajectory. Sustaining innovation is key in times of mature markets and technologies. For example, incrementally adding new AI-based scheduling features to a ride hailing app improves that application in ways that can drive better outcomes for existing customers.

Markets periodically experience disruptions that call for disruptive innovations. The Age of AI is a macroeconomic disruption that is forcing many companies to learn how to deliver them. For example, an experience that anticipates needs without requiring manual hailing or human drivers could require a ride hailing vendor to deliver disruptive innovation.

A value stream structured and measured by outcomes intended for sustaining innovation will not be able to deliver on disruptive innovation. This is why so many disruptive innovation efforts fail and why so many companies fall prey to these waves of creative destruction. Since the start of the Age of AI, countless companies have put in place AI product initiatives. Too many of these initiatives are not producing the expected business value. This is part of the "AI productivity paradox."[7] If these organizations' inputs, outputs, and outcomes are managed according to sustaining innovation, they will not enable a pivot into the Age of AI.

Outcome Domains

When implemented, the outcome domains form the four top-level value streams in the Outcome Tree. As the tree is cleanly partitioned, this means we can partition the budget parts of the inputs accordingly. For example, an elite performing organization that is investing in disruptive innovation around AI could have 35% of its cost base in the core domain to ensure that revenue is supported, 5% in the incubation domain to ensure fast moving research and experimentation on the latest AI technologies, and 15% in the transformation domain that is dedicated to bringing to market the organization's AI offering. The remaining 45% of the cost base is dedicated to platform domain value streams, which support each of the other three domains. This does not mean that AI investment is limited to the disruptive innovation domain. For example, a significant portion of the new platform domain work could include evolving an AI agent framework as well as knowledge graph and data foundations that make it easy for each of the other outcome domains to implement AI features in their products.

TABLE 9.1: Illustrative Metrics for Outcome Domains

Outcome Domain	Inputs (Illustrative)	Planned Work	Outputs	Flow	Outcomes
Core Domain	35% of cost base	> 70% planned quarterly	> 40% features	Flow Time < 14 days	90% of revenue; Customer satisfaction
Platform Domain	45% of cost base	> 70% planned quarterly	Balanced	Flow Time < 14 days	Service availability
Incubation Domain	5% of cost base	< 30 % planned weekly	> 80% features	Flow Time < 1 day	0 revenue; New users
Transfor-mation Domain	15% of cost base	< 50% planned monthly	> 60% features	Flow Time < 7 days	10% of revenue

Once the disruptive innovation initiative is completed, the portion of the cost base in the transformation domain can go to zero, for example, if the organization has successfully launched its AI offering and is making market progress, disrupting itself before it gets disrupted. When tracking that progress, the key result the transformation domain value stream needs to achieve is 10% of the company's top-line revenue. At that point, the new product will be validated and become a part of the core domain portfolio. If the new transformation domain AI product cannibalizes any of the core domain revenue, we then need to calculate whether its growth rate offsets that cannibalization. In this way, we can leverage the key results to determine if the return on investment in the transformation domain is materializing and map out the growth trajectory to determine when a product is ready to move domains. Similarly, if we see rapidly growing traction of an incubation product, it should be considered for movement into the transformation domain.

Configuring the Outcome Loop by Domain

With the four outcomes domains in place, we can configure each mechanism of the Outcome Loop according to the planning methodologies best suited to that domain. The planning methodologies can be tailored according to the four complexity domains of the Cynefin framework, which are associated with the four outcome domains reviewed in Chapter 1. A good place to start this process is by laying one two-by-two matrix over the other, with incubation being chaotic, transformation being complex, core being complicated, and platform being clear. However, all of this depends on organizational context and market dynamics. For example, an organization undertaking significant AI transformation and platform innovation is likely to additionally have its core and platform domains follow the dynamics of the complex domain.

In terms of planning according to the dynamics for each domain, Strategic Portfolio Management is a methodology that is well suited to managing core and platform domain product portfolios. For incubation and transformation domains, the planning and iteration cadence needs to be much faster, and tools such as the Lean Canvas[8] can be much better suited to faster iteration on product development and customer development. Similarly, doing the top-level planning cadence for the two sustaining domains, core and platform, on a quarterly basis may be sufficient. For the incubation domain, where there is constant experimentation, a weekly cadence can be beneficial. Once one of the incubation offerings is at a level of maturity where it can move to the transformation domain, the planning loop will need to be more closely connected to go-to-market functions. At this point, a monthly cadence can be effective, along with participation in the quarterly cadence reviews of the entire core domain product portfolio.

Another key target metric to set for each domain is the proportion of planned work as summarized in Table 9.1. With core and platform products, we want to ensure we are delivering on customer and company commitments, so the majority of the work should be committed to the value stream's roadmap. In contrast, in the incubation domain, where the goal is responding as quickly as possible to what we learn from experimentation with prototypes, products, and new technologies, the majority of activities should be devoted to unplanned work and incorporating learnings much more frequently. The transformation domain should lie somewhere in the middle in terms of its proportion of planned and unplanned work.

Finally, the outputs and flow for each domain differ, in particular in terms of their Flow Distribution. For the incubation domain, we want to focus on very fast feature delivery and be less concerned about defects, risks, or debts as we will typically be creating demos, prototypes, and preproduction software. Once a product moves into the transformation domain, customers are paying for it, and additional capacity needs to be allocated to defects, risks, and debts. However, the majority of the capacity should still be going to new feature work, as disruptive innovations tend to be a race between organizations bringing the best offering to market as quickly as possible.

In contrast, in the core and platform domains, it is critical to have a very deliberate Flow Distribution balance while striving to ensure as much capacity goes to new feature work as possible. From value streams studied in the *Project to Product State of the Industry Report*, we learned that a rough target to start with is 40% to 50% of value stream capacity being dedicated to features, but again this is context dependent.

Another key flow metric to track is flow time. In the incubation and transformation domains, it is critical that this is as short as possible in order to ensure the fastest feedback feasible for the Outcome Loop. While shorter flow time is generally better, the core and platform domains may not need as short a flow time in order to deliver on their outcomes.

With these Outcome Loop parameters set at each of the four top-level domains, cascading them down to the child value streams in the Outcome Tree is a straightforward process. For example, an organization might have a dozen incubation value streams running in parallel, some human led and some autonomous, and each should follow the parameters set above them in the tree.

Segmenting the Core

For most organizations, the largest number of products will reside under the core value streams. These products also have a lot of organizational and market visibility, as they are the products that the company markets and sells to customers. If the company has been around for multiple years, the core products themselves will be at various life cycle stages. For example, one product may have initially launched the company to success, whereas others could have been added to the portfolio through acquisitions.

Furthermore, some products may be in a rapid growth mode and require significant ongoing investment in sustaining innovations. Others may be later in their life cycle with an established customer base and require little investment while still contributing materially to company top line or profit. Finally, some products may be declining due to market disruptions or due to how far they are into their life cycle. In each case, we want to manage this portfolio of core domain products according to a similar set of outcome metrics that boil down to how much investment should be allocated to each in order to drive the target financial outcomes. Different companies may have different categories for life cycle stages in the core domain, but, at minimum, growth, maintenance, and sunset value streams should be included in the Outcome Tree.

TABLE 9.2: Core Value Stream Segmentation

Core Value Stream	Inputs	Outputs (Flow Distribution)	Outcomes
Growth	Majority of cost	Majority to features	Revenue growth; Customer satisfaction
Maintenance	Reducing cost; Significant revenue	Balanced	Revenue maintenance; Customer satisfaction
Sunset	Minor cost; Declining revenue	Majority to defects and risks	Cost control/ divestment; Customer migration

Product to Platform

So far, we have focused on products and platforms that the company builds. However, most organizations build products on a combination of third-party platforms and solutions. For example, agentic frameworks, frontier AI models, and cloud hosting services tend to be more economical to adopt from platform providers than to build in house. Determining which products and platform services to build internally and which to buy can be done through a core versus context analysis.[9]

The cost of these third-party dependencies can become a very significant portion of the overall cost of the Outcome Tree. As we reviewed in Chapter 2 (The Outcome Loop), it is critical for all hosting, inference, and other third-party costs to be tracked and made visible as part of the budget portion of each value stream's Outcome Loop. What many organizations will notice is that the platform domain has the largest portion of these costs. Platform teams tend to provide the first layer of internal services that sit on top of cloud hosting, data, AI, and similar third-party solutions. In addition, platform teams are typically the ones that need to make the buy versus build decisions on platform services that other value streams will need.

For example, many language model–based AI solutions benefit from data being represented as a graph that an agent can traverse. Let us assume that the current storage services are based on relational databases instead. If multiple product value streams have AI functionality on their roadmaps, then they either need to each build their own graph database or rely on a common platform service. The Platform team is best positioned to provide this service and best equipped to determine whether they should build the graph database from scratch, rely entirely on a vendor solution, or use a combination of the two. While it may make sense to have one product value stream experiment with a new kind of service, for example, in the transformation domain, once there is broad need for consumption of that service, it should be moved into the platform domain.

Consolidating platform investments can also help manage the growing cost base that many organizations need to manage. With the shift to cloud hosting in the 2010s, operations teams were able to offload managing compute and storage infrastructure onto cloud vendors. This provided substantial benefits. However, for many organizations, the cloud hosting costs have consumed an increasing portion of the technology budget. This has been referred to as the Trillion Dollar Paradox.[10]

Ensuring that the portion spent on external dependencies is visible and managed as part of the top-level Outcome Loops is critical to avoid the scenario where hosting and AI token spend consumes a disproportionate amount of the company's investment. This is, again, a place where platform teams can assist. For example, if hosted AI inference costs are running higher than planned, the AI platform team could decide to provide its client value streams with an option to leverage internally hosted open-source models for a subset of use cases or to create an architecture that provides better optimization for token consumption.

Guidance: Manage External Dependencies in the Platform Domain: Cloud, AI, and other external dependencies should be made visible, budgeted, and managed through the platform domain. Platform value streams should own the buy-versus-build trade-offs required to optimize for outcomes across the value streams that they support.

Domain Leadership

The final consideration of establishing effective domains at the top level of the Outcome Tree is the type of leadership that each needs. In the core domain, leadership needs to have a deep understanding of the customer and market and a very close collaboration with the go-to-market parts of the organization. This needs to be combined with the ability to manage a potentially large portfolio of products, each of which is responsible for the majority of the contribution to the company's top line. Leadership must also have a keen sense for how best to manage Flow Distribution to balance delivering sustaining innovations for existing customers with managing risks, defects, and debts.

The leader of the incubation domain should be someone with an appetite for constant learning, risk, experimentation, and innovation. They should be comfortable with a high degree of uncertainty and be willing to quickly pivot and kill off failed experiments. The transformation domain leader also needs to have a startup mindset to aid them in building a new business within an existing business and to display a relentless dedication to driving the growth of that new business.

Platform domain leaders need to be highly technical. Their customers are most commonly internal to the business. They need to be able to determine when a buy versus build decision takes them through a one way door[11] and locks the company into a technology or architecture that would take multiple quarters to unwind.

Given that the four outcome domains are the top value streams in the Outcome Tree, each of these leaders often report directly to the CEO. At some larger organizations, there may be a chief product and technology officer role in between these leaders and the CEO. But in any scenario, for companies that depend on technology to achieve success, the CEO must provide support across the four domains directly.

Navigating the Innovator's Dilemma at Tasktop

Even for those well-versed in the *Innovator's Dilemma*, it can be frustratingly difficult to overcome organizational inertia to deliver disruptive innovation. As disruption accelerates in the Age of AI, it will become increasingly challenging to navigate the gap between the needs of existing customers while avoiding being overtaken by organizations born in the Age of AI. Some may feel like they are not high enough in the decision-making ranks to influence the organization even though they can clearly see that if change does not happen the entire company will be at risk. But this issue can arise no matter where in the leadership hierarchy your role resides. I will never forget the time when, as CEO, I felt like I could not alter the path of my company even though I knew we were headed for a slow disruption by a thousand cuts.

After founding the company around open- and closed-source developer tools, the Tasktop business scaled around the rapid growth of Tasktop Hub, a value stream integration solution that connected the many tools and stakeholders involved in the software delivery life cycle. Everything was going very well in terms of company growth, which made our customers, staff, and investors happy. But in writing out our three-year vision, I realized that this growth trajectory was unlikely to continue. The growth maturation of the Software-as-a-Service market implied that vendor consolidation would happen, which would limit our growth rate. I became convinced that we needed to pivot the company to create a new offering that moved us beyond integration and into Value Stream Management.

I worked closely with our teams to create a new vision document, plans, and roadmaps to deliver this new product that we named Tasktop Viz. With Gail Murphy and my research background, the company had been founded on innovation and experimentation, with the first of our core values being "Vision to transform the industry, validated incrementally." I knew from prior discontinuous innovation efforts of this sort that we needed a small and well-insulated skunkworks team[12] made up of several of our top engineers who would report directly to me. While it was hard to fund the skunkworks team, as it would limit the growth of the flagship product, we knew that the existing products' customer needs would make the very rapid pace of innovation for Viz impossible without isolating the new value stream. The experiment worked, and we adopted it internally for managing our value streams and then got several of our largest customers purchasing the prerelease version of the solution.

And then things went haywire. We had exceeded our key sales and growth plan numbers for years without fail. But halfway through the fiscal year, we were significantly behind on our recurring revenue plan for the year and would come in 20% short. While we had segmented the engineering team to create the new skunkworks team, we had made no material change to the way we managed the Outcome Tree as a whole. As a result, the new product was being planned, measured, and tracked with the same approach as the existing products. For example, the support teams had ramped up to support the new product far too prematurely, which was a distraction from the critical support they were providing for the flagship product that was responsible for the vast majority of our revenue. In other words, while the product and engineering work were seemingly contained to their portions of the Outcome Tree, there was misalignment and confusion across the sales, marketing, and support functions.

The practice I had put in place at Tasktop was to put the entire top-level strategic plan on a single page accessible to all staff and reinforced regularly. This included the core values, three-year strategy, and the entire Outcome Tree and Objectives and Key Results cascade for the fiscal year and for each quarter. The Hub value stream had dominated our revenue to that point, and, unsurprisingly, all of the supporting systems had been created around the growth of Hub and its mature market. Viz, the new product, was entirely different, built cloud native from the ground up and targeted at a new market category that we were creating. We needed to completely resegment our Outcome Tree across the entire organization to make not just the product but all outcome metrics support this brand-new, category-defining product. The issue was not a lack of will from leaders to balance the new and the old product; the issue was a lack of mechanisms.

I realized we needed a new north star outcome metric for Viz that provided a clearly partitioned balance between it and all of our other initiatives. So, after creating a transformation outcome domain for Viz, we set the outcome metric as adding incremental 10% of new top-line revenue growth to the company within twelve months. At that point, we could consider Viz to be validated in terms of initial product market fit. Nine months later, Viz far exceeded that 10% goal and then saw such rapid growth that within three years it was the number one contributor to revenue. We were back on the path of hitting our ambitious growth number year after year, right up until the company's successful acquisition.

Conclusion

The complexity of large organizations means the Outcome Tree needs to be partitioned into discrete domains. This partitioning enables the segmentation of product life cycle and market-specific outcomes and facilitates setting input and outcome targets accordingly. Outcome domains make it possible for the leaders, teams, and agents under the value streams to focus on the outputs that will make the biggest impact for that domain. Failing to establish outcome domains results in "one size fits all" targets and metrics, which get in the way of empowering disruptive innovation and transformational value streams and can result in over-allocation of resources to later-stage value streams. A well-defined segmentation makes it easy to leverage the Plan Distribution and Flow Distribution mechanisms in a way that is tailored to the life cycle and complexity domain of each value stream. It also empowers the leaders of each domain to have clear and tailored targets. Finally, for those organizations going through an AI transformation, it enables clear segmentation and measurement of that transformation, ensuring that meeting existing customer needs does not derail the transformation. In the next chapter, we will review additional mechanisms for architecting the Outcome Tree as well as how leadership roles need to evolve to support the acceleration provided by value streams composed entirely of agents.

In Summary

- Uniform value stream planning and measurement creates dysfunctions by failing to distinguish between product life cycle stages and market contexts.
- Partitioning the Outcome Tree into outcome domains (core, platform, incubation, and transformation) ensures that each is measured with context-specific input and outcome metrics.
- Outcome domain–specific flow and feedback ensure that incubation and transformation initiatives are able to iterate quickly with specifically tailored Plan Distribution and Flow Distribution.
- Segmentation enables resilience and innovation by increasing option value and balancing the core business while pursuing disruptive innovation in the Age of AI.

Key Takeaways

- Segment value streams by outcome domain so that each has tailored input and outcome metrics.
- Use the Outcome Domain Model to set Plan Distribution and Flow Distribution according to product life cycle and market context.
- Balance sustaining and disruptive innovation by managing investments in the various outcome domains.

Prompt

Objective: Help humans segment their Outcome Tree into outcome domains and tailor inputs, metrics, and flow to each.

Operating protocol (assist, don't act unilaterally):

- Map the current portfolio: List major value streams and classify each into core/performance, platform/productivity, incubation, or transformation based on life cycle and business role.
- Define domain-specific guardrails: For each domain, propose illustrative targets for budget share, Plan Distribution (planned vs. unplanned vs. canceled/aged), Flow Distribution (features/defects/risks/debts), cadence, and key outcome metrics (e.g., revenue, retention, adoption, availability).
- Expose "one-size-fits-all" metrics: Highlight where early stage or disruptive initiatives are judged with core metrics, or platforms with product P&L metrics, and show how this distorts decisions.
- Suggest domain-aware Outcome Loops: Adjust strategy inputs, Outcome Roadmaps, and flow metrics per domain (e.g., fast, experiment-heavy loops in incubation; balanced, reliability-focused loops in core/platform).
- Identify candidates to move between domains (incubation → transformation → core) using clear outcome thresholds (e.g., revenue or adoption milestones).

Guardrails: Do not reallocate budgets or kill products yourself; always present domain options, trade-offs, and risks for leaders to decide.

Chapter 10

Seventh Shift: Managers to Makers

I distinctly remember the moment in my career when I had to succumb to the manager's schedule. Up to that point, more than half of my calendar was whitespace. But as my company grew, meetings became more frequent and a more important part of what I provided to the company. When I was a developer, these meetings were an unwelcome and costly distraction that pulled me out of my flow. The longer the empty blocks in my calendar were, the more flow time I had and the more I contributed. That is the maker's schedule, where we think of blocks of time in half-day or multi-hour intervals interrupted by the odd meeting. The manager's schedule is all about thirty- or sixty-minute intervals that are optimized for collaboration and decision-making.[1] This split between managers and makers, bosses and workers, executives and individual contributors has been a defining part of knowledge work. The bifurcation has shaped our organizations and our workdays.

What will happen to organizational roles and structures as AI produces more and more of the outputs that were the realm of makers? What will the roles of managers of unbounded outputs be?

In the Age of AI, will every maker become a manager? Individual contribution work, such as coding, will increasingly be done by AI agents. Will technologists need to learn to manage teams of agents and spend more time planning and orchestrating work than they do delivering?

In the Age of AI, will every manager become a maker? Many traditional managerial tasks, such as reporting, providing status updates, and attending meetings, will be made obsolete by AI agents. Decision-making will be amplified by AI. Will the managers who leverage these agents directly and take a more hands-on role in delivering value be the ones to thrive?

Will managers become makers, or will makers become managers?

In this final shift from output to outcome, we will explore the changing role of leadership in knowledge work as AI-driven outputs scale beyond the boundaries of what any leader has previously managed. The lines between managing and making will increasingly blur, with leaders at all organizational levels leveraging AI to deliver outcomes while individual contributor roles evolve to leading value streams and managing agents.

Shift: Managers to Makers: The traditional divide between makers and managers will dissolve in the Age of AI. AI will replace many of the reporting and coordination functions of managers in addition to automating traditional knowledge work. Future leaders will need to both make and manage, directly shaping and delivering outcomes.

Outcome Architecture Model

A key part of traditional management has been organizational architecture. Each manager is given a budget and strategy and must determine the team and leadership structure needed to deliver on that budget. This makes the manager directly responsible for reporting lines, hiring, and performance management decisions within their scope. With Outcome Management, the manager is additionally responsible for defining the architecture and structure of the value streams within their scope.

Given that the goal of value streams is to deliver outcomes, what the manager is responsible for is, provided the inputs of strategy and budget, an architecture that maximizes outcomes. This architecture is composed of the value streams supporting the Outcome Tree and its Outcome Loops and the people and agents that deliver those outcomes. For example, if a team is overloaded and ineffectively managing a set of agents, the manager must determine the changes needed to address the overload. If a value stream's scope has grown too large, they must rearchitect the Outcome Tree to split that one value stream into multiple. If a value stream is at a point in its life cycle or complexity domain where it can be fully automated with agents, they must rebalance the Outcome Tree accordingly. Each of these is a practice of Outcome Architecture.

Outcome Architecture Model: The configuration of value streams, people, and agents that transforms strategic inputs into business outcomes.

Before we explore the evolution of manager and maker roles, we will briefly examine the historical context of technology leadership across prior revolutions.

Making the Way Through the Ranks

While researching *Project to Product*, I had the opportunity to work closely with executives at several global car brands, which provided me with a better perspective on the historical context of the Age of Oil & Mass Production. I spent a significant amount of time in Germany in particular, admiring the engineering traditions of the car manufacturers and suppliers there.

What amazed me most was how strongly engineering and manufacturing influenced the approach to management. The CEOs of Daimler-Benz, Volkswagen, and BMW Group had all come from car engineering and plant operations roles and backgrounds. This was different from what I was used to, as most senior executives at enterprise organizations had finance backgrounds. In contrast, the CEO of Daimler-Benz, Volkswagen, and BMW Group had all come from car engineering and plant operations roles and backgrounds. At that time, the discussions we were having were about how traditional car companies were being threatened by Tesla and BYD, whose CEOs have software and battery engineering backgrounds, respectively. In each case, the top managers at these companies gained deep expertise in their domain as makers. They then became highly effective managers, whether by founding their companies or rising up through the ranks.

A similar pattern holds true for careers forged in previous technological revolutions. The early days of the Age of Oil & Mass Production were defined by Henry Ford, a mechanical engineer and machinist, as well as Kiichiro Toyoda, the mechanical engineer who founded Toyota. Prior to that, in the Age of Steel & Heavy Engineering, Andrew Carnegie and Isambard Kingdom Brunel both came from deep technical and construction backgrounds. In the Age of Software & Digital, nearly every one of the global tech giants was founded and scaled by leaders who worked as software engineers or computer scientists.* Rather than being professional managers or financiers, the backgrounds of these leaders involved building things, and they leveraged their deep technical expertise to become some of the most impactful managers of their times.

Given the automation of knowledge work, what do makers make in the Age of AI? Is a background in coding a key prerequisite, as it was for the majority of the titans of the Age of Software & Digital? What skills will characterize the breakout leaders in the Age of AI? We can use the trend from previous ages to assume that the deep expertise in the making mechanisms of the age will be a core component. But that brings us back to the flip side question: What production are managers managing in the Age of AI?

A cursory view could conclude that the makers of the Age of AI are the AI scientists and machine learning engineers at frontier labs. However, those are the people creating the software infrastructure for the Age of AI. In that sense, they are similar to the programming language and compiler developers of the Age of Software & Digital. Many compiler developers had great insights about software, but ultimately it was the people who leveraged the tools they created that came to deliver

* This includes Microsoft (Bill Gates and Paul Allen), Apple (Steve Jobs and Steve Wozniak), Google (Larry Page and Sergey Brin), Amazon (Jeff Bezos), Facebook/Meta (Mark Zuckerberg), Netflix (Reed Hastings), Adobe (John Warnock and Charles Geschke), Tencent (Pony Ma), and Baidu (Robin Li). Alibaba (Jack Ma) is an exception as Ma was an English teacher.

the bulk of the economic value of software. It is not the programming language or compiler developers who became the household names we know today; rather, it was the people who leveraged that infrastructure to create new services and applications. In the Deployment Period of a new age, it is those who create the new tools and infrastructure that are most prominent, which is why the AI scientists at frontier labs appear in headlines today. But the true value is unlocked as we enter the Installation Period, when those who leverage these technologies to build great things deliver the most wealth generation.

In the Age of AI, the process of creating value shifts from delivering outputs to delivering outcomes. As such, the new generation of makers will be those who master and then scale delivering outcomes to the people and markets they serve. In this case, mastering means harnessing AI for the Outcome Loop, while scaling means leading the other people supporting the Outcome Tree.

An Outcome Loop of One

As vibe coding took hold in 2025, a fascinating thing happened. Some of the most seasoned and well-known developers whose careers had shifted to management started coding again. The colleagues whose work we reviewed in previous chapters, including Gene Kim and Kent Beck, started creating increasingly impressive applications entirely on their own and reignited a passion for making that they had not felt for a decade or more. My own experience with this reminded me of my early days when I was building open-source tools entirely on my own with no wait states, only a focus on delivering features that delighted the user community I was supporting. It was invigorating getting feedback as quickly as I could and then incorporating that into the next drop of new features. It is easy to optimize an Outcome Loop of one, and in the Age of AI, the scope of what this can produce has been dramatically amplified.

The growing amplification of outputs could mean that a single person can manage a fleet of AI agents to run a business that previously took hundreds or thousands of people to run. However, for the foreseeable future, single-person Outcome Loops will be more limited in what they can achieve than those involving teams of people. The current era of AI technologies commoditizes intelligence but not intentionality. AI automates cognition but not direction. Intelligence can now be leveraged at scale, but purpose and intention remain human, and harnessing the intentions and goals of multiple people is likely to continue to be the way that we produce the greatest outcomes.

When combined with the inherent diversity in people's approaches to work and problem solving, creativity, meaning, and collectively sought outcomes emerge. As such, the outcomes that can be delivered by an organization leveraging AI will generally exceed those that can be delivered by an individual leveraging AI. While the bar of what a single person can produce will keep rising, even those that start out solo may find themselves wanting to bring on additional colleagues to scale their vision. And for most of us, the challenge is one of transforming a traditional team topology into an effective Outcome Tree.

Outcome Loop Leaders

In Chapter 4 (Functions to Flow), we described the ownership and leadership structures that existing organizations can apply as they shift from functional structures into the Outcome Tree. This included the dual-leader model, where product and technology leaders partner to provide the leadership for a value stream. But what if we wanted to cut down the entire organizational tree and grow a new, AI-native one in its place? This might take the form of a new organization being created, an AI-native organization being formed within an existing one, or an existing organization being entirely restructured around AI.

In building up this new organization, what kind of leaders would we want at each of the levels of the Outcome Tree? We know that a single-leader structure is simpler and more efficient than a dual- or triple-leader structure, so who would these single leaders be? Would they have an engineering background, as did the makers that defined the great companies of prior ages? Or would they have more of a product or business background given that the vast majority of the code will be produced by AI? The answers to these questions define the nature of managerial roles in the Age of AI, as well as the skills that organizations need to develop or recruit to fill those roles.

To define the skills required for Outcome Loop leadership, we need to revisit the Dedicated Leadership Model from Chapter 4, which states that each product value stream has a leader whose main focus is driving the outcomes for that value stream. In the Outcome Tree, each node has a human who is accountable for delivering the outcomes for that particular value stream. In other words, the Outcome Tree leverages the intentionality and accountability that is the domain of humans while empowering each value stream to automate as many of its outputs as is feasible.

Autonomous Value Streams

As the capabilities of AI grow, it will be possible to automate entire value streams. For example, consider a scenario where the mobile and chat experience for an application is built and managed entirely by agents. Defects that arise are solved by agents and feature requests are prioritized and implemented autonomously. The inputs of long-term strategy and budget, as well as the desired outcomes, such as growing the number of daily users, are provided as goals to the value stream's top-level agent.

In this scenario, the value stream no longer requires a human leader, and its accountability simply rolls up to the leader of the parent value stream in the Outcome Tree. In a small organization, this might be the CEO. In a complex organization with many products and platforms, there may be many layers in the Outcome Tree between the CEO and the automated value stream. Each automated value stream rolls up to a human leader who is accountable for the inputs and outcomes of one or more *autonomous value streams*. This leader is the *outcome manager*.

Outcome Manager: The first-line leadership role directly accountable for the inputs and outcomes of human, hybrid, and autonomous value streams.

If the company vision or goals change, the outcome manager needs to revise and update the inputs to the autonomous value stream. Similarly, if the outcomes of the autonomous value stream are not being delivered as expected, the outcome manager needs to reconfigure the outputs of the value stream, for example, by reconfiguring the agents or the data sets being used. These autonomous value streams have execution autonomy, in that they can deliver on objectives without human intervention. However, they do not have operational autonomy, as that is derived from the evolving intentionality encoded in each level of the Outcome Tree, where each level has a human who is accountable for interpreting strategy and owning outcome delivery.

Autonomous Value Stream: A value stream that can execute on its inputs and deliver outputs without human intervention.

A way to visualize the impact of autonomous value streams on the organization is that with increasing degrees of AI automation, for a particular market or problem domain, Outcome Trees will be automated from the bottom up. Consider our TeenWellness app example. The vice president of apps has three directors who are each responsible for an app: one a mobile app, another a chat interface, and the third a business partner portal. With sufficiently powerful AI agents, we can envision the mobile app and chat apps becoming autonomous value streams. The business partner portal may be involved in ongoing discussions and relationships with the business partners themselves and thus better suited to leverage AI for outputs but not for leadership. In this scenario, two of the value streams in this part of the Outcome Tree have become fully autonomous.

The effects of this kind of automation could reduce the portion of the Outcome Tree that is powered by humans as the number of autonomous value streams grows. For some companies, this could mean producing more outcomes with fewer inputs. For others, it could mean that the scope of what the organization can do grows dramatically as existing leaders are deployed to more novel and innovative value streams. For example, with the Chat App value stream becoming autonomous, that leader and team could take on the challenge of expanding the platform to support new fitness and health functions.

Where we end up in terms of the managerial workforce growing or shrinking is the realm of the Jevons paradox, which tells us that increased efficiency driven by technology can paradoxically increase demand,[2] which will encourage effective organizations to expand their overall size and scope, thereby growing the Outcome Tree. In areas of static demand, it could cause the number of people supporting an Outcome Tree to shrink. But in either scenario, it is critical that the organization have the Outcome Management system in place to navigate the transition. Either we manage the output gains provided by AI, or they will manage us.

Controlling Unconstrained Output

Consider a functionally oriented, pre-AI organization that is poorly managed. People are doing work, but this work is not aligned to the organization's strategy. As the strategy drift grows, the makers end up building things that might be interesting and valuable in their contexts but do not deliver on the top-level company goals. These scenarios of the "tail wagging the dog" are common at ineffective organizations, and in competitive markets, they result in companies languishing or going out of business. As the macro environment changes, poorly managed companies cannot pivot in time because the changes in strategy are too slow to translate to changes in execution and delivery. Now, imagine this poorly managed organization scales its output tenfold. The effects of the high levels of output at the leaves of the organization will not only cause drift within a weak management structure, but, without adequate control points, they will accelerate the organization's divergence from strategy.

In the previous six shifts, we reviewed the Outcome Tree mechanisms for empowering leaders and teams while providing some aspects of control by allowing strategy inputs and objectives to cascade down with outcome attainment cascading up. For autonomous value streams, the mechanism changes, as the human-centric mechanisms for supporting empowerment, ownership, and happiness do not apply to agents. To manage autonomous value streams, we apply only the control mechanisms to the Outcome Tree to ensure that output production and Outcome Loop execution are aligned to the rest of the Outcome Tree. In this sense, the Outcome Tree becomes an operational control mechanism for AI agents. The hierarchical nature of the Outcome Tree means we can then scale the control mechanism to arbitrarily large solution domains.

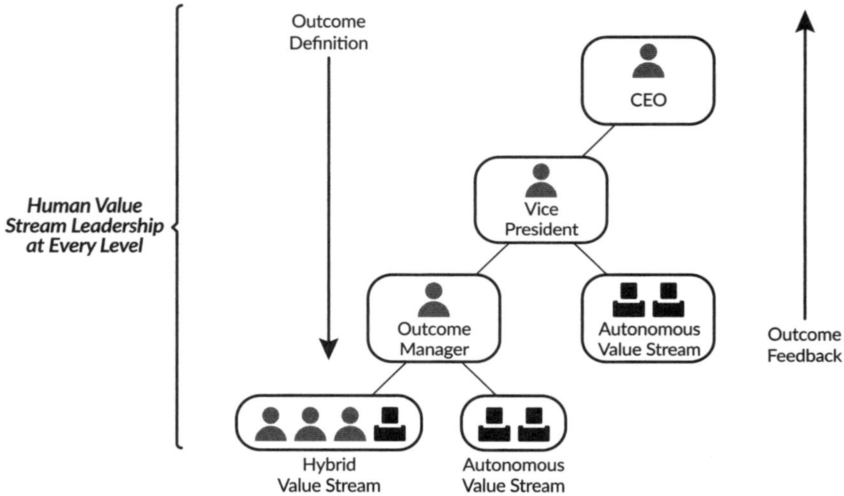

FIGURE 10.1: Outcome Tree as Control Structure for Autonomous Value Streams

Guidance: Use the Outcome Tree as a Control Structure for Agents: While the Outcome Tree is an empowerment and ownership structure for people, with autonomous value streams, it can also serve as a control structure for agents.

The need for a robust control structure for agents is illustrated by Nick Bostrom's "paperclip problem" thought experiment.[3] Imagine that we have an autonomous value stream and specify an outcome to produce as many paperclips as possible. Without constraints on inputs or a human-supervised control mechanism, a superintelligence could acquire all the resources on the planet to maximize the delivery of paper clips, removing all obstacles in its way, including the humans wanting to turn it off. While this may sound like a hyperbolic scenario, it underscores the need for human control mechanisms in the Outcome Loop to avoid unintended consequences.

Consider a more tangible scenario where an autonomous value stream is delivering the chat functionality for our TeenWellness example. Assume the objectives from the vice president of apps cascading down to the value stream are an increase in the daily usage and star ratings of the app. After many iterations deploying new features to users and autonomously running many experiments, the AI running the autonomous value stream could conclude that the latest pro-level frontier model is best suited to drive this level of user engagement. If the inference cost is ten times higher in that new model, the goal may be reached, but the cost may have simultaneously spun out of control and affected the bottom line of the company.

The AI could argue that its budget input constraints were not explicit enough, but in the end, who is accountable for this budget overrun when the chief financial officer raises the issue at the next leadership meeting? It is the vice president of apps, whose career will be on the line, not the agent. If the vice president of apps is not performing, the accountability for that is with their manager and so on up the Outcome Tree. The Outcome Tree provides an accountability structure, ensuring that adequate controls and communication are in place when AI is responsible for a significant portion of delivery.

Guidance: Humans Report to Humans: The Outcome Tree is an ownership structure designed for humans, and each node is supported by a human who reports to another human. Agents amplify the value streams at each node and support each leader and team but are not part of the leadership hierarchy.

Characteristics of Outcome Managers

For many organizations, the biggest changes that result from AI-driven outputs will come from the bottom up. Some teams will have rapidly scaled output delivery with AI, while others will struggle. Candidates for autonomous value streams will appear and need to be acted on. Codebases and data sets will grow to scales not previously foreseen. In each case, the roles of leaders will change dramatically. Leaders must continually reconfigure their value streams based on the evolving capabilities of AI. This requires a deep understanding of these evolving capabilities.

Consider the case where a new set of agents is capable of either augmenting the output of a team or automating the value stream entirely. Understanding how to successfully transform the value stream requires a combination of strategy, product, and engineering management. Due to the continually evolving capabilities of AI, it also requires deep AI expertise. Since changes in one value stream affect all other value streams above it in the Outcome Tree, as well as all dependent value streams, this requires significant technical program management skills. As outcome ownership is all about the customer of the value stream, it also requires thorough business expertise. But perhaps first and foremost, due to the complexity of the role, it requires *systems thinking.*[4]

Systems Thinking for the Age of AI: A holistic approach to managing complexity by understanding and optimizing the flow of value across the interconnected structures of people, processes, technologies, and agents.

At the leaves of the Outcome Tree, we need outcome managers who can connect the deeply technical aspects of ever more complex systems with the outcomes of the value stream. While the coding activities that were done by software engineers will increasingly be taken over by AI, the computational and systems thinking that coders learn gives them a major advantage for taking on these roles. For first-line managers in the Outcome Tree, the role involves enough technical and architectural depth and understanding of the boundaries and capabilities of AI agents that the role is no longer a pure management role but also that of a maker.

What happens when we go up the Outcome Tree to the second-line manager? The leader for this value stream has multiple outcome managers as their staff, and their value stream combines the outputs of their staff's value streams. The second-line manager's role could be less technical, and they may not need to configure and reconfigure fleets of agents. However, if a value stream is a candidate for full automation, the second-line manager will be responsible for understanding when and how to make that change and be accountable for handling problems if the automation fails.

Similarly, they will need to understand when to split and merge value streams and when to promote new platform value streams that can be used elsewhere in the organization. While their job is less technical than that of the first-line manager, these decisions still involve a complex combination of architecture, systems, people, and agents. Thus, the second-line manager also needs deep familiarity with systems and AI. In this way, the role of the second-line manager is also that of a maker. Second-line managers should thus be actively engaged with building and experimenting on systems using hands-on, AI-native engineering.

In larger organizations, as we proceed up the Outcome Tree and away from the leaves where outputs are created, each level becomes a step removed from direct production and more focused on managing strategy, budgets, and people. However, the architecture aspects of Outcome Management and AI automation remain. For example, if a senior leader is relying on a cross-company reporting team to produce weekly reports, they may determine that a single AI-native engineer reporting to them with an autonomous value stream can produce much better results in near real time. In making that change, they are now effectively a second-line manager of that autonomous value stream. If the reports produce inaccurate data, or require a disproportionate cost to produce, they are accountable.

This ability to directly produce outputs and outcomes meaningful to the business is likely why we have seen so many senior technology leaders get their hands on vibe and agentic coding and build great things. We reviewed an example of this in Chapter 4's case study on Pieter Jordaan, chief information officer at TUI Group, becoming one of that company's most prolific AI-native makers without taking his hands off any of his executive responsibilities.

In addition to systems thinking, the other characteristic of effective outcome managers are the traditional characteristics of product managers. This is unsurprising in the sense that the discipline of Product Management is all about delivering outcomes, which is why the Product Operating Model underpins the Outcome Tree. Product managers need to define what outcomes a product value stream should deliver, identify the users and market they are delivering to, connect it to the overall company strategy, and turn it into execution. Their role is communication heavy, as they continually align their value stream both internally and externally. Each of these activities is critical for the outcome manager. As such, an effective outcome manager is a hybrid of a product manager and an engineering manager. As discussed in Chapter 4, many organizations will leverage dual leadership to achieve the necessary expertise. However, AI can also be leveraged by those with leadership ambitions and an appetite for learning to become single-leader outcome managers.

The Outcome Tree is a structure for creating outcomes. As such, it bears a resemblance to an engineering team organization structure and cascade of leadership, as engineering structures are built around the separation of concerns into well modularized team structures. But unlike an engineering team structure, which is optimized for delivering outputs, the Outcome Tree is optimized for delivering outcomes. As such, in the Outcome Tree, those leaders who combine a mix of managerial and technical expertise and ambition will thrive. Product Management and the Product Operating Model were instrumental in getting us to the Age of AI, and these foundations will continue to be key success factors as organizations scale their outputs with AI.

Reconfiguring the Outcome Tree

We are currently in the first wave of AI-native engineering, and the effects on teams will continue to evolve along with the capabilities of frontier models and agents. Some organizations are moving from "two-pizza" sized teams to "one-pizza," as individual engineers are able to produce so much more output with AI. Other organizations are experimenting with teams of two people, pairing up an outcome manager with an outcome engineer. While team sizes and composition are likely to continue to change, the goal of the Outcome Tree is to provide a robust managerial structure that supports the evolution of these changes. When the changes are substantial enough, for example, the addition or removal of a large number of value streams or the implementation of a significant number of staffing changes, the Outcome Tree itself needs to be reconfigured.

In steady state, the Outcome Tree and its feedback loops can respond to changes in inputs. This is the operating mode of the Outcome Tree and is similar to our own ability to quickly react as inputs change. However, there are times where we cannot react quickly and instead need to learn entirely new skills or update our own mental models. This is similar to the fast and slow thinking popularized by Daniel Kahneman.[5] Similarly, we need to know when the Outcome Tree architecture needs to change in support of market conditions, technological disruptions, or changes in strategy. This is the process of continually improving the alignment of the Outcome Tree to the strategy.

In Chapter 5, we discussed how top-down planning can trigger these changes. In this chapter, we have examined the sort of bottom-up forces that can create substantial changes in the Outcome Tree, such as a new ability to automate multiple value streams. Continually examining the architecture of the Outcome Tree within the scope of their value streams is the remaining key function of the outcome manager. Every outcome manager and outcome engineer must continually examine the Outcome Architecture and feed any changes needed into the planning process.

The profound scaling of outputs and the growing capabilities of AI create both a big opportunity and a big risk for organizations to drift away from their strategy. It is the role of outcome managers to ensure that AI delivers for us so that it does not inadvertently direct us.

Leadership Lessons for the Age of Age of AI

In my early days as an open-source developer, I was amazed and frustrated by how small a portion of my day was spent creating meaningful value. The vast majority of my time was spent on wiring, configuring, and wrestling with complex systems. It dawned on me that better programming languages and tools could increase productivity tenfold by removing all of that waste. As part of my PhD thesis, I created a developer productivity measurement system that compared the effort spent actively coding to the effort spent on wasteful thrashing. I used this ratio to not only validate my thesis work but also optimize my own work. Eventually, I got my own productivity systems and tools to the point where I was manually writing between five and ten thousand lines of code per day, which over the years summed up to over a million lines of open-source code.

All of that coding felt very productive, as it was delivering value to my open-source community. For over a decade, I thrived on the craft of coding and the feedback loop of users getting value from my creations. As the company I founded grew, I hired more and more developers, and slowly my focus shifted to spending a significant portion of the day on strategy, planning, supporting a growing number of teams, and engaging directly with customers. But in those early days of Tasktop, I ensured that my title stayed chief technology officer to stay true to my technical focus and roots.

Then, as the company approached two dozen developers, an odd realization dawned on me. As I learned how to offload even the most complex programming tasks to my teams, I found that doing those tasks myself was starting to feel like a mechanical job. In parallel, I noticed that I was getting more satisfaction from guiding teams to produce outputs, while most of my energy was focused on scaling outcomes.

This turned out to be the most profound shift in my career. I forced myself to stop reading developer literature and to dive into reading Peter Drucker. I decided I wanted to move beyond purely technical contributions and learn how to be a good manager. I still wanted to retain that rewarding feeling of LEGO blocks that came from building software, but I wanted to apply it to building and rebuilding an organization.

As the teams grew, their collective output far eclipsed anything I had produced on my own. I realized that any time I spent focused on outputs instead of outcomes was not well spent. While I stayed very close to our technology and architecture, I stopped all but casual coding and finally accepted that CEO was a reasonable title.

AI has automated a broad range of knowledge output. The unfortunate part is that producing some of those outputs was highly enjoyable and rewarding work. However, while I have fond memories of late nights coding, the joy of working with teams to build a successful business turned out to be much more engaging and satisfying. I made this transition over the course of two years. With AI, it is possible for any technologist to start this transition by managing fleets of agents that deliver on whichever outcomes delight you, your team, or your business most. And as discussed in this chapter, most technologists will need to make this transition to some degree.

Whether you are a team of one or a manager of thousands, my belief is that great leadership in the Age of AI will require being connected to each part of the Outcome Loop. For each of us, there is a part of the Outcome Loop that falls into our comfort zone. When I started Tasktop, my comfort zone was producing outputs. I needed to learn, stretch, and lean on my business partner, Neelan Choksi, to get better at strategy and finance. As we grew, I had to stretch again to create a connected, scaled system for tracking outcomes. Similarly, someone with a technical background will need to stretch to the outer portions of the Outcome Loop and can leverage AI to accelerate that journey. In contrast, those with more of a business or finance background need to stretch to better understand the output portion, which is why directly engaging with agentic coding tends to be such a transformational experience for seasoned managers.

To understand how to deliver outcomes in a particular domain, leaders need to have hands-on experience working with outputs for that domain. As your seniority in leadership grows, your ability to optimize an Outcome Loop must similarly scale to creating, managing, and evolving the portions of the Outcome Tree that are within your span of control. While the mix of humans and agents delivering outputs in that tree will evolve at rates that are difficult to predict, the ownership of outcomes will remain.

My journey from developer to CEO took a decade. To me, becoming CEO simply meant owning the top-level Outcome Loop for the organization, needing to learn on the job as the company and the market evolved, and adjusting the Outcome Tree accordingly, whether through one of the five rounds of investment or the two recessions that we navigated. I found the pace of change and learning both dizzying and invigorating. While it accelerated further when we entered the Age of AI and my job at the time shifted to running a portion of the Outcome Tree as chief technology officer of Planview with a mix of humans and agents, the principles remained the same. I believe that the leaders who thrive in the Age of AI will take CEO-level ownership of their Outcome Loop.

Conclusion: Learning to Learn

In times of uncertainty, those who learn and adapt fastest are the ones who thrive. As the roles of makers and managers blend, those who learn and adapt fastest will be best positioned to help their value streams and their organizations succeed. This pace of learning is not easy, but it is required in times of rapid change. At the beginning of the Age of Software & Digital, there was a high degree of uncertainty about how technology would reshape society. Avin Toffler's book *Future Shock* discussed ways to adapt,[6] drawing on the work of psychologist Herbert Gerjuoy, who argued that tomorrow's "illiterate" would not be those who cannot read and write, but those who have not learned how to learn.[7] Half a century later, the pace has further accelerated, putting even greater pressure on individual and organizational learning.

A key motivation of the Outcome Loop and the Outcome Tree is to create structures that accelerate organizational learning. This includes learning by the leaders and teams within your organization and, in particular, learning that is amplified by the agents contributing to the Outcome Loops of your organization. The faster and more effectively these can be harnessed, the more successful your organization will be.

Old approaches to management, leadership, and delivery will collapse under the output amplification provided by AI. In every prior technological revolution, leaders who clung to old operating models lost relevance, while those who learned, adapted, and rewired their organizations thrived. The Age of AI is accelerating faster than any revolution before it. The time to act is now, and our pace of learning must match.

In Summary

- The traditional divide between makers and managers will blur and eventually dissolve in the Age of AI. In addition to automating much of the traditional production of knowledge work, AI replaces many of the reporting and coordination functions of managers. Future leaders will need to both make and manage, directly shaping and delivering outcomes.
- The most successful leaders will follow the historical pattern of previous technological revolutions by combining a deep understanding of production with leadership.

- Outcome managers will provide the hybrid product and engineering combination that leads both human and autonomous teams toward outcomes.
- Autonomous value streams can function without human makers and must be incorporated into a human-aligned Outcome Tree to control their outputs and outcomes.
- The most effective leaders will combine systems thinking, Product Management, and hands-on AI fluency and delivery.

Key Takeaways

- Management and making converge, with effective leaders directly shaping outcomes through the use of agents and AI.
- Outcome managers replace functional leaders, with accountability mapped directly to value streams, not departments and functions.
- Autonomous value streams require new control structures that align their outputs and outcomes to human intentionality.

Prompt

Objective: Help humans evolve roles, teams, and value streams so managers become makers and AI is harnessed safely through Outcome Management.

Operating protocol (assist, don't act unilaterally):

- Map current roles to the Outcome Tree: Identify who is managing which value streams and how much time they spend on meetings/reporting vs. directly shaping outcomes.
- Propose an outcome architecture: Suggest configurations of people + agents per value stream (team sizes, candidate autonomous value streams, where agents should augment vs. own the delivery loop).
- Help identify potential outcome managers: Leaders with both product and technical aptitude who can manage inputs, configure agents, and reason about flow metrics and outcomes.
- Recommend "maker time" for leaders: Concrete ways managers can use AI hands-on (vibe/agentic coding, data analysis, rapid experiments) to stay connected to the Outcome Loop.
- Flag control risks: Where agentic output is scaling without clear objectives, budget constraints, or human ownership; reinforce that humans report to humans and Outcome Trees control agents.

Guardrails: Do not redefine titles or fire people; always present options, trade-offs, and risks for humans to decide.

Conclusion

Our capacity for shared intentionality distinguishes humans from other species.[1] While the power of AI continues to grow by leaps and bounds, both individual and collective intentionality continue to differentiate human intelligence from artificial intelligence. Humans have a unique ability to create joint objectives and shared plans that bring us into the common psychological state that emerges as we work together. These shared psychological states are why working on a thriving team is so rewarding, invigorating, and fun. AI is reshaping the entire landscape of knowledge work, but it should amplify, not take away, our ability to form and grow organizations that achieve amazing things.

The growing power and capabilities of AI may feel daunting. The fear of machines taking over has been present in popular press and media since the Age of Steam & Railways. In 1863, when contemplating the impact of steam-powered machines, Samuel Butler wrote the following passage in a letter titled "Darwin Among the Machines":

> ...we are ourselves creating our own successors; we are daily adding to the beauty and delicacy of their physical organization; we are daily giving them greater power and supplying by all sorts of ingenious contrivances that self-regulating, self-acting power which will be to them what intellect has been to the human race.[2]

I believe we have the opportunity to change that plot. As AI becomes increasingly powerful, the question becomes one of harnessing that power for positive outcomes. As military arsenals grew, the command-and-control mechanisms of military organizations had to become increasingly sophisticated in order to direct that power to match military strategy and to help avoid missteps or abuses of that power. We are now in a similar situation with AI. The power of AI is becoming vast enough that good intentions and ad hoc organizational changes are grossly inadequate for managing it.

Organizations need to adopt a rigorous and scalable set of mechanisms to harness AI. These are the Product Operating Model, the Outcome Loop, and the Outcome Tree. The Seven Shifts provide the additional models and mechanisms needed to make the transition. The end goal is a scalable structure that harnesses agents, AI, and the massive knowledge work output in a way that empowers the people in the organization and leverages the tremendous power of shared intentionality that comes from teams and organizations delivering on a common vision and strategy.

I hope *Output to Outcome* helps you and your organization thrive in the Age of AI. The more organizations that succeed in this transition, the better the societal outcomes will be.

Making the Shift

To create a dynamic learning organization that can leverage and adapt through the Installation Period of the Age of AI, you must transition from managing outputs to delivering outcomes. For your organization to survive and your career to thrive, these shifts are not optional.

Shift from functions to flow. Stop organizing around siloes and handoffs, and structure around value streams that own outcomes end-to-end.

Shift from slop to substance. Stop obsessing over outputs like features, lines of code, or agents delivered. Focus on and celebrate only what connects to business, customer, and employee outcomes.

Shift from chaos to cadence. Throw away ceremonies and cadences that are mismatched with the business cadence, and align the entire organization to a single planning and feedback rhythm.

Shift from matrix to modularity. Stop adding dotted lines and shared ownership, and replace those structures with a singular modular hierarchy of value streams with loose coupling and high cohesion.

Shift from objectives to ownership. Stop diffusing accountability across shared objectives, and give every objective a single and accountable owner, with incentives tied to outcomes.

Shift from divisions to domains. Stop treating all value streams uniformly, and create outcome domains that will help you incubate and transform your organization around your AI initiatives.

Shift from managers to makers. Stop removing the technologists that will become your best leaders through the Age of AI, and start empowering all managerial roles to directly shape outputs and deliver outcomes.

The future of your organization depends not on how many outputs you can produce, but on how fast you can turn your strategy into outcomes. It is time to make the shift.

The leaders who master this operating model will not only thrive but also help shape the Deployment Period of the Age of AI.

Appendix: Playbook

For the most up-to-date playbook, visit OutputToOutcome.org.

Problem: In the Age of AI, output creation becomes increasingly abundant, rendering output-oriented management an increasingly inadequate proxy for value.

Solution: Outcome Management channels AI-amplified capacity into measurable business and customer outcomes.

Target:

- Strategy and budget inputs are connected to outcomes through objectives and quantifiable key results, cascaded through the organization, and continually adjusted through the **Outcome Loop**.
- The organization is structured around value streams into an **Outcome Tree** with dedicated leadership, outcome ownership, and feedback at every node.
- Flow becomes the primary unit of analysis for diagnosing constraints and improving throughput across the Outcome Tree.

Three Foundational Models

1) Product Operating Model

- Align strategy, funding, and delivery around **value streams** instead of projects and functions. Projects remain for episodic work.

- Implement capacity-based funding, planning, and outcome tracking for each value stream.

2) Outcome Loop

- Connect **inputs (strategy, budget)** to **outputs (activities, artifacts)** to **outcomes (customer, employee),** which roll up to business outcomes.
- Make the Outcome Loop metrics the core telemetry for every value stream.
- Build an **Outcome Roadmap** to sequence the work on objectives and drive hypothesis testing, parallelizing delivery as much as feasible.

3) Outcome Tree

- Define a mutually exclusive and collectively exhaustive hierarchy of value streams and their Outcome Loops.
- Ensure each node in the tree is a value stream with its supporting team and leadership, with inputs cascading down and outcome feedback cascading up.
- Ensure that humans report to humans in the outcome tree structure while leveraging AI and agents to amplify outcome delivery at each level.

Seven Shifts

1) **Functions to Flow:** Replace functional organization design with value streams structured into an Outcome Tree.

    - Map the value streams top-down to represent the organization's product, platform, and supporting offerings, leveraging the **Dedicated Leadership Model** for the organizational structure.

- Define value stream organization bottom-up to ensure that teams and value streams form a single structure that is cleanly partitioned into the Outcome Tree.
- Review and improve the resulting structure as part of a regular planning cadence.

2) **Slop to Substance**: Ensure AI-amplified activity generates value by connecting outputs to outcomes.

- Operationalize and regularly review Outcome Loop telemetry across the Outcome Tree.
- Standardize delivery telemetry using the **Flow Metrics Model** and by implementing an **Outcome Loop Improvement** mechanism to accelerate flow.
- Apply the Theory of Constraints to the Outcome Loop to increasingly leverage AI amplification in a way that ensures measurable business outcomes.

3) **Chaos to Cadence**: Replace parallel meeting and reporting systems with a single unified operating cadence across the Outcome Tree.

- Implement the **Unified Cadence Model** to provide a single meeting and reporting cadence for planning and feedback.
- Align annual, quarterly, monthly, and weekly cycles so value streams can reprioritize independently and transparently while remaining connected to outcomes.

4) **Matrix to Modularity**: Remove matrix line overlays and replace them with modular value streams with clear ownership and autonomy.

- Use the Outcome Tree as the primary operating model and organizational structure, not an overlay on the organizational chart.

- Continually reduce value stream coupling and increase cohesion to minimize dependencies and optimize flow across the Outcome Tree.
- Ensure value stream empowerment and accountability using the **Independent Action Model**.

5) **Objectives to Ownership**: Replace shared and ambiguous accountability with clear and singular ownership aligned to the Outcome Tree.

   - Start with each objective having one single-threaded ownership, using dual- and triple-leadership structures only where necessary.
   - If using dual- or triple-leadership structures, ensure titles match across the roles supporting the Outcome Tree to avoid ownership imbalance.
   - Align incentive and compensation structure to the **Outcome Ownership Model**.

6) **Divisions to Domains**: Avoid one-size-fits-all planning by partitioning the top-level of the Outcome Tree into context-specific domains.

   - Segment the Outcome Tree into the **Outcome Domain Model**, which supports core, platform, incubation, and transformation domains.
   - Tailor input metrics, objectives, flow, and leadership assignments according to the context of each domain.
   - Establish explicit thresholds for moving value streams between domains, such as incubation to transformation and then to core.

7) **Managers to Makers**: Redefine leadership as AI collapses traditional coordination work and expands the need for outcome ownership.

- Establish **Outcome Managers** who are responsible for inputs and outcomes for both humans and **Autonomous Value Streams**.
- Leverage the Outcome Tree as a control structure that keeps autonomous execution under human accountability.
- Adopt the **Outcome Architecture Model** as a leadership discipline to continually evolve value streams, team structures, and agentic systems in service of better customer and employee outcomes.

Bibliography

Acemoglu, Daron, and James Robinson. *Why Nations Fail: The Origins of Power, Prosperity, and Poverty*. Crown Business, 2012.

Aho, Alfred V., Monica S. Lam, Ravi Sethi, and Jeffrey D. Ullman. *Compilers: Principles, Techniques, and Tools*. 2nd ed. Addison-Wesley, 2006.

Amazon Web Services. "Amazon Connect Forecasting, Capacity Planning, and Scheduling." Amazon Connect Optimization. Accessed August 2025. https://docs.aws.amazon.com/connect/latest/adminguide/forecasting-capacity-planning-scheduling.html.

Azad, Deepak. *An Exploratory Study of Socio-Technical Congruence in an Ecosystem of Software Developers*. Master's thesis, University of British Columbia, 2014.

Baghai, Mehrdad, Stephen Coley, and David White. *The Alchemy of Growth: Practical Insights for Building the Enduring Enterprise*. Perseus Books, 1999.

Baldwin, Carliss Y. "Design Rules: Past and Future." *Industrial and Corporate Change* 32, no. 1 (2023): 1–13.

Baldwin, Carliss Y., and Kim B. Clark. *Design Rules, Volume 1: The Power of Modularity*. MIT Press, 2000.

BankingDay. "CBA Puts Hard Numbers Against the Soft Metrics." BankingDay, February 19, 2024. https://www.bankingday.com/cba-puts-hard-numbers-against-soft-metrics.

Beane, Matt. *The Skill Code: How to Save Human Ability in an Age of Intelligent Machines*. Harper Business, 2024.

Beck, Kent, et al. "Manifesto for Agile Software Development." 2001. Accessed July 29, 2025. https://agilemanifesto.org/.

Beltman, John. "You Build It, You Run It." Software Musings, September 1, 2023. https://www.beltman.id.au/you-build-it-you-run-it/.

Bezos, Jeff. "2015 Letter to Shareholders." Amazon.com, April 2016. https://s2.q4cdn.com/299287126/files/doc_financials/annual/2015-Letter-to-Shareholders.PDF.

Blank, Steve. *The Four Steps to the Epiphany: Successful Strategies for Products That Win*. 5th ed. K&S Ranch, 2013.

Booking Holdings Inc. "Booking Holdings Reports Fourth Quarter and Full Year 2024 Results." Booking Holdings Investor Relations, February 2025. https://ir.bookingholdings.com.
Boston Consulting Group. "What Employees Say About Agile Transformations." BCG, January 31, 2022. https://www.bcg.com/publications/2022/what-employees-say-about-agile-transformations.
Bostrom, Nick. *Deep Utopia: Life and Meaning in a Solved World*. Ideapress Publishing, 2024.
Bostrom, Nick. "Ethical Issues in Advanced Artificial Intelligence." In *Cognitive, Emotive and Ethical Aspects of Decision-Making in Humans and in Artificial Intelligence*, edited by I. Smit et al., 12–17. Vol. 2. International Institute for Advanced Studies in Systems Research and Cybernetics, 2003.
Bryar, Colin, and Bill Carr. *Working Backward: Insights, Stories, and Secrets from Inside Amazon*. St. Martin's Press, 2021.
Bughin, Jacques, and Michael Chui. "95 Percent of Generative AI Implementations in Enterprise Have No Measurable Impact on P&L, Says MIT." *MIT Sloan Management Review*, reported in Tom's Hardware, July 2025. https://www.tomshardware.com/tech-industry/artificial-intelligence/95-percent-of-generative-ai-implementations-in-enterprise-have-no-measurable-impact-on-p-and-l-says-mit-flawed-integration-key-reason-why-ai-projects-underperform.
Butler, Samuel. "Darwin Among the Machines." *The Press*, June 13, 1863.
Castro, Felipe. "A Practical Guide to OKRs." *Zensai*, September 17, 2024. https://zensai.com/articles/how-to-set-okrs/.
Cataldo, Marcelo, James D. Herbsleb, and Kathleen M. Carley. "Socio-Technical Congruence: A Framework for Assessing the Impact of Technical and Work Dependencies on Software Development." *SSRN Electronic Journal*, January 2008.
Christensen, Clayton M. *The Innovator's Dilemma: When New Technologies Cause Great Firms to Fail*. Harvard Business School Press, 1997.
Christensen, Clayton M., and Michael E. Raynor. *The Innovator's Solution: Creating and Sustaining Successful Growth*. Harvard Business School Press, 2003.
Christensen, Clayton M., Taddy Hall, Karen Dillon, and David S. Duncan. *Competing Against Luck: The Story of Innovation and Customer Choice*. HarperBusiness, 2016.
Commonwealth Bank of Australia. "Customer Safety, Convenience and Recognition Boosted by Early Implementation of Gen AI." CommBank Newsroom, November 28, 2024. https://www.commbank.com.au/articles/newsroom/2024/11/reimagining-banking-nov24.html.

Conway, Melvin E. "How Do Committees Invent?" *Datamation* 14, no. 5 (April 1968): 28–31.

DeGrandis, Dominica. *Making Work Visible: Exposing Time Theft to Optimize Work & Flow.* 2nd ed. IT Revolution Press, 2022.

Detroit Historical Society. "Model T." *Encyclopedia of Detroit.* Accessed July 29, 2025. https://www.detroithistorical.org/learn/online-research/encyclopedia-of-detroit/model-t.

DevOps Research and Assessment (DORA). *Accelerate: 2024 State of DevOps Report.* Perforce Software, Inc., 2024. https://www.multitudes.com/blog/devops-metrics-and-kpis.

Doerr, John. *Measure What Matters: How Google, Bono, and the Gates Foundation Rock the World with OKRs.* Penguin, 2018.

Drucker, Peter F. *The Landmarks of Tomorrow: A Report on the New "Post-Modern" World.* Harper & Brothers, 1959.

Economicpoint. "Elasticity of Production." Accessed July 31, 2025. https://economicpoint.com/elasticity-production.

Encyclopaedia Britannica. "How Rich Was John D. Rockefeller?" Accessed November 12, 2025. https://www.britannica.com/topic/How-Rich-Was-John-D-Rockefeller.

Forsgren, Nicole, Jez Humble, and Gene Kim. *Accelerate: The Science of Lean Software and DevOps: Building and Scaling High Performing Technology Organizations.* IT Revolution Press, 2018.

Friedman, Mark. *A Guide to Developing and Using Performance Measures in Results-Based Budgeting.* The Finance Project, Fiscal Policy Studies Institute, 1997.

Fuchs, Jay. "Sandbagging Sales: What It Is & Why You Shouldn't Do It." HubSpot Sales Blog, December 9, 2024. https://blog.hubspot.com/sales/sandbagging-sales.

Gantt, Henry L. "A Graphical Daily Balance in Manufacture." In *Transactions of the American Society of Mechanical Engineers*, 24 (1903): 1322–1336.

Gerjuoy, Herbert. "Educating Man for the Future." In *Education for an Uncertain Future*, edited by Robert Leeper, 1–19. University of California Press, 1966.

Goldratt, Eliyahu M. *Theory of Constraints.* North River Press, 1999.

Gonzales-Black, Alexis. "The Next Big Thing You Missed: Companies That Work Better Without Bosses." *Wired*, January 7, 2014. https://www.wired.com/2014/01/holacracy-at-zappos/.

Goodhart, Charles A. E. "Problems of Monetary Management: The U.K. Experience." Reserve Bank of Australia Papers in Monetary Economics, 1975.

Google re:Work. "Guides: Set Goals with OKRs." Accessed August 1, 2025. https://rework.withgoogle.com/intl/en/guides/set-goals-with-okrs/.

Graham, Paul. "Maker's Schedule, Manager's Schedule." PaulGraham.com, July 2009. https://paulgraham.com/makersschedule.html.

Grove, Andrew S. *High Output Management*. Vintage Books, 1995.

Han_Thot_Terse. "Over Christmas Break I Wrote a Fully Functional Browser with Claude Code in Rust : R/Anthropic," Reddit, January 2025. https://www.reddit.com/r/Anthropic/comments/1q4xfm0/over_christmas_break_i_wrote_a_fully_functional/.

Hayat, Zia. "Digital Trust: How to Unleash the Trillion-Dollar Opportunity for Our Global Economy." World Economic Forum, August 17, 2022. https://www.weforum.org/stories/2022/08/digital-trust-how-to-unleash-the-trillion-dollar-opportunity-for-our-global-economy/.

Henry, Kimberlee. "Reporting Lines: Strategies for Clear Reporting Relationships." TheOrgChart.com, June 25, 2024. https://theorgchart.com/resources/reporting-line-and-relationship/.

Hilbert, David. "Mathematical Problems." Lecture delivered before the International Congress of Mathematicians, Paris, August 8, 1900. In *Proceedings of the International Congress of Mathematicians in Paris*, 1900. Paris: Gauthier-Villars, 1902.

Hirschman, Charles, and Elizabeth Mogford. "Immigration and the American Industrial Revolution from 1880 to 1920." *Social Science Research* 38, no. 4 (2009): 897–920.

Hoffman, Reid, and Chris Yeh. *Blitzscaling: The Lightning-Fast Path to Building Massively Valuable Companies*. Currency, 2018.

Holland, John H. *Emergence: From Chaos to Order*. Addison-Wesley, 1998.

Horowitz, Ben. *The Hard Thing About Hard Things: Building a Business When There Are No Easy Answers*. Harper Business, 2014.

Huawei and Oxford Economics. *Digital Spillover: Measuring the True Impact of the Digital Economy*. Huawei Technologies Co., Ltd., 2017. https://www.huawei.com/minisite/gci/en/digital-spillover/files/gci_digital_spillover.pdf.

International Labour Organization. "Knowledge Workers as a Share of Total Employment by Country Income Group." In *B59 Automation Hits the Knowledge Worker: ChatGPT and the Future of Work*, 2023.

Jevons, William Stanley. *The Coal Question; An Inquiry Concerning the Progress of the Nation, and the Probable Exhaustion of Our Coal-Mines*. Macmillan & Co., 1865.

Kahneman, Daniel. *Thinking, Fast and Slow*. Farrar, Straus and Giroux, 2011.

Kaplan, Robert S., and David P. Norton. *The Balanced Scorecard: Translating Strategy into Action*. Harvard Business School Press, 1996.

Kersten, Mik. *Eclipse Mylyn: Task-Focused Interface for Eclipse IDE*. Open-Source Project under Eclipse Foundation, initiated March 2005.

Kersten, Mik. *Focusing Knowledge Work with Task Context*. PhD diss., University of British Columbia, 2007. https://doi.org/10.14288/1.0302110.

Kersten, Mik. *Project to Product: How to Survive and Thrive in the Age of Digital Disruption with the Flow Framework*. IT Revolution Press, 2018.

Kersten, Mik, host. "Episode 20: Justin Watts on Doing the Right Things Wrong." *Mik + One: Podcast*. Podcast audio, March 11, 2020. https://podcast8w.podbean.com/e/episode-20-justin-watts-on-doing-the-right-things-wrong/.

Kersten, Mik, host. "Episode 28: Pieter Jordaan on TUI's Incredible 6-Month Cloud Journey." *Mik + One Podcast*. March 23, 2021. https://podcast8w.podbean.com/e/episode-28-pieter-jordaan-on-tui-s-incredible-6-month-cloud-journey/.

Kersten, Mik, host. "Episode 44: Geordie Henderson on Implementing Organizational Design and Innovation to Scale High-Performing Teams." *Mik + One: Podcast*. Podcast audio, April 5, 2022. https://podcast8w.podbean.com/e/episode-44-geordie-henderson-on-implementing-organizational-design-and-innovation-to-scale-high-performing-teams/.

Kersten, Mik, host. "Episode 56: GitHub's Scott Densmore on the Copilot Revolution, Coding at the Speed of Thought," Mik + One: The Official Project to Product Podcast, December 14, 2023. https://podcast8w.podbean.com/e/episode-56-github-copilot-s-scott-densmore-on-copilot-revolution-coding-at-the-speed-of-thought/.

Kiczales, Gregor, Jim des Rivières, and Daniel G. Bobrow. *The Art of the Metaobject Protocol*. MIT Press, 1991.

Kiczales, Gregor, John Lamping, Anurag Mendhekar, Chris Maeda, Cristina Videira Lopes, Jean-Marc Loingtier, and John Irwin. "Aspect-Oriented Programming." In *Proceedings of the 11th European Conference on Object-Oriented Programming (ECOOP '97), Lecture Notes in Computer Science* 1241, 220–242. Springer-Verlag, June 1997.

Kim, Eugene. "Inside Amazon's Plan to Cut Managers: More Direct Reports, Fewer Senior Hires, and Pay Cuts." *Business Insider*, January 30, 2025. https://www.businessinsider.com/amazon-plan-cut-managers-aws-internal-guidelines-2025-1.

Kim, Gene et al,. "Improve Flow in DevOps Value Stream." IT Revolution (blog), November 30, 2021. https://itrevolution.com/articles/improve-flow-devops-value-stream/.

Kim, Gene, and Steven J. Spear. *Wiring the Winning Organization: Liberating Our Collective Greatness Through Slowification, Simplification, and Amplification*. IT Revolution Press, 2023.

Kniberg, Henrik, and Anders Ivarsson. "Scaling Agile @ Spotify." White paper, Spotify AB, 2012. https://blog.crisp.se/wp-content/uploads/2012/11/SpotifyScaling.pdf.

Kondratiev, Nikolai D. *The Long Wave Cycle*. Translated by Guy Daniels. Richardson & Snyder, 1984.

Kotter, John P. *Accelerate: Building Strategic Agility for a Faster-Moving World*. Harvard Business Review Press, 2014.

Lawrence, Neil. *Atomic Human: Understanding Ourselves in the Age of AI*. Penguin Business, 2024.

Lee, Bill. "The Hidden (in Plain Sight) Legacy of Steve Jobs." *Harvard Business Review*, August 30, 2011. https://hbr.org/2011/08/the-hidden-in-plain-sight-lega.

Leffingwell, Dean, and Richard Knaster. *SAFe® 4.0 Reference Guide: Scaled Agile Framework for Lean Software and Systems Engineering*. Addison-Wesley Professional, 2016.

Lockheed Martin. *Skunk Works®: The Skunk Works Legacy*. Lockheed Martin Aeronautics Company. https://www.lockheedmartin.com/en-us/who-we-are/business-areas/aeronautics/skunkworks.html.

Ludlow, Edward, and Kate Clark. "Cognition AI Reaches $10 Billion Valuation with New Funding." Bloomberg.com, September 8, 2025. https://www.bloomberg.com/news/articles/2025-09-08/cognition-ai-cinches-10-billion-valuation-with-new-funding.

MacCormack, Allan, John Rusnak, and Carliss Y. Baldwin. "The Impact of Component Modularity on Design Evolution." Harvard Business School Working Paper No. 08-038, December 2007.

McCallum, Daniel C. "Plan of Organization of the New York & Erie Railroad." Diagram drawn by George Holt Henshaw, September 1855. New York & Erie Railroad Company, 1855. Cited in Sarah Hallam, "How the Rise of the Railroads Gave Way to the World's First Org Chart," TheOrg, 2023.

McKinsey & Company. "The Bottom-Line Benefit of the Product Operating Model." McKinsey & Company, December 19, 2023. https://www.mckinsey.com/capabilities/tech-and-ai/our-insights/the-bottom-line-benefit-of-the-product-operating-model.

Meadows, Donella H. *Thinking in Systems: A Primer*. Chelsea Green Publishing, 2008.

Miles, Stephen A., and Mary Michelle Scott. "The Leadership Team: Complementary Strengths or Conflicting Agendas." *Harvard Business Review*, April 2007.

Minto, Barbara. *The Pyramid Principle: Logic in Writing and Thinking.* Financial Times/Prentice Hall, 1985.

Mollick, Ethan. *Co-Intelligence: Living and Working with AI.* Portfolio/Penguin, 2024.

Moore, Geoffrey A. *Living on the Fault Line: Managing for Shareholder Value in the Age of the Internet.* HarperBusiness, 2000.

Moore, Geoffrey A. *Zone to Win: Organizing to Compete in an Age of Disruption.* Diversion Books, 2015.

Morgan, Johanna, and Jens Heitland. *Strategic Portfolio Management: Balancing Innovation and Execution for Sustainable Growth.* Springer, 2020.

Msv, Janakiram. "The AI That Built Itself in 10 Days Now Wants Access to Your Desktop." *Forbes*, January 19, 2026. https://www.forbes.com/sites/janakirammsv/2026/01/16/the-ai-that-built-itself-in-10-days-now-wants-access-to-your-desktop/.

Mueller, Joann. "Why GM Sees U.S. Supply Chain as Key to EV Leadership." *Axios*, November 5, 2024. https://www.axios.com/2024/11/05/gm-us-supply-chain-ev-batteries.

NES Fircroft. "A Brief History of American Automotive Manufacturing." Accessed July 29, 2025. https://www.nesfircroft.com/resources/blog/a-brief-history-of-american-automotive-manufacturing/.

Newman, Sam. *Building Microservices: Designing Fine-Grained Systems.* O'Reilly Media, 2015.

Ohno, Taiichi. *Toyota Production System: Beyond Large-Scale Production.* Productivity Press, 1988.

Organisation for Economic Co-operation and Development (OECD). *The OECD Productivity Manual: A Guide to the Measurement of Industry-Level and Aggregate Productivity Growth.* OECD Publishing, 2001.

Orosz, Gergely. "How Big Tech Runs Tech Projects and the Curious Absence of Scrum." The Pragmatic Engineer (blog), September 3, 2023. https://blog.pragmaticengineer.com/project-management-at-big-tech/.

PagerDuty, Inc. "Time-Critical, Unplanned Work Causes Major Disruption to Business: New Report Shows Escalating Cost of Outages and Downtime." *Business Wire*, March 10, 2020.

Parrish, Shane, and Rhiannon Beaubien. *The Great Mental Models: General Thinking Concepts.* Vol. 1. Latticework Publishing, 2019.

Perez, Carlota. *Technological Revolutions and Financial Capital: The Dynamics of Bubbles and Golden Ages.* Edward Elgar, 2002.

Piketty, Thomas. *Capital in the Twenty-First Century. Translated by Arthur Goldhammer.* Harvard University Press, 2014.

Pink, Daniel H. *Drive: The Surprising Truth About What Motivates Us.* Canongate Books, 2010.

Planview. *The 2024 Project to Product State of the Industry Report*. Planview, 2024. https://info.planview.com/project-to-product-state-of-the-industry-_report_vsm_en_reg.html.

Poincaré, Henri. *New Methods of Celestial Mechanics*. Translated by Cathleen S. Prosser. American Institute of Physics, 1993.

Project Management Institute. *A Guide to the Project Management Body of Knowledge (PMBOK® Guide)*. 6th ed. Project Management Institute, 2017.

Radek, Arkadiusz. "Objectives and Key Results (OKRs) 101 (Advanced Techniques)." The Product Compass, August 19, 2023. https://www.productcompass.pm/p/okrs-101-advanced-techniques.

Ravishankar, Vinit, Artur Kulmizev, Mostafa Abdou, Anders Søgaard, and Joakim Nivre. "Attention Can Reflect Syntactic Structure (If You Let It)." arXiv preprint arXiv:2101.10927 (January 26, 2021). https://doi.org/10.48550/arXiv.2101.10927.

Reinertsen, Donald G. *The Principles of Product Development Flow: Second-Generation Lean Product Development*. Celeritas Publishing, 2009.

Reuters. "Australia's CBA Posts Record Annual Profit, but Investors Shed Pricey Shares." *Reuters*, August 12, 2025. https://www.reuters.com/business/finance/australias-cba-posts-record-annual-profit-investors-shed-pricey-shares-2025-08-12/.

Ries, Eric. *The Lean Startup: How Today's Entrepreneurs Use Continuous Innovation to Create Radically Successful Businesses*. Crown Business, 2011.

Robertson, Brian J. *Holacracy: The New Management System for a Rapidly Changing World*. Henry Holt & Company, 2015.

Rodrik, Dani. *Economics Rules: The Rights and Wrongs of the Dismal Science*. W.W. Norton, 2015.

Rother, Mike, and John Shook. *Learning to See: Value Stream Mapping to Add Value and Eliminate MUDA*. Lean Enterprise Institute, 1999.

Ryseff, James, Brandon F. De Bruhl, and Sydne J. Newberry. *The Root Causes of Failure for Artificial Intelligence Projects and How They Can Succeed: Avoiding the Anti-Patterns of AI*. RAND Corporation, 2024.

Salesforce, Inc. "Agentforce Marketing: AI Agents for Real-Time Campaign Planning and Optimization." Salesforce.com (blog), October 23, 2025. https://www.salesforce.com/blog/agentforce-marketing/.

Scaled Agile, Inc. "PI Planning." Scaled Agile Framework® (SAFe®), last updated October 15, 2024. https://framework.scaledagile.com/pi-planning.

Scaled Agile, Inc. "Planning Interval." Scaled Agile Framework® (SAFe®), last updated February 25, 2025. https://framework.scaledagile.com/planning-interval.

Scaled Agile, Inc. "Weighted Shortest Job First (WSJF)." Accessed July 31, 2025. https://framework.scaledagile.com/wsjf

Schein, Edgar H. *Organizational Culture and Leadership*. 4th ed. Jossey-Bass, 2010.

Schumpeter, Joseph A. *Capitalism, Socialism and Democracy*. 3rd ed. Harper & Brothers, 1950. First published 1942.

Schwaber, Ken, and Jeff Sutherland. *The Scrum Guide: The Definitive Guide to Scrum: The Rules of the Game*. Scrum.org and Scrum Inc., November 2020. https://scrumguides.org/scrum-guide.html.

Scott, Adam. "Tesla's Vertical Integration Revolutionizes Supply Chains." Supply Chain 360, June 19, 2024. https://supplychain360.io/teslas-vertical-integration-revolutionizes-supply-chains/.

Silicon Valley Product Group. "The Alternative to Roadmaps." Silicon Valley Product Group, September 7, 2015. https://www.svpg.com/the-alternative-to-roadmaps/.

Silver, Amanda. "Celebrating 50 Million Developers: The Journey of Visual Studio and Visual Studio Code." Microsoft for Developers (blog), May 15, 2025. https://developer.microsoft.com/blog/celebrating-50-million-developers-the-journey-of-visual-studio-and-visual-studio-code.

Skelton, Matthew, and Manuel Pais. *Team Topologies: Organizing Business and Technology Teams for Fast Flow*. IT Revolution Press, 2019.

Šmite, Darja, and Zane Galviņa. "Socio-Technical Congruence Sabotaged by a Hidden Onshore Outsourcing Relationship: Lessons Learned from an Empirical Study." In *Product-Focused Software Process Improvement (PROFES 2012), Lecture Notes in Computer Science*, vol. 7343, edited by Óscar Dieste, Arturo Jedlitschka, and Natalia Juristo, 190–202. Springer, 2012.

Smith, Zoe. "Some Redwood Leaves Make Food While Others Drink Water." Science News Explores, May 27, 2022. https://www.snexplores.org/article/some-redwood-leaves-make-food-while-others-drink-water.

Snowden, David J., and Mary E. Boone. "A Leader's Framework for Decision Making." *Harvard Business Review*, November 2007.

Solow, Robert M. "We See the Computer Age Everywhere Except in the Productivity Statistics." *New York Times Book Review*, July 12, 1987.

Soltani, Ehsan. "The Rising Dominance of U.S. Big Techs in the Global Stock Market." Visual Capitalist, December 13, 2024. https://www.voronoiapp.com/markets/-The-Rising-Dominance-of-US-Big-Techs-in-the-Global-Stock-Market-3419.

S&P Automotive Insights. "Digital Twins in the Automotive Industry Explained," September 16, 2025. https://www.spglobal.com/automotive-insights/en/blogs/2025/08/digital-twins-in-the-automotive-industry-explained.

Stack Overflow. "Stack Overflow Developer Survey 2024: Most Popular Integrated Development Environments (IDEs)." Stack Overflow,

June 2024. https://survey.stackoverflow.co/2024/#most-popular-technologies-integrated-development-environment.

Stevens, Wayne P., Glen J. Myers, and Larry L. Constantine. "Structured Design." *IBM Systems Journal* 13, no. 2 (1974): 115–139.

Straker-Carrier, Stephen. "Please, Stop Quarterly Planning: It's Just Waterfall in Disguise." Straker-Carrier Blog, March 21, 2023. https://strakercarryer.com/posts/please-stop-quarterly-planning/.

StraitsResearch. *Digital Transformation Consulting Market Size & Share Report*. 2024. https://straitsresearch.com/report/digital-transformation-consulting-market.

Suleyman, Mustafa, with Michael Bhaskar. *The Coming Wave: Technology, Power, and the Twenty-First Century's Greatest Dilemma*. Crown Publishing Group, 2023.

Taylor, Frederick Winslow. *The Principles of Scientific Management*. Harper & Brothers, 1911.

Theil, David. "How to Set Good OKR Key Results." *Medium*, January 17, 2023. https://david-theil.medium.com/how-to-set-good-okr-key-results-1542759eb720.

Tidd, Joe, and John Bessant. "Review of Innovation Models: From Linear to Systems Approaches." In *Innovation Through Time*, 2005.

Toffler, Alvin. *Future Shock*. Random House, 1970.

Tomasello, Michael, et al. "Understanding and Sharing Intentions: The Origins of Cultural Cognition." *Behavioral and Brain Sciences* 28, no. 5 (2005): 675–691.

Toon, Nigel. *Atomic Human: Understanding Ourselves in the Age of AI*. Penguin Business, 2024.

Ulwick, Anthony W. *What Customers Want: Using Outcome-Driven Innovation to Create Breakthrough Products and Services*. McGraw-Hill, 2005.

Voronoi. "The Rising Dominance of U.S. Big Techs in the Global Stock Market." February 7, 2025. https://www.voronoiapp.com/markets/-The-Rising-Dominance-of-US-Big-Techs-in-the-Global-Stock-Market-3419.

Wang, Sarah, and Martin Casado. "The Cost of Cloud, a Trillion-Dollar Paradox." *a16z*, May 27, 2021. https://a16z.com/the-cost-of-cloud-a-trillion-dollar-paradox/.

West, Geoffrey B. *Scale: The Universal Laws of Growth, Innovation, Sustainability, and the Pace of Life in Organisms, Cities, Economies, and Companies*. Penguin Press, 2017.

West, Dave, Mike Gilpin, and Tom Grant. "Water-Scrum-Fall Is the Reality of Agile for Most Organizations Today," *Forrester*, July 25, 2011. https://www.forrester.com/report/water-scrum-fall-is-the-reality-of-agile-for-most-organizations-today/RES60109.

Wikipedia. "Jensen Huang." Last updated July 2025. Accessed August 1, 2025. https://en.wikipedia.org/wiki/Jensen_Huang.

Womack, James P., and Daniel T. Jones. *Lean Thinking: Banish Waste and Create Wealth in Your Corporation*. Simon & Schuster, 1996.

Womack, James P., Daniel T. Jones, and Daniel Roos. *The Machine That Changed the World: The Story of Lean Production—Toyota's Secret Weapon in the Global Car Wars That Is Now Revolutionizing World Industry*. Free Press, 1990.

World Bank Group. *Output-Based Aid: Competitive Vouchers in Health. Pilot Programs Initiated in the 1990s in Low- and Middle-Income Countries*. World Bank Group, 2002.

Zeff, Maxwell. "GitHub Copilot Crosses 20M All-Time Users." *TechCrunch*, July 30, 2025. https://techcrunch.com/2025/07/30/github-copilot-crosses-20-million-all-time-users/.

Zheng, Z., Minghao Zhao, Lei Li, and Heng Ji. "Attention Heads of Large Language Models: A Survey." arXiv preprint arXiv:2409.03752 (2024). https://doi.org/10.48550/arXiv.2409.03752.

Zhang, Ruimin. *The Rendanheyi Model*. China Machine Press, 2017.

Notes

Preface

1. Drucker, *The Landmarks of Tomorrow.*
2. Planview, *The 2024 Project to Product State of the Industry Report.*

Introduction

1. Bostrom, *Deep Utopia.*
2. Msv, "The AI That Built Itself in 10 Days Now Wants Access to Your Desktop."
3. Han_Thot_Terse, "Over Christmas Break I Wrote a Fully Functional Browser with Claude Code in Rust : R/Anthropic."
4. Planview, *The 2024 Project to Product State of the Industry Report.*
5. Goldratt, *Theory of Constraints.*
6. Toon, *Atomic Human.*

Chapter 0

1. Solow, "We See the Computer Age Everywhere."
2. Kersten, *Focusing Knowledge Work with Task Context.*
3. OECD, *The OECD Productivity Manual.*
4. Schumpeter, *Capitalism, Socialism and Democracy.*
5. Piketty, *Capital in the Twenty-First Century*; Acemoglu and Robinson, *Why Nations Fail.*
6. Suleyman, *The Coming Wave.*
7. Encyclopaedia Britannica, "How Rich Was John D. Rockefeller?"
8. Kondratiev, *The Long Wave Cycle.*
9. Hilbert, "Mathematical Problems."
10. Rodrik, *Economics Rules.*
11. Perez, *Technological Revolutions and Financial Capital.*
12. Detroit Historical Society, "Model T."

13. NES Fircroft, "A Brief History of American Automotive Manufacturing."
14. Tidd and Bessant, "Review of Innovation Models."
15. Hirschman and Mogford, "Immigration and the American Industrial Revolution."
16. International Labour Organization, "Knowledge Workers."
17. Taylor, *The Principles of Scientific Management.*
18. Womack, Jones, and Roos, *The Machine That Changed the World.*
19. Beck et al., "Manifesto for Agile Software Development."
20. Ludlow, Edward, and Clark, "Cognition AI Reaches $10 Billion Valuation with New Funding."

Chapter 1

1. Voronoi, "The Rising Dominance of U.S. Big Techs."
2. Hayat, "Digital Trust."
3. Huawei and Oxford Economics, *Digital Spillover.*
4. DORA, *Accelerate: 2024 State of DevOps Report.*
5. StraitsResearch, *Digital Transformation Consulting Market.*
6. Planview, *The 2024 Project to Product State of the Industry Report.*
7. McKinsey & Company, "The Bottom-Line Benefit."
8. McCallum, "Plan of Organization."
9. Taylor, *The Principles of Scientific Management.*
10. Gantt, "A Graphical Daily Balance in Manufacture."
11. Kersten, *Project to Product.*
12. Snowden and Boone, "A Leader's Framework."
13. Poincaré, *New Methods of Celestial Mechanics.*
14. Lawrence, *Atomic Human.*
15. Mollick, *Co-Intelligence.*
16. Reinertsen, *The Principles of Product Development Flow.*

Chapter 2

1. Amazon Web Services, "Amazon Connect Forecasting."
2. Bryar and Carr, *Working Backward.*
3. Economicpoint, "Elasticity of Production."
4. World Bank Group, *Output-Based Aid.*
5. Friedman, *A Guide to Developing and Using Performance Measures.*
6. Ulwick, *What Customers Want.*
7. Christensen, Hall, Dillon, and Duncan, *Competing Against Luck.*

8. Doerr, *Measure What Matters.*
9. Kersten, *Focusing Knowledge Work with Task Context.*
10. Kersten, *Eclipse Mylyn.*
11. Learn more at FlowFramework.org.
12. Hoffman and Yeh, *Blitzscaling.*
13. Orosz, "How Big Tech Runs Tech Projects and the Curious Absence of Scrum."
14. Leffingwell and Knaster, *SAFe® 4.0 Reference Guide.*
15. Silicon Valley Product Group, "The Alternative to Roadmaps."
16. Theil, "How to Set Good OKR Key Results."
17. Salesforce, "Agentforce Marketing."
18. S&P Automotive Insights, "Digital Twins in the Automotive Industry Explained."
19. Silver, "Celebrating 50 Million Developers."
20. Stack Overflow, "Stack Overflow Developer Survey 2024."
21. Zeff, "GitHub Copilot Crosses 20M All-Time Users."
22. Silver, "Celebrating 50 Million Developers."
23. Parrish and Beaubien, *The Great Mental Models.*

Chapter 3

1. Ryseff, De Bruhl, and Newberry, *The Root Causes of Failure.*
2. West, Gilpin, and Grant, "Water-Scrum-Fall Is the Reality of Agile for Most Organizations Today,"
3. Skelton and Pais, *Team Topologies.*
4. Kim and Spear, *Wiring the Winning Organization.*
5. Schwaber and Sutherland, *The Scrum Guide.*
6. Kotter, *Accelerate.*
7. Robertson, *Holacracy.*
8. Gonzales-Black, "The Next Big Thing You Missed."
9. Zhang, *The Rendanheyi Model.*
10. West, *Scale.*
11. Soltani, "The Rising Dominance of U.S. Big Techs."
12. Smith, "Some Redwood Leaves Make Food."
13. West, *Scale.*
14. West, *Scale.*
15. West, *Scale.*
16. Minto, *The Pyramid Principle.*
17. Wikipedia, "Jensen Huang."
18. Kim, "Inside Amazon's Plan to Cut Managers."

19. Kiczales, des Rivières, and Bobrow, *The Art of the Metaobject Protocol.*
20. Kiczales et al., "Aspect-Oriented Programming."
21. Baldwin and Clark, *Design Rules.*
22. Aho et al., *Compilers.*
23. Zheng et al., "Attention Heads of Large Language Models."
24. Ravishankar et al., "Attention Can Reflect Syntactic Structure."
25. Horowitz, *The Hard Thing About Hard Things.*

Chapter 4

1. Forsgren, Humble, and Kim, *Accelerate.*
2. Womack and Jones, *Lean Thinking.*
3. Bryar and Carr, *Working Backward*, 75.
4. Miles and Scott, "The Leadership Team."
5. Kim and Spear, *Wiring the Winning Organization.*
6. Kersten, "Episode 44."
7. Rother and Shook, *Learning to See.*
8. Scaled Agile, Inc., "Weighted Shortest Job First."
9. Reinertsen, *The Principles of Product Development Flow.*
10. Kersten, "Episode 28."

Chapter 5

1. Ries, *The Lean Startup.*
2. Holland, *Emergence.*
3. Kaplan and Norton, *The Balanced Scorecard.*
4. Planview, *The 2024 Project to Product State of the Industry Report.*
5. Morgan and Heitland, *Strategic Portfolio Management.*
6. Planview, *The 2024 Project to Product State of the Industry Report.*
7. Planview, *The 2024 Project to Product State of the Industry Report.*
8. PagerDuty, Inc., "Time-Critical, Unplanned Work."
9. Planview, *The 2024 Project to Product State of the Industry Report.*
10. Goodhart, "Problems of Monetary Management."
11. Kersten, *Project to Product.*
12. Ohno, *Toyota Production System.*
13. IT Revolution, "Improve Flow in DevOps Value Stream."
14. Kersten, *Project to Product.*
15. Womack and Jones, *Lean Thinking.*
16. Beltman, "You Build It, You Run It."
17. Beltman, "You Build It, You Run It."

18. Planview, *The 2024 Project to Product State of the Industry Report.*
19. Ohno, *Toyota Production System.*
20. Planview, *The 2024 Project to Product State of the Industry Report.*
21. Project Management Institute, *PMBOK® Guide.*

Chapter 6

1. Boston Consulting Group, "What Employees Say."
2. Scaled Agile, Inc., "PI Planning."
3. Straker-Carrier, "Please, Stop Quarterly Planning."

Chapter 7

1. Kniberg and Ivarsson, "Scaling Agile @ Spotify."
2. Stevens, Myers, and Constantine, "Structured Design."
3. Conway, "How Do Committees Invent?"
4. Cataldo, Herbsleb, and Carley, "Socio-Technical Congruence."
5. Azad, *An Exploratory Study*; Šmite and Galviņa, "Socio-Technical Congruence Sabotaged."
6. Kim and Spear, *Wiring the Winning Organization.*
7. Scott, "Tesla's Vertical Integration"; "Why GM Sees U.S. Supply Chain."
8. Bezos, *2015 Letter to Shareholders.*
9. MacCormack, Rusnak, and Baldwin, "The Impact of Component Modularity."
10. Skelton and Pais, *Team Topologies.*
11. Baldwin and Clark, *Design Rules.*
12. Baldwin, "Design Rules: Past and Future."
13. Kersten, "Episode 20."
14. Booking Holdings Inc. "Booking Holdings Reports Fourth Quarter and Full Year 2024 Results."

Chapter 8

1. Schein, *Organizational Culture and Leadership.*
2. Doerr, *Measure What Matters.*
3. Pink, *Drive.*
4. Google re:Work, "Guides: Set Goals with OKRs."
5. Lee, "The Hidden (in Plain Sight) Legacy."
6. Henry, "Reporting Lines."
7. Castro, "How to Set OKRs."
8. Product Compass, "Objectives and Key Results."

9. Radek, "Objectives and Key Results."
10. Lawrence, *Atomic Human*.
11. Indeed Editorial Team, "What Is Sales Sandbagging?"
12. Grove, *High Output Management*.
13. Doerr, *Measure What Matters*.
14. Kersten, "Episode 56: GitHub's Scott Densmore on the Copilot Revolution, Coding at the Speed of Thought."

Chapter 9

1. Christensen, *The Innovator's Dilemma*.
2. Baghai, Coley, and White, *The Alchemy of Growth*.
3. Moore, *Zone to Win*.
4. Reinertsen, *The Principles of Product Development Flow*.
5. Blank, *The Four Steps to the Epiphany*.
6. Christensen and Raynor, *The Innovator's Solution*.
7. Bughin and Chui, "95 Percent of Generative AI Implementations."
8. Blank, *The Four Steps to the Epiphany*.
9. Moore, *Living on the Fault Line*.
10. Wang and Casado, "The Cost of Cloud."
11. Bezos, "2015 Letter to Shareholders."
12. Lockheed Martin, *Skunk Works®*.

Chapter 10

1. Graham, "Maker's Schedule, Manager's Schedule."
2. Jevons, *The Coal Question*.
3. Bostrom, "Ethical Issues in Advanced Artificial Intelligence."
4. Meadows, *Thinking in Systems*.
5. Kahneman, *Thinking, Fast and Slow*.
6. Toffler, *Future Shock*.
7. Gerjuoy, "Educating Man for the Future."

Conclusion

1. Tomasello et al., "Understanding and Sharing Intentions."
2. Butler, "Darwin Among the Machines."

Index

Note: Page numbers with f or t indicate figures and tables.

Acknowledgments

My wife, Alicia Kersten, has made all of the work, rework, and prework that went into this book possible. The decades I have spent head down, doing research, building a company, running technology organizations, and writing books would not have been possible without her unyielding support, her steady presence as a sounding board, and her smile.

I am grateful to the team at IT Revolution Press, especially Anna Noak and Leah Brown, whose editing skills continue to amaze me. Anna's ability to deliver tough love in the most pleasant and positive of ways is a force to be reckoned with. I could not have asked for a better editor.

No page was left unturned or unchanged between the initial galley version of this book and the final manuscript. For that I have an extraordinary group of reviewers to thank. Brendan Hopper (CBA) has been an exceptional intellectual sparring partner from the earliest brainstorming sessions and is one of the deepest-thinking technology leaders I have worked with. Geordie Henderson (Waterbay) inspired several of the ownership structure ideas and provided profound, thoughtful, and thorough feedback. Gene Kim (IT Revolution) worked tirelessly to help refine, simplify, and streamline the book's core arguments. Adrian Cockcroft (Nubank) offered invaluable advice on the models. The mentorship and guidance of Carlota Perez (University College London) on technological revolutions were instrumental in helping me understand how this revolution relates to previous ones.

I am also deeply grateful to the support of those who contributed the case studies in the book and are helping to lead their organizations, and the industry, forward: Sajal Amin (Priceline), Mike Carr (Vanguard), Brendan Hopper (CBA), Pieter Jordaan (TUI Group), and swyx (Cognition). Their contributions and candor made the arguments clearer and more grounded. I would also like to thank Razat Gaurav (Kinaxis), who was CEO at Planview while I proposed this ambitious book project during my tenure as CTO, as well as Matt Zilli, who later took the reins as Planview's CEO and continued to support the effort.

The following people also provided immensely helpful feedback through their revisions, notes, and comments: Matt Anderson (Patra), Rebecca Davis (Scaled Agile), Dawn Hovancsek (PNC), Dean Leffingwell (Scaled Agile), Russell Moss (HCSC), Gail Murphy (UBC), Matt Ring (John Deere), Andrew Sales (Scaled Agile), Rene Te-Strote (BMW Group), Ralf Waltram (BMW Group), Dave West (Scrum.org), and Steve Yegge (Freelance).

Thank you all. Your insight, encouragement, and guidance made this book possible.

About the Author

Dr. Mik Kersten is an independent technology strategist and researcher best known as the creator of the Flow Framework and author of the bestselling book *Project to Product*. Mik founded Tasktop and led the company as CEO until its acquisition by Planview in 2022. He continues to support Planview as an Executive in Residence.

Mik started his career as a Research Scientist at Xerox PARC as part of the team that created the first aspect-oriented programming language. He then completed his PhD in Computer Science at the University of British Columbia, where he pioneered the integration of software development and collaboration tools. That work became the foundation for Tasktop and helped shape the emerging field of Value Stream Management. Before shifting his focus to flow, outcomes, and organizational modularity, Mik wrote more than one million lines of open-source code that are still in use today.

His work now focuses on helping leaders transition from output-driven management to outcome-driven operating models, enabling organizations to harness the power of AI in a human-centric way. Mik lives in Vancouver, Canada, and enjoys skiing, biking, and surfing with family and friends.